Black Music Biography

An Annotated Bibliography

Black Music Biography

An Annotated Bibliography

SAMUEL A. FLOYD, JR.
MARSHA J. REISSER

KRAUS INTERNATIONAL PUBLICATIONS

White Plains, New York

A Division of Kraus-Thomson Organization Limited

First printing 1987

Printed in the United States of America

The paper used in this publication meets the
minimum requirements of American National
Standard for Information Science—Permanence of
Papers for Printed Library Materials, ANSI Z39.48-
1984. This book is Smyth sewn and casebound in
F-grade library buckram, which contains no
synthetic fibers.

Library of Congress Cataloging-in-Publication Data

Floyd, Samuel A.
   Black music biography.

   Includes index.
   1. Afro-American musicians—Biography—
Bibliography.   I. Reisser, Marsha J.   II. Title.
ML128.B3F6 1987   780'.92'2 [B]   86-27827
ISBN 0-527-30158-2 (alk. paper)

Contents

Contents

Contents

Introduction

Biography is "life-writing." To be effective, it should provide insight into and information about a musical subject's personality and character, trials and tribulations, hopes and joys, personal motivations and accomplishments, preferences and prejudices, and in the case of a musician, his/her musical influences, education, tendencies, uniqueness, achievements, and impact, weaving all of this into a narrative that tells the story of a subject's life. Such works, to be used successfully as research resources, should offer even more: bibliographies, discographies, photographs, chronologies, and indexes are all important features of definitive biographies. From our point of view, good biographies have both immediate and far-reaching applications and implications; they are both literary and scholarly, musically competent, and appreciable by both scholars and laymen.

Unique among our titles is James Doran's Erroll Garner, an effective oral history of a life based on a technique that might be called "life-telling" as opposed to life-writing, in that interviews of a variety of informants have been carefully arranged to tell the story of Garner's life. A book using a related technique is Mabel Rowland's Bert Williams, in which Rowland's commentary serves to connect into an integrated whole the numerous stories and remembrances of Williams's friends and colleagues. The titles by Cazort and Hobson, Southall, and Green (see name index) are not, strictly speaking, biographies but rather "chronicles": they present running commentary on the chronology of events in the individuals' lives. The books in the Kings of Jazz

Introduction

Series are career sketches--G. E. Lambert's Johnny Dodds, for example.

The books annotated here demonstrate, for various reasons, a wide range of effectiveness. For some of the books, the use of primary sources has been abundant; for others, nil. The same is true of secondary sources. Some books are filled with easy explanations of complex behavior and events and are therefore not extremely reliable. Some are naive and uninformed; others are based on faulty and questionable psychological interpretations. As far as such interpretation is concerned, some authors do it well, others poorly. In the process of preparing their books, some authors had the advantage of direct observation and access to information about their subjects, as well as observations by protagonists' intimate associates (e.g., David Ritz, for Divided Soul: The Life of Marvin Gaye), while others had remote or little access to such observation and information (e.g., James Lincoln Collier, for Louis Armstrong). The results are comparatively different and comparatively valid. Some of the books are based on thorough research (Geneva H. Southall's Blind Tom series) and extensive interviews (Timothy White's Catch a Fire: The Life of Bob Marley), while others are based on superficial and scant research and are purely anecdotal (Robert Goffin's Horn of Plenty: The Story of Louis Armstrong). Another factor in the quality of some of the biographies is the lack of candor that has often prevailed on the part of the musicians in interview situations. Ritz, for example, tells of Marvin Gaye's deception of a journalist:

> He painted an idealized version of his childhood, a version which he thought would be acceptable to a white audience, the pop market which he had worked so long to sell. Gaye wasn't prepared, not in front of these new fans, to wash his dirty laundry. As though he were trying to convince himself that his childhood was really not a nightmare, he glossed over his pre-adolescent conflicts. Ray Charles had played the same trick on Whitney Balliet in The New Yorker. But even in ignoring the pain of his past, Gaye revealed a great deal (Ritz, Divided Soul, p. 156).

Jack Bradley's anecdote about Erroll Garner is typical of the jazz musician's stance when he tires of answering questions that he deems ridiculous and silly:

> One of Erroll's fans asked him how he got his name. Erroll replied, "I was named after Erroll

Flynn." He said it with such seriousness I
thought I'd just witnessed a great historical
jazz fact. Later, when I started to think about
it, I realized that Erroll Flynn must have been
a mere baby when Erroll Garner was born. He was
just putting the fan, me, and everybody else on
(Doran, Erroll Garner, p. 103).

As complete life writings, many of the books included
here have shortcomings. Don George's Sweet Man, for
example, sheds no light on the musical genius of Duke
Ellington, while Ellington's own autobiography tells us
nothing about Ellington the man. Charles Blancq's Sonny
Rollins tells us much about the subject's musical style
but little about Rollins himself. Some of the books are
filled with dates and are also otherwise well documented;
others have few dates, with the chronology only implied.
For example, W. C. Handy's autobiography, Father of the
Blues, presents a running record of the development of his
life and career, but does not indicate when, specifically,
many of the events in his life took place.

Some authors effectively place their subjects' lives and
careers within the social, cultural, economic, and
political climates of the periods, blending historical,
human, and artistic considerations into narratives that
both inform and entertain. A case in point is Virginia
Hamilton's Paul Robeson: The Life and Times of a Free
Black Man. In a similar vein, Lyon, in treating Leontyne
Price's life in the context of the social attitudes of the
time of her development and emergence as an opera star,
tells how the singer's great art triumphed over racial
prejudice, leading a La Scala official to assert that her
race would be no problem there and that "the public will
have to get used to it. If she sings Butterfly and
anybody objects, we'll say she's a suntanned Butterfly"
(Lyon, Leontyne Price, p. 94).

Some works avoid aesthetic evaluation (e.g., Arnold
Shaw's Belafonte), while others make it an integral part
of their narratives (e.g., Martin Williams's King Oliver,
David Ritz's Divided Soul, and James Lincoln Collier's
Louis Armstrong). In writing of Oliver's improvising
around 1930, Williams gives the following critical
comment:

King Oliver might follow a recording on which
he did not play with one on which he played very
well, and follow that with one on which he
falters badly. That is about the best that one
can make of the difficult tangle of Oliver's
cornet and trumpet solos in these years. He

could follow dates with no solos or simple,
quiet ones by taking those really bravura solos
on Too Late and New Orleans Shout for himself.
But it is that kind of pride that he was made of
(Williams, King Oliver, pp. 76-77).

And in another place:

All of these recordings show, I think, how the
vocal-instrumental blues was dealing with the
very difficult problem of balancing poetry,
singer, and instrument. There is always a clash
among the three in any coming together they may
have: the opera librettist knows he cannot make
his lines too good or they draw too much
attention to themselves as poetry. And the
operatic composer knows he has got to balance
his singers and his instruments so that one does
not overshadow the others. And the so-called
"country blues" singer knows that he had best
keep his guitar simple and appropriately
functional for he is primarily a poet. If that
kind of balancing of the arts of poetry-
song-instruments has ever been better handled in
jazz it is surely only the best of the Joe Smith
and Louis Armstrong accompaniments. The
interplay of Lester Young and Billie Holiday in
the mid 'thirties might sometimes surpass it in
some ways, but there is no question of any
"poetry" in A Sailboat in the Moonlight (and
You), so the problem has changed. And today for
a Mahalia Jackson, the problem is even simpler.
She is primarily a singer and both the verses
and the accompaniment take second place to her
voice and delivery. The most advanced blues
artists of the 'twenties--writers, singers,
instrumentalists--obviously solved a subtle
artistic problem for themselves that few have
even dealt with since--and which perhaps only
German lieder solved before it. And George
Thomas's Morning Dove Blues as performed by
Sippie Wallace and Joseph Oliver is a classic,
and almost self-explicating, example of what
they achieved (Williams, King Oliver, pp.
84-85).

Bessie Jones's For the Ancestors: Autobiographical
Memories and William Broonzy's Big Bill Blues give
insights into the dating process of the oral tradition,
as, for example, when the latter writes:

xii

Introduction

> In them times every year something strange
> would happen--a drought, a flood or a picnic, or
> some Negro would get killed in some strange way,
> and so you see you can't forget when your child
> is born in the South. If you had ever been in a
> flood or a storm over there, or if you could
> have been at one of our camp meetings or our big
> picnics where everything was free, you wouldn't
> never forget it (Broonzy, <u>Big Bill Blues</u>, p.
> 7).

The poetic license taken by some writers has, on
occasion, served to obscure both facts and the lack of
them. Ann Fairbairn's work on George Lewis is a case in
point. Take, for example, the following passage, in which
the author/narrator has been asked the source of Lewis's
clarinet tone:

> "Where does George's tone come from?" I might
> have replied . . . "It comes from where, please
> God, no jazz man's tone will ever come again,
> but it comes from it in beauty. . . . It comes
> from the sound of the horns on the balcony of
> Hopes Hall, and the strength of the yearning in
> a boy's heart to tell his story as they were
> telling theirs. It comes from the grief of a
> young man, standing on a street corner, watching
> as his baby's body was placed in a vault in a
> cheap pine coffin. It comes from the strength
> within him, that kept him blowing, night after
> night, half dead with sickness and exhaustion.
> It comes from the sound of women weeping at a
> graveside and in a funeral service. It comes
> from the shouting, leaping, happy antics of the
> children in the second line, following the
> horns, as the children of Hamelin followed the
> Pied Piper. It comes from the sensitiveness
> within him, that flinches from a hurt and will
> not let him hurt another. It comes from many
> things and it tells of many things, and the
> greatest of the things of which it tells are the
> sorrows of his people, the triumphs of his race,
> and his faith in God. Where else could it have
> come from? Where else?" (Fairbairn, <u>Call Him
> George</u>, pp. 13-14).

On the other hand, the scholars among our authors tend
to eschew the poetic license and the colorful language of
the aesthete in order to give a more accurate account of
phenomena and events. The following statement, while it
does contain metaphor, is a good example of the scholar's
approach.

Introduction

> Joe Smith was, without question, a fine jazz
> musician. In particular, he was admired for the
> great beauty of his tone, which was clear and
> pure, a ribbon of silver. He often worked with
> a coconut shell as a plunger mute, but even then
> his tone remained bright and clean. His attack
> was sharp and his playing delicate, precise, and
> occasionally elegant (Collier, Louis Armstrong,
> p. 146).

Speaking of language, some of the books are heavily
scatalogical. Charles White, for example, lets Little
Richard tell his story in his own tasteless fashion with
descriptions of biological and sexual functions that, in
our opinion, go beyond the erotic and are merely
pornographic.

Some critics complain that works that expose human
weaknesses (e.g., Don George's Sweet Man) denigrate the
individuals about whom they are written. In our opinion,
however, they portray the humanity of their subjects,
making it easier for us to identify with them. As long as
the line is drawn at the tasteless, all other matters are
appropriate information for discussion. (Of course, it is
up to the reader to decide for him/herself what is
tasteless and what is not, as we have done for ourselves
here.) We can learn from our knowledge and awareness of
specific human fallibilities. Some would have us read
only "dates, facts, and didactic Kitsch" as in accounts of
the life of Bach, along with equal doses of musical
analysis, suppressing the individual's human and personal
essence.[1] It is the biographer's duty to record the
complete record of his/her subject's life and career as
far as it can be determined. What matters is that the
task be accomplished with honesty, sympathy, and
understanding.

Some of the biographers whose works appear in the
following pages do not establish or maintain the critical
equilibrium necessary for sound biographical writing.
This will be evident in the reading of the annotations.
Among those who do, however, are Brian Priestly, Laurraine
Goreau, and Sammy Davis, Jr. (an autobiographer!) and his
collaborators.

Naturally, the portraits of our protagonists are
distorted by the filtration processes of time and distance

---

[1] Wolfgang Hildesheimer, Mozart (New York: Farrar,
Straus, Giroux, 1982), p. 362.

Introduction

(both psychical and spatial), by the prejudices and perceptions of their biographers, and by the writing itself, including both the narrative construction/development and the editing process. Our images of historic and contemporary musical figures are usually formed on the basis of what we hear and think of their music and through what we hear and experience in casual conversation, none of which can give us a complete picture of an individual. Nor can biographical writings themselves give us a complete picture, for a biographer, too, will only receive partial information, choosing even from among what he/she receives. Factual omissions are often many because the written record is sparse. But biographical studies do illuminate, in varying degrees, the external and internal circumstances of their subjects' lives, however obscured these may be.

In our reading of these biographies of black musicians, we have noticed that nearly all of them have in common one omission: references to letters written by and to the subjects. A powerful source of information and interpretation in life-writing, items of correspondence are extremely valuable tools. Two examples of this, involving white subjects, are the reliance of Mozart's various biographers on letters written to and received by him and John Tasker Howard's use of the Foster family's letters in his biography of Stephen Foster where he relates that "it is possible to trace little Stephen's babyhood and his early years closely through the family letters."[2] Contrast this with Collier's statement to the effect that almost nothing is known of Louis Armstrong's life before he was fourteen years old. Later, Armstrong himself was an avid letter writer, although it seems that not much use has been made of his letters by his biographers. While correspondence from Jimi Hendrix to his father is included in Jerry Hopkins's _Hit and Run_, the sketchy nature of that correspondence does not shed the kind of light on his inner thoughts and feelings that the letters of Mozart and other eighteenth- and nineteenth-century white composers shed on theirs. For most black musicians, it may be that the letters are not readily available or do not exist. However, the black musicians whose biographies are annotated in this book have seldom expressed themselves in writing. A notable exception is Marian Anderson, whose correspondence totals

---

[2] John Tasker Howard, _Stephen Foster: America's Troubador_ (1943, reprint, Darby, Pa.: Arden Library, 1982), p. 68.

eighty boxes.[3] Unfortunately, they were not available when existing works were written about her.

So, most of the biographies about our musicians have shortcomings, and many of the subjects warrant better treatment, especially those in the field of concert music. But biographical studies of many significant figures are yet to appear, while the lives and works of still others will forever remain obscure because the informants and the documents needed for the chronicling and illuminating of these latter lives no longer exist. The possibility remains that good life-works can be written about William Grant Still, James P. Johnson, and Howard Swanson, individuals whose stories would make splendid biographies but whose lives still remain largely undelineated. Some lives are too impalpable, or information about them is too meager, to yield solid biographies; examples are those of Johnny Hodges, Wendell Phillips Dabney, and Tommy Johnson (in spite of the fact that career sketches of Dabney and Johnson are included in the present work).

Many of the works included here are autobiographies--memoirs--about which Sam Vaughan tells us: "The value of a memoir is not whether it is accurate. It's a picture of what the man wants you to think. Memoirs are all flawed by self-service." So, too, are biographies, but "they still have their value."[4] The didactic value of both biographies and autobiographies can be high. We can observe how a life can change and how perspectives on life can shift by comparing autobiographies written by a single individual at different times in his/her life. Ethel Waters's His Eye Is on the Sparrow and To Me It's Wonderful are instructive and revealing in this regard. In addition, aspiring concert and opera singers can gain insight, inspiration, and knowledge from reading the life-writings of Roland Hayes, Paul Robeson, Marian Anderson, and Leontyne Price.

We can learn much about inter- and intra-racial prejudice from the life-writings of musicians such as Lena Horne and Eartha Kitt, each of whom has suffered discrimination at the hands of both blacks and whites. There were also efforts to suppress and deny the

[3] See Neda M. Westlake and Otton E. Albrecht, Marian Anderson: A Catalog of the Collection at the University of Pennsylvania Library (Philadelphia: University of Pennsylvania Press, 1981), pp. 3-16.

[4] Sam Vaughan, publisher of Doubleday, quoted in Sweet Man by Don George (Putnam, 1981), p. 238.

outstanding achievements and abilities of William Grant Still, as when he ran into difficulty in his attempt to get his opera Troubled Island produced and when "plans were . . . afoot for 'the boys' [critics] to pan the opera, even before they heard it" (Verna Arvey, In One Lifetime, p. 143). Many of these lives, like David Ritz's Marvin Gaye and Paul Oliver's Bessie Smith, have "all the elements of high drama and great tragedy" (Oliver, Bessie Smith, p. 71). Gaye's life, in fact, does read like a Greek tragedy--in modern black, of course. The day-to-day insults suffered by black musicians who lived in and on the fringes of white society between 1930 and 1970 are vividly portrayed and explained in Sammy Davis, Jr.'s Yes I Can; this book provides tremendous insight into the nature and reality of racial prejudice and discrimination, as well as racial preferences and ironies in the United States as the nation moved toward a more equitable society. Dorothy Dandridge's Everything and Nothing exemplifies and details that "two-ness" of which W.E.B. DuBois wrote in The Souls of Black Folk. But it goes even further; it is a brutally frank revelation of the contradictory currents, the psychological stresses and strains, of looking white and being black in white society in the 1950s and early 1960s. Dandridge tells us that "some figures, involved in that way [blacks working in a white world], smoke heavily, from the tensions involved. Like Nat King Cole. Others privately drank or even took drugs. I had no such habits at the time. But whenever I returned to Los Angeles I hastened to my psychiatrist. There I received consolation and relief" (p. 101).

Some of our protagonists were victims of varying degrees of unusual Establishment oppression, suppression, and ostracism. Paul Robeson, Lena Horne, and Eartha Kitt all suffered at the hands of citizen witch-hunters and public officials. Others were initially most appreciated by white audiences: Little Richard, Chuck Berry, Jimi Hendrix, Eartha Kitt, and Donna Summer, for example.

Normally, we are interested in musicians' lives because of their artistic accomplishments. We would not care or know about Louis Armstrong or Duke Ellington, for example, had they not accomplished great things musically. With Paul Robeson, however, it may be that the opposite is the case: it is possible that we still care so much about his artistry because of his accomplishments and the conditions that prevailed in other aspects of his life. This is not to denigrate his art; it is just in the nature of things that he might have remained as unheralded, say, as Jules Bledsoe had his professional life not had more variety. As it is, however, at least seven books have been written about him. In some cases, the lives of individuals exceed their importance as musical figures (e.g., Pearl Bailey); in other cases, the musical significance of the individuals transcends the biographical information presented (e.g., William Grant Still).

From a strictly musical standpoint, a few of the books can provide insight into the spontaneous high-level music-making of groups who never rehearsed their music, jazzmen who played jobs and recording sessions without ensemble preparation--e.g., the Miles Davis Quintet and the Erroll Garner Trio--and the magically polished and aesthetically refined results they produced because of their leaders' artistry and guidance. Insights can be gained into musical-technical evolution and innovation: "Henderson's real career begins when he takes a dance band and tries to make a jazz band out of it. Oliver, who had a jazz band, wanted to keep it that, while he borrowed a section from a conventional dance band. . . . Ellington began at a different point. For it was not until he had a 'show' or 'pit' band to convert into a jazz orchestra that Ellington began to find his way" (Williams, King Oliver, p. 58).

THE USE OF THIS BIBLIOGRAPHY

In one sense, Black Music Biography is a kind of survey of the history of the music of black Americans and of race relations in the United States, for all of the musicians whose life-writings are included here experienced significant change and development in the two inescapable conditions of their lives--the making of music and the sting of racism in its various forms and guises.

The body of writing reviewed in this book also reveals: 1) the wide and large amount of interaction that has always taken place among black musicians and entertainers, no matter how diverse their fields--relationships, for example, between Bessie Smith and J. Rosamond Johnson, Bessie Smith and Will Marion Cook, Bessie Smith and Charles A. Tindley, Ethel Waters and Paul Robeson, William Grant Still and W. C. Handy, Harry T. Burleigh and Florence Mills, Marvin Gaye and Bo Diddley, Leontyne Price and Margaret Bonds, the Commodores and the Jackson Five, and Harry Belafonte, Odetta, and Miriam Makeba; 2) the large number of musicians whose fathers were preachers, e.g, Fats Waller, Pearl Bailey, Otis Redding, Marvin Gaye, and Paul Robeson, to name just a few; 3) the ways in which black musicians use humor as a way of stressing and articulating--both directly and obliquely--the weight of living as Afro-Americans in a racist society, (e.g., Duke

Introduction

Ellington's response when his nomination for a Pulitzer Prize in 1965 was denied: "Fate is being very kind to me; Fate doesn't want me to be too famous too young" [Ellington, Music Is My Mistress, p. 286]); and 4) the history of black music in the United States and associated and parallel events outside the United States. As a body of literature the life-writings listed in this work constitute a history of black music, touting many of the significant figures of the culture and telling who did and said what, when, where, and how.

Black Music Biography can be read as a collection of brief career vignettes that give essentials and highpoints of the subjects' professional and sometimes their personal lives. It can also serve as a kind of biographical dictionary in storybook form. Read in the chronological order of the musicians' birth dates, the book can give one a sense of the evolution of Afro-American music (although the events as they happen from book to book will not consistently appear as they actually occurred). To facilitate this approach, we provide here the birth dates of all the musicians whose life-writings are annotated in these pages. The majority of the dates were taken from Eileen Southern's Biographical Dictionary of Afro-American and African Musicians (Greenwood Press, 1982).

1849 Blind Tom	1893 Gordon, Taylor
1854 Bland, James A.	1894 Jenkins, Edmund Thornton
1864 Blind Boone	1894 Bricktop
1865 Dabney, Wendell Phillips	1894 Smith, Bessie
1868 Joplin, Scott	1895 Still, William Grant
1871 Johnson, James Weldon	1896 Johnson, Tommy
1873 Fletcher, Tom	1896 Waters, Ethel
1873 Handy, W. C.	1897 Bechet, Sidney
1874 Williams, Bert	1897 Henderson, Fletcher
1875 Coleridge-Taylor, Samuel	1897 Smith, Willie the Lion
1877 Bolden, Buddy	1898 Dodds, Baby
1879 Johnson, Bunk	1898 Robeson, Paul
1882 Dett, R. Nathaniel	1899 Ellington, Duke
1883 Blake, Eubie	1900 Armstrong, Louis
1883 Harrison, Hazel	1900 Lewis, George
1885 Morton, Jelly Roll	1901 Collins, Lee
1885 Oliver, King	1902 Anderson, Marian
1886 Rainey, Ma	1902 Jones, Bessie
1887 Hayes, Roland	1904 Basie, Count
1887 Patton, Charley	1904 Hawkins, Coleman
1889 Sissle, Noble	1904 Waller, Fats
1892 Dodds, Johnny	1906 Baker, Josephine
1892 Foster, Pops	1907 Calloway, Cab
1893 Bradford, Perry	1907 Carter, Benny
1893 Broonzy, Big Bill	1909 Wells, Dicky

Introduction

1912	Jackson, Mahalia	1926	Berry, Chuck
1915	Holiday, Billie	1926	Coltrane, John
1917	Gillespie, Dizzy	1926	Davis, Miles
1917	Horne, Lena	1926	Short, Bobby
1918	Bailey, Pearl	1927	Belafonte, Harry
1919	Cole, Nat King	1927	Price, Leontyne
1919	Gonzales, Babs	1928	Dolphy, Eric
1920	Parker, Charlie	1928	Hawes, Hampton
1921	Garner, Erroll	1928	Kitt, Eartha
1922	Mingus, Charles	1930	Charles, Ray
1923	Dandridge, Dorothy	1930	Rollins, Sonny
1925	Davis, Sammy, Jr.	1932	Little Richard
1925	King, B. B.	1932	Schuyler, Philippa
		1939	Gaye, Marvin
		1941	Redding, Otis
		1942	Crouch, Andrae
		1942	Hendrix, Jimi
		1944	Ross, Diana
		1945	Marley, Bob
		1948	Summer, Donna
		1949	Richie, Lionel
		1950	Wonder, Stevie
		1958	Prince
		1959	Jackson, Michael

The reader will notice that the annotations in this work vary in length. Our experience with our first annotated bibliography, _Black Music in the United States: An Annotated Bibliography of Selected Reference and Research Sources_ (Kraus, 1983), made us well aware of the inevitability of this condition. Aside from the obvious reasons for such length differences (the varying lengths, quality, depth, and content of the books annotated), there are other reasons that are related specifically to the matter of genre. For example, there is more to say about biographies than chronicles, and more to say about profound works than superficial ones. Another matter has also affected the lengths of certain of the annotations; when a later-dated biography of a given subject has repeated much of the information that appeared in an earlier one, the later annotation usually will be shorter, except in the few cases where a later biography had to be annotated before the earlier one (for logistical reasons). Later biographies, of course, often contain newer and updated information. For example, the writers of the later biographies of Armstrong and Ellington have had much to build on as well as opportunities to correct errors, interpretations, and omissions. (Sometimes, of course, the shortcomings are only perpetuated.)

In writing our annotations, we used three basic approaches in an effort to provide variety for the

reader. Some of our annotations, therefore, are brief
descriptions of the books they treat (e.g, Jeffrey P.
Green's Edmund Thornton Jenkins); others are
mini-summaries (e.g., Arnold Shaw's Belafonte); and still
others are mini-condensations (e.g., David Ritz's Divided
Soul). We have freely quoted from many of the books to
give the reader an idea of the various writing styles and
narrative flavors and to reflect authors' insights into
their subjects' varied lives. Of course, the character
and style of the books' narratives have determined, to
some degree, the varying styles of the annotations. We
have tried not to make judgments on such matters as
quality (although we have slipped here from time to time),
accuracy, or scholarship. We have tried simply to
communicate what the books are about, what and how they
function, and what they have to offer the reader. Quoted
remarks should not be taken as authoritative, only as
indicative of an author's approach, attitude, or claims,
as with Al Rose's statement that Eubie Blake's "Charleston
Rag" "would establish a basis for the Eastern style of
piano playing" (Rose, Eubie Blake, p. 26).

ON THE BOOKS INCLUDED

In planning and preparing for this work, titles of books
to be considered for inclusion were gathered from perusal
of the catalogs of publishers known to produce books in
the area of black music, from the bibliographies of many
of the biographies that are included here, from searches
of selected out-of-print bookstores, from the
bibliographic listings that appear in Eileen Southern's
Biographical Dictionary of Afro-American and African
Musicians, and from a search of the 1985-1986 edition of
Books in Print and of Biographical Books 1950-1980
(Bowker, 1980). The number of books included is 147.
Thirty-two of the books are autobiographies. The number
of different authors and co-authors represented is 153.
Fourteen of them have written more than one book. The
most prolific author is James Haskins with six books. The
various musical genres are represented as follows:

Jazz	58	Religious	8
Blues	14	Rhythm & Blues	
Ragtime	5	and Pop	38
Folk	2	Concert/Opera	22

In the spring of 1985 the book-gathering research for
the project was halted, and no new books were added to our
list. This practical consideration necessitated the

exclusion of a number of worthy books from the present work. Among them are: Stephen Ivory's biography of Tina Turner, Tina (Perigee Books, 1985); Count Basie and Albert Murray's Good Morning Blues: The Autobiography of Count Basie (Random House, 1985); and the several slim volumes of the Jazz Masters series, published jointly by Spellmount (Tunbridge Wells, England) and Hippocrene Books (New York), including Billie Holiday by Burnett James (1984), Oscar Peterson by Richard Palmer (1985), Count Basie by Alun Morgan (1984), and Lester Young by Dave Gelly (1985). Each of the books in the latter series consists of an article-length career sketch and a selected discography of the recordings of the book's subject.

Collections of biographical writings on individual musicians and collections of writings on several musicians have not been included. Therefore, works such as, in the first case, Peter Gammond's Duke Ellington: His Life and Music (Phoenix House, 1958) and Stanley Dance's The World of Earl Hines (Scribner's, 1977) and, in the second, Mildred Green's Black Women Composers: A Genesis (Twayne, 1983) have been omitted. Annotations of such works can be found in our Black Music in the United States.

Some books about musicians do not qualify as life-writings at all, although they may be books about the subjects' careers. For example, Graham Collier's book about Cleo Laine and her husband (Cleo and John: A Biography of the Dankworths, Quartet Books, 1976) consists of a series of quotations from newspaper articles and from the subjects and their friends connected by a thread of the author's narrative. Also, some of them contain information so scant that they cannot be considered as books at all, as in the case of Samuel Charters' Robert Johnson (Oak Publications, 1973) and Joe McEwen's Sam Cooke: The Man Who Invented Soul (Chappell & Co., 1977). All such writings have been omitted here.

Also absent are the extremely brief commentaries about black musicians written for elementary-school children. These biographical sketches are shorter than article length and are extensively illustrated by drawings of the artist or of events in the artist's life. Examples of these books for children are: Stevie Wonder by Beth P. Wilson (Putnam, 1979); Roberta Flack by Charles and Ann Morse (Creative Education, 1974); Charley Pride and Duke Ellington: Ambassador of Music by Pamela Barclay (Creative Education, 1974 and 1975, respectively); Aretha Franklin by James T. Olsen (Creative Education, 1974); Mahalia Jackson: Young Gospel Singer by Montrew Dunham (Bobbs, 1974); and Make a Joyful Noise Unto the Lord! by Jesse Jackson (Thomas Y. Crowell, 1974). Likewise, novels written for young readers and based on the events of a musician's life have been excluded. An example is Jeannette Eaton's Trumpeter's Tale: The Story of Young Louis Armstrong (William Morrow, 1955).

Black Music Biography is organized alphabetically by the names of the subjects of the biographies. We have used the most recent headings in the Library of Congress Name Authority File as the source for the nameforms used as section headings. For example, Thomas Greene Wiggins Bethune is here listed as Blind Tom in accordance with LC practice. Nameforms for many of the jazz musicians were taken from the (Rutgers University) Institute of Jazz Studies' IJS Jazz Register and Indexes. This project works with the Library of Congress to establish consistent, authoritative nameforms. In a few cases a musician's name was not found in either source. In these cases the nameform was chosen according to with the principles exhibited in the LC File. For example, John W. "Blind" Boone is here listed as Blind Boone to conform to the use of a commonly used nickname without setting it off in quotation marks. We hope that our use of authoritative nameforms will be of assistance to others.

Under the subjects' names, the entries for the biographies themselves are arranged alphabetically by the authors' names. Each book annotation is accompanied by a listing of the book review citations given in the following indexes: Book Review Digest, Book Review Index, Current Book Reviews, National Library Service Cumulative Book Review Indexes, 1950-1974, and Music Index. Each index was searched for the year of the book's publication and the two following years. In the case of reprints, citations have been included for the original edition when they appeared in the process of searching for citations. Each of the citations includes the following information as it is applicable: name of periodical; volume number; page number; and the month, date, and year of publication, or series number and year of publication. Periodical titles are given as they appear in the source index, except that subtitles have been deleted. The basic information contained in the citations is also retained from the source index.

Selective discographies have been included for each of the subjects who recorded during his/her lifetime (many of the books themselves carry discographies). Selective listening to the musical output of a subject prior to the reading of his/her biography, we believe, will give the reader insight, perspective, and aural orientation that will aid his/her understanding and effective comprehension. Thus, our selective discographies can be considered as recommended pre-reading listening lists. Similarly, such listening during and after the reading will illuminate the text. For the purpose of reviewing a musician's recorded work, selective compilations--albums and sets--are the most convenient and effective resources. For some musicians, however, no such collections exist. In the case of many "classical" musicians, we have listed either their entire recorded output or selected representative recordings. For example, Roland Hayes's brief discography allowed us to list it entirely and completely; William Grant Still's more extensive oeuvre required selectivity. In most cases the sound recordings listed in the "Selective Discography" sections of the entries were chosen to give a comprehensive view of each individual's lifetime output. A few of the discographies, however, were selected on the basis of information available in the standard discographies and do not necessarily reflect a representative sample of the musician's recorded output. Dates are given when they have been available; most are release dates, although, because of the inconsistency in the date information provided by the diverse sources from which the information was taken, the events to which the dates refer will vary from annotation to annotation, some being release dates while others are composition or session dates. Therefore, the items in the discographies are arranged in alphabetical order rather than chronological order, as we might have preferred.

The book's index is not meant to be all-inclusive. It contains only: 1) the names of authors and co-authors; 2) the names of the writers of the books' introductions, prefaces, and forewords; 3) titles of books, with subtitles only when necessary to distinguish between two or more biographies; 4) designations of biographees' performing media, i.e., trumpeter, singer, etc.; and 5) designations of the genre in which the musicians performed.

Using this work as a point of departure, researchers will be able to widen the scope and deepen the extent of their research on a single individual or group of individuals by consulting journal articles or chapters in collective works with guidance from Skowronski's <u>Black Music in America: A Bibliography</u> (Scarecrow Press, 1981) and the "Biographies" volume of de Lerma's <u>Bibliography of Black Music</u> (Greenwood, forthcoming). Skowronski's volume is limited to selected musicians and compiled from the entries in eleven different information sources. De Lerma's work was compiled from all available sources, including bibliographies of various kinds, other book lists, and library card catalogs.

Introduction

Another category of works related to life- and career-writing will be useful to researchers: biblio-discographies and research guides on individual musicians are becoming vogue. Works such as Lenwood G. Davis's <u>A Paul Robeson Research Guide: A Selected Annotated Bibliography</u> (Greenwood Press, 1982), Janet L. Sims's <u>Marion Anderson: An Annotated Bibliography and Discography</u> (Greenwood Press, 1981), and Morroe Berger, Edward Berger, and James Patrick's <u>Benny Carter: A Life in American Music, Volume II</u> (Scarecrow Press and the Institute of Jazz Studies, 1982) are examples. Such works are indispensable supplementary tools, and their availability enhances research in this area of scholarship.

Also of assistance to researchers are the lengthy discographies of the subjects' recorded performances contained in several of the books. The second volume of the Berger/Berger/Patrick biography of Benny Carter, cited above, is one such example. James Doran's extensive discography of Erroll Garner's recorded output, which does not include titles of his albums, would be useless to a novice investigator or casual reader but is invaluable for a Garner scholar.

Many of the new readers of these books will encounter terms with which they are not familiar--terms that emerged from, and many of which remain exclusively a part of, black culture in general and the jazz life in particular. In addition, names of unfamiliar but important musicians will be encountered frequently. For such readers we recommend as tableside references Robert S. Gold's <u>Jazz Talk</u> (Bobbs-Merrill, 1975) and Eileen Southern's <u>Biographical Dictionary of Afro-American and African Musicians</u> (Greenwood Press, 1982).

<u>Black Music Biography</u> is the first of a kind. Nowhere else does there exist even a list of black musicians on whom book-length biographical studies have been written. Based on our perusals of pertinent research sources, we estimate that approximately 100 of the 1,500 musicians cited in Southern's <u>Biographical Dictionary</u> have been the subjects of book-length biographies. Although more notable black musicians have existed than Southern lists in her selective work, we can assume that it does include most of the black musicians on whom book-length biographical studies have been written.

We hope that our book will stimulate work in this important area of scholarship. Interested scholars will want to read the following exploratory articles for introductions to this relatively uninvestigated region: Bruce Tucker's "Recent Black Music Biography," <u>Black Music</u>

Introduction

Research Journal (1983, pp. 58-69) and "Prejudice Lives: Toward a Philosophy of Black Music Biography," Black Music Research Journal (1984, pp. 1-21); and Richard Long's "Black Music Biography," Black Music Research Journal (1986, pp. 49-56). Perhaps through these scholars, the dearth of scholarly literature in the area will begin to be remedied.

We would like to thank Kraus International Publications's former Editor-in-Chief, Marion Sader, for encouraging the writing of this work; Barry Katzen, Managing Editor at Kraus, for working with us as editor; Paula Epstein, reference/special projects librarian, and Dorothy Dryden, librarian, both at Columbia College, for their assistance in locating and acquiring many of the books for us to read; Barbara Strauss, librarian at the University of Wisconsin at Madison, for logistical support; and Antonio Greene, Terry S. Koger, James Nichols, and Jacqueline Wheeler for assistance in the preparation of the review citations and the discographical information. Special thanks go to Ralph Eastman, David Evans, Deborra Richardson of the Moreland-Spingarn Collection at Howard University, and Suzanne Steel of the University of Mississippi's Blues Archive for providing us with discographical information.

Annotated
Bibliography

Marian Anderson

Anderson, Marian. <u>My Lord, What a Morning: An Autobiography</u>. New York: Viking Press, 1956. 312 pp. photographs.

In this book the renowned singer reveals details of her personal and professional lives, beginning with her modest but happy childhood and ending with her residency with the Metropolitan Opera in 1955. In the process, she discusses her billing as "the baby contralto, ten years old" when she was actually eight, her training in church choirs and her singing at church and other functions in her home city of Baltimore, and her first encounter with a promoter (p. 14). She treats of the short singing tours she took when she was still in high school, her vocal teachers and the details of their methods, and the development of her vocal technique. At the same time, she tells of her first encounter with the cruelty of racism, the disappointment of her Town Hall debut, her participation in and winning of a Philharmonic Society contest, and her subsequent appearance with the New York Philharmonic in 1925. She then goes on to detail her first recording and her reactions to it, her marriage, the kindness of individuals who helped her along the way, and encounters and friendships with musicians such as Harry T. Burleigh, Lawrence Brown, Roland Hayes, and Amanda Ira Aldridge. Her trips to Europe beginning in 1931, the receptions she received there, and the acceptance of her by Scandinavian audiences prepared her to "face the challenge of bigger

things" (p. 145). She also discusses her feelings,
perceptions, and actions on the occasion of the
refusal of the Daughters of the American Revolution
to allow her to perform at Constitution Hall in
Washington, D.C. Anderson provides insights into
her philosophy on and approach to programming and
preparing a repertoire; notes on caring for the
voice, on music criticism, on wardrobe
considerations, and on touring; her accompanists
and companions on tour; the experience of being an
"exception"; and comments on "Those Who Listen,"
the commercial recordings of her music, and
"Husband and Home."

> Reviews: Booklist 53:11 S 1 '56; Booklist 53:91
> O 15 '56; Bookmark 16:30 N '56; Canadian Forum
> 37:47 My '57; Chicago Sunday Tribune p4 O 28
> '56; Christian Science Monitor p4 O 25 '56;
> Kirkus Reviews 24:619 Au 15 '56; Library Journal
> 81:1984 S 15 '56; Library Journal 81:2734 N 15
> '56; Music Clubs Magazine 36:18-19 N '56;
> Musical Courier 154:39 D 1 '56; Musical America
> 76:28 D 1 '56; Musical Times 99:83 F '58; New
> York Herald Tribune Book Reviews pl O 28 '56;
> New York Times p14 N 11 '56; New Yorker 32:239 N
> 17 '56; Notes 14:266 Mr '57; Opera (London)
> 8:517 Au '57; Pan Pipes 50:31+ Ja '58; San
> Francisco Chronicle p29 D 5 '56; Saturday Review
> 39:22 N 3 '56; Wisconsin Library Bulletin 53:309
> Ja '57

Newman, Shirlee P. Marian Anderson: Lady from Philadelphia. Philadelphia: Westminster Press, 1966. 175 pp.
photographs. bibliography. index.

> About the content of this book, the author says,
> "It's all true, based on actual happenings. And
> fortunate, indeed, is the biographer who need not
> make up incidents to make exciting reading.
> Occasionally, toward the beginning of the book, I
> have switched the sequence of events a bit, but for
> the most part, I have simply reported what took
> place, using actual dialogue whenever possible, as
> remembered by Marian Anderson herself or someone
> who was there" (p. 167). Anderson was early
> involved with music in the church and in the south
> Philadelphia community where she was raised. Near
> the end of her high school years, she was able to
> study with Guiseppe Boghetti, who taught her
> correct breathing and worked to "develop an even,
> unbroken vocal line from her lowest tone to her
> highest" (p. 27). In her increasingly frequent

performances, she began to be accompanied and managed by Billy King, a noted local pianist. "With Billy at the piano, she appeared at churches, in theaters, schools, halls, clubs, and at parties in private homes. Often she and Billy were invited to perform at Negro schools in the South, from big colleges like Hampton Institute and Howard University, down to one-room schoolhouses in the backwoods, where they accepted a small fee or none at all" (p. 31). She made her Town Hall debut at twenty, singing art songs as well as spirituals, as she would continue to do throughout her career; however, the audience was small and the reviews were poor.

In 1925, after almost a year's hiatus from singing, Anderson won a competition for which the prize was a performance with the New York Philharmonic Orchestra at Lewisohn Stadium. Shortly after, she began to be managed by the Arthur Judson agency. After a year of little progress with her career, she decided to travel to Europe for a time to gain experience and to learn languages. A Rosenwald grant allowed her to return to Europe to continue her studies and concertizing. She made a preliminary tour of Scandinavia which led to a second, more extended tour of Scandinavia, Europe, and Russia with her Finnish accompanist, Kosti Vehanen. Sol Hurok heard her perform and took her under his management. She was booked for a tour that covered the whole of the United States. At first she played to segregated houses. "Later, Marian insisted on 'vertical seating'--that is, she asked that Negro ticket buyers, although seated apart from whites, be allotted seats in every part of the auditorium and not only in the balcony. As she became more renowned, white people were sold tickets first and the Negro section grew smaller and smaller. Marian asked that Negroes be given a chance to buy seats first come, first served. Finally she refused to appear in segregated halls" (p. 100). In 1939 the D.A.R. refused to rent Constitution Hall in Washington, D.C., to Anderson for a performance. After an outcry by many prominent performers, Eleanor Roosevelt led "a wave of others" who resigned from that organization (p. 106). The concert was held on Easter Sunday at the Lincoln Memorial before a crowd of 75,000 people. In that same year, Anderson sang a command performance at the White House before the king and queen of England, and she received the NAACP's Spingarn Medal for the "American Negro achieving most during the year. . . . Her nation and her own people honored her; so did the city in which she was born. On March 18, 1941, Marian was given the Bok Award, presented annually to the citizen of which Philadelphia is proudest. She was the first Negro and the second woman to receive the award" (pp. 113-114). The year 1943 saw her marriage to Orpheus "King" Fischer.

"Marian had come a long way since those early days in the church choir. She had sung on almost every continent in the world, for kings and presidents, for mighty and humble. She had, however, never sung in opera" (p. 131). In 1955 she sang the part of "Ulrica, the Negro sorceress in Verdi's opera The Masked Ball," being the first black artist to perform with the Metropolitan Opera (p. 132). In 1957 she made a tour of Asia, the Orient, and the Middle East for the State Department. The following year she was made a United States Delegate to the United Nations. Other honors came her way: election to the American Academy of Arts and Sciences (1959) and the Presidential Medal of Freedom (1963). Anderson sang her Farewell Concert at Carnegie Hall in 1965.

Reviews: Best Sellers 26:102 Ju 1 '66; Booklist 63:57 S 1 '66; Christian Science Monitor p8B My 5 '66; Commonwealth 84:290 My 27 '66; Instructor 76:217 Au '66; Kirkus Reviews 34:115 F 1 '66; Library Journal 91:3545 Jy '66; New York Times Book Review 71:38 Jy 10 '66; Publishers Weekly 189:80 My 16 '66; Saturday Review 49:42 My 14 '66

Vehanen, Kosti. Marian Anderson: A Portrait. New York: McGraw-Hill; London: Whittlesy House, 1941. 270 pp. photographs.

Marian Anderson's accompanist and companion of ten years gives a memoir of the singer's professional life during the period of their association, beginning with their meeting in 1931 and their subsequent appearance in Scandinavia, and ending with the American tours of 1938-1941. The author tells of their travels and performances in Finland, Norway, Denmark, Sweden, Holland, Belgium, England, France, Spain, Italy, Switzerland, Czechoslovakia, Poland, Austria, Hungary, Latvia, Estonia, and Russia, giving details of their first of three tours in the latter country, the first in Scandinavia, those in England and France, and of later tours in Brazil and

Argentina. The author presents facts and insights related to: how the singer "always rejected . . . operatic engagements" early in her career (p. 65); adventures on the road; picturesque descriptions of the lands they visited; the beginning of Anderson's worldwide reputation in Paris in 1934; the development of her song repertoire; her method of studying songs and of programming them; the development of her taste in clothes and her becoming a "well-dressed woman of excellent taste" (p. 166); her two appearances at the White House during this period; and the beginning of her "sensational success" in the United States in 1935 in the midst of great prejudice and discrimination (p. 231). Filled with anecdotes, the book also reveals something of Anderson's character; her moral and religious beliefs; her generosity to charity; her aesthetic orientation; her philosophy of life; and her relationship with her family.

Reviews: Booklist 37:514 Jy 1 '41; Commonweal 34:213 Ju 20 '41; Library Journal 66:356 Ap 15 '41; New York Times p6 Ju 15 '41; Saturday Review 24:21 Ju 21 '41; Springfield Republican p6e Ju 22 '41

SELECTIVE DISCOGRAPHY

Alto Rhapsody, Op. 53. Johannes Brahms. RCA SP 33-555, 1969.
Un Ballo in Maschera, Selections. Giuseppe Verdi. RCA LM-1911, 1955.
Beloved Schubert Songs. Franz Schubert. RCA LM-98, 1951.
Christmas Carols. RCA LM/LSC-2613, 1962.
Farewell Recital. RCA LM/LSC-2781, 1964.
First Recordings of Marian Anderson. Halo 50281, 1956.
"He's Got the Whole World in His Hands." RCA LM/LSC-2592, 1962.
Lady from Philadelphia. RCA LM-2212, 1958.
"The Lord's Prayer" and Other Songs of Faith and Inspiration. RCA VCS-7083, 1971.
Marian Anderson Sings. Varsity 6986.
Marian Anderson Sings Spirituals. RCA AVMI-1735, 1976.

Louis Armstrong

Armstrong, Louis. Satchmo: My Life in New Orleans. New York: Prentice-Hall, 1954. 240 pp. photographs.

Armstrong's early life was one in which he "did a whole lot of singing" in Sunday school and church and listened to the music coming from the honky tonks of his immediate neighborhood, including that from the famous Funky Butt Hall where he claims to have heard the legendary Buddy Bolden (p. 11). In his impoverished childhood, Armstrong sang in a quartet which performed "for pimps and whores" in his neighborhood (p. 32). In this book he details his quartet activity; his arrest for firing a pistol during New Orleans's end-of-year celebrations and his subsequent arrest and assignment to a "waif's home"; and his education, musical training, and happy life during his exposure to Bunk Johnson, Freddie Keppard, and Joe Oliver. He tells of his teen years in the toughest district in New Orleans; his first professional job as a blues player when he was fifteen and the subsequent one-nighters in honky-tonks; and his serving as the sole financial support of his family when he was seventeen. Moving toward treatment of his adulthood and professional life, he details his performing with the Kid Ory Band and the Tuxedo Brass Band; his joining the Fate Marable Band to play aboard the Mississippi River excursion steamer Sidney and a subsequent stint on the steamer Saint Paul; his making the rounds of New Orleans honky-tonks on a drinking spree with his mother; and his move from New Orleans to Chicago in 1922 to

- 8 -

join Joe Oliver's band, finally hitting "the big time" (p. 240).

Reviews: Booklist 51:105 N 1 '54; Chicago Sunday Tribune p3 O 10 '54; Down Beat 21:1+ N 3 '54; High Fidelity 4:129 F '55; Jazz Journal 8:25 Ap '55; Kirkus Reviews 22:607 S 1 '54; Library Journal 79:2336 D 1 '54; Melody Maker 30:3 N 27 '54; New York Herald Tribune Book Reviews p4 O 17 '54; New York Times p7 O 10 '54; New Yorker 30:165 O 16 '54; Newsweek 44:96+ O 18 '54; Orkester Journalen 22:27 D '54; Record Changer 14:6 N 2 '55; San Francisco Chronicle p19 O 31 '54; Saturday Review 37:54 N 27 '54; Variety 196:50 S 29 '54

Collier, James Lincoln. Louis Armstrong: An American Genius. New York: Oxford University Press, 1983. ix, 383 pp. photographs. bibliography. discography. index.

This book is intended to support and substantiate the author's opening statement that

> Louis Armstrong was one of the most important figures in twentieth-century music, . . . that he was the most im-portant of them all, for almost single-handedly he remodeled jazz and, as a consequence, had a critical effect on the kinds of music that came out of it: rock and its variants; the music of television, the movies, the theater; the tunes that lap endlessly at our ears in supermarkets, elevators, factories, offices; even the "classical" music of Copland, Milhaud, Poulenc, Honegger, and others (pp. 3-4).

Contrary to the prevailing myth, he was born Louis Armstrong in 1898; due to a dearth of records of black residents from the turn of the century, the exact date cannot be established, but the author's documentation makes clear the fact that Armstrong was not born on July 4, 1900, as he stated on his draft card at the beginning of World War I. Armstrong was raised largely by his paternal grandmother in the midst of New Orleans's black Storyville, near the Funky Butt and Odd Fellows halls where Buddy Bolden regularly played the new music that was to become jazz. When he was seven he returned to his mother's home to become, in large part, responsible for the care of his mother and younger sister. His early musical experiences also included performing on street corners in a quartet of local boys. His first experience with brass instruments came in the Colored Waif's Home where he had been sent in 1912 or 1913--which, the author theorizes, possibly restricted the development of his technical ability.

The book traces Armstrong's early musical development and Joe Oliver's sponsorship of him in his early New Orleans career; the possible musical influences on him of blues bands and the musicians Freddie Keppard, Buddy Bolden, and Buddie Petit; his playing on excursion riverboats with Fate Marable's band, where he learned to read music; his several unaccepted opportunities to leave New Orleans with bands led by Kid Ory and Fletcher Henderson; his move to Chicago in 1922 to join his mentor, Joe Oliver; his marriage to Lil Hardin and his leaving Oliver's band; his joining the Henderson band in New York in 1924 at the height of the Harlem Renaissance; his performance and recording as an accompanist for blues singers, including Bessie Smith; and his return to Chicago in 1925. In the latter year occurred the recording of the famous Hot Fives and Hot Sevens that were to influence the subsequent development of jazz. The late 1920s saw Armstrong's developing friendship and collaboration with Earl Hines and Zutty Singleton; the increasing frequency of his vocal performances; his return to New York to perform briefly with the Henderson orchestra; and his becoming a member of the band and a feature soloist with a show called Hot Chocolates.

After 1930 "the entertainer in Armstrong [often] took precedence over the jazz musician" (p. 219). He made the first two of his many international tours in 1932 and 1933. During the second tour he found himself stranded in Europe without a passport, but made an extended tour of England, Holland, and Scandinavia until he could return to the United States in 1935. During the rest of his career Armstrong continued to record and tour the United States and the world. He also starred in more than sixty films and made regular appearances on nationally broadcast radio and television shows, "including all of the most famous ones" (p. 312). He was made a State Department Ambassador of Goodwill beginning in 1960.

The book is filled with informative, effective, and revealing analyses of Armstrong's recorded output from the early 1920s to the late 1950s, including the Creole Jazz Band recordings (1923), recordings with the Fletcher Henderson band (1924), the Bessie Smith recordings (1925), the Hot Fives and Hot Sevens (1925-1928), the big band recordings (1929-1932), the 1933 Victor recordings, the Decca big band recordings (1935-1947), the All Star recordings of the Town Hall and Carnegie Hall concerts (1947), and the four Decca albums titled "Satchmo: A Musicial Autobiography of Louis Armstrong" (1956-1957). In the process the author examines Armstrong's playing and improvising style and the ongoing development of and changes in his style. The book includes discussions about how Armstrong's production of his music relates to who he was as a person.

In developing the story, the author corrects errors that abound in previous biographies of Armstrong and also successfully debunks several cherished myths of jazz history. Among the theories discussed in the book are: the nature of the origins of jazz in New Orleans; the development of jazz as an entertainment music for white audiences; the influence of radio on the development of jazz as early as 1923; the intertwining of the histories of jazz and the recording industry; the practice in jazz of detaching the melody line from the ground beat; the critical importance of the blues to the development of jazz; the influence of organized crime on the development of jazz and the interactions between gangsters and musicians; the notion that early jazz was appreciated only by blacks and European whites and that the socialist-oriented left-wing press contributed to the creation and continuation of that notion; and the process of the fall of the big bands in favor of small groups and vocalists. The author's ongoing discussions of jazz rhythm are an informative and provocative bonus.

Reviews: Best Sellers 43:326 D '83; Billboard 96:38 Ja 14 '84; Booklist 80:125 S 15 '83; Canadian Forum 63:35 F '84; Choice 21:830 F '84; Christian Science Monitor 75:B6 N 4 '83; Down Beat 51:69 Ju '84; Jazz Studies 3:193-198 '85; Jazz Times p12 F '84; Kirkus Reviews 51:858 Au 1 '83; Library Journal 108:2161 N 15 '83; Los Angeles Times Book Review p12 N 20 '83; Nation 237:675 D 24 '83; New Leader 66:11 D 26 '83; New

Louis Armstrong

Republic 190:34 Ja 30 '84; New Statesman 107:29
My 11 '84; New York Times 133:13 O 8 '83; New
York Times Book Review 88:12 O 30 '83; Newsweek
102:83 O 10 '83; Publishers Weekly 224:376 Au 26
'83; Times Literary Supplement p490 My 4 '84;
Village Voice 29:44 Ap 3 '84; Wall Street
Journal 202:28 O 27 '83 West Coast Review of
Books 9:40 N '83;

Collier, James Lincoln. Louis Armstrong: An American
Success Story. New York: Macmillan, 1985. 165 pp.
photographs. index.

Written for younger readers, this book treats
Armstrong's life from his youth to the early 1940s,
with a postscript statement about events at the end
of his life. The reader learns of Armstrong's
childhood in New Orleans; his schooling at the Fisk
School and the Colored Waif's Home; his early
musical experiences in the band at the Waif's Home
and in New Orleans after his release from the
home. Later-life experiences treated include his
becoming a protégé of Joe Oliver; his experiences
playing on Mississippi riverboats with Fate
Marable; his move to Chicago to join Oliver's band;
his marriage to Lil Hardin; his short tenure with
Fletcher Henderson's New York orchestra and the
recordings with Bessie Smith; his return to Chicago
and the Hot Five and Hot Seven recordings; his
second move to New York, to perform in Connie's
Inn; his tours of Europe in 1932 and 1933; and the
beginnings of his film career with Pennies from
Heaven (1936). In addition to information about
Armstrong and his career, the young reader will
learn about the circumstances and conditions of
being black and poor in America at the turn of the
century; the musical traditions of New Orleans,
including marches, quadrilles, popular songs,
ragtime, and the blues; and the development of
ragtime and jazz to the 1920s.

Reviews: Best Sellers 45:237 S '85; Booklist
82:219 O 1 '85; Center for Children's Books
Bulletin 39:44 N '85; Horn Book Magazine 61:462
Jy '85; Jazz Journal International 38:24 Jy '85;
Kirkus Reviews 53:J20 Mr 1 '85; Public
Administration Review 60:66 N '85; Publishers
Weekly 227:68 Jy 5 '85; School Library Journal
32:169 O '85; Voice of Youth Advocates 8:330 D
'85

Louis Armstrong

Goffin, Robert. <u>Horn of Plenty: The Story of Louis</u>
<u>Armstrong</u>. Translated by James F. Bezou. New York: Allen,
Town & Heath, 1947. 304 pp. photographs.

This somewhat fanciful, patronizing, and factually
unreliable book tells of the trumpeter's birth and
early life in squalid circumstances; his first job,
selling newspapers, when he was seven; his growing
up as a "street urchin" who spent most of his spare
time listening to the music of early jazzmen such
as Buddy Bolden, Bunk Johnson, and Freddie Keppard;
details of his singing-quartet activities as a
youth; events of and surrounding his detention in a
"waif's home" and the musical precocity he revealed
and developed while there; the ups and downs of his
pre-professional career; his meeting and
relationship with Joe Oliver; and his start as a
professional at Matranga's Saloon.

Following discussions of voodoo and other
matters, the author treats Armstrong's rise "to the
pinnacle of local fame" when he joined the Kid Ory
Band (p. 32); his period on the riverboats during
which he "learned to read music, . . . perfected
his technique," and established his reputation
along the Mississippi (p. 140); and his joining Joe
Oliver's band in Chicago, his life there, and the
fame he achieved as "the best trumpet player in the
country" (p. 177). In 1924 Armstrong joined the
Fletcher Henderson band in New York. The details of
that short stint are discussed, as well as
Armstrong's influence on other musicians of that
period. The author discusses the apparent thoughts
and motivations of the trumpeter; his permanent
move to New York, where he starred in musicals and
revues and fronted a new band; his triumphant
return to New Orleans as an internationally famous
personality; and his subsequent and highly
successful trips to England and the continent in
1932 and 1933.

Reviews: Chicago Sun Times Book Week p6 Ju 1
'47; Library Journal 72:641 Ap 15 '47; New York
Times p32 My 4 '47; San Francisco Chronicle p24
My 25 '47

Hoskins, Robert. <u>Louis Armstrong: Biography of a Musician</u>.
Los Angeles: Holloway House, 1979. 222 pp. filmography.
discography.

Written in the form and style of a novel, this book
is somewhat derivative, but it points out,

Louis Armstrong

corrects, reconciles, and synthesizes conflicting versions of events among previous writings. The work effectively compresses the events in Armstrong's life and career--information that is included in previous versions of the Armstrong story--and also presents new information, including a third version of how Armstrong got his first cornet and the name of the first feature movie in which Armstrong appeared--Ex-Flame. A single chapter is devoted to Armstrong's activities as an "ambassador of jazz," a goodwill representative of his country on trips to Europe, Africa, South America, and the Far East, where he performed for massive audiences. The author also tells of the 1947 formation of the Louis Armstrong All-Stars and how they toured the world from 1961 on--"Africa, Australia, New Zealand, Mexico, Iceland, India, Singapore, Korea, Hawaii, Japan, Hong Kong, Formosa, East and West Germany, Czechoslovakia, Romania, Yugoslavia, Hungary, France, Holland, Scandinavia, and Great Britain" (p. 197). The film-ography comprises annotations of "almost forty motion pictures, ranging from one-reel short subjects and animated cartoons to major musicals" (p. 209). The discography is an extremely brief sampling of the "more than twenty-five hundred sides [that Armstrong cut] during his long recording career, including hundreds of appearances as a back-up man for other artists" (p. 221).

Reviews: Billboard 92:118 Mr 29 '80; Orkester Journalen 49:2+ F '81

Jones, Max, and John Chilton. Louis: The Louis Armstrong Story, 1900-1971. London: Studio Vista, 1971. 256 pp. photograph. filmography. index.

This book compresses, streamlines, expands upon, debunks, confirms, and convincingly corrects various of the events and information contained in previous writings on the subject. It begins with a review of Armstrong's activities and musical contributions as an Ambassador of Jazz and of his childhood in New Orleans. While stressing the details of his association with Joe Oliver, the authors also present Armstrong in his early career as "moving steadily up a ladder whose base was held by Lil Armstrong, watching him climb" (p. 79); as a jazz innovator during 1922-1925, when he played with Fletcher Henderson and made the Blue Five and Red Onion Jazz Babies recordings, and during 1925-1928 when he "cut more than 60 titles with his own small groups" and as a sideman on dates of other musicians (p. 94); as an "interpreter of popular songs" during 1929-1931 (p. 105); and as an individual name attraction. The reader glimpses Armstrong's stay in Chicago during 1930-1931, his return to Chicago in the latter year, and his episodes with gangsters. The authors demonstrate that Armstrong, by 1933, was famous in England while "virtually unknown to the theater public here" (p. 144); in this regard, details of and insights into his 1934 visit to Europe are revealed. There are also discussions of: the formation of the Louis Armstrong All-Stars and their impact on the trumpeter's art and career; Armstrong as goodwill ambassador; Armstrong's handling of his public relations, his rehearsals, and his health; and his attachment and ritualistic relationship to his instrument.

Following treatment of the final chapter of Armstrong's life and his funeral, the authors review their subject's impact as one who was known and loved, for most of his working life, "as much for his stagecraft and humor as for his musicality . . . [as one who] possessed immense personal charm and a special kind of courtesy which enabled him to get on well with people of almost every type and nationality" (p. 202). This section consists of stories and anecdotes of events of a personal nature, meant to reveal Armstrong's humanity. Then the authors allow Armstrong to present his own severely condensed but effective overview of his life and career, with comments on his social and religious values. Finally, in a chapter titled "Louis On Record," Chilton briefly reviews and evaluates Armstrong's entire recorded output. The book ends with an almost-fifty-year chronology of Armstrong's activities as a jazzman and with a "Film List" that covers the years 1931-1969, when the trumpeter appeared in thirty-seven short and feature films.

Reviews: Best Sellers 31:347 N 1 '71; Choice 9:655 Jy/Au '72; Crescendo International 10:15 N '71; Down Beat 39:37 Ap 13 '72; Guardian Weekly 105:24 O 30 '71; Jazz & Blues 1:9 Ja '72; Jazz Forum n21:71 F '73; Jazz Research 3/4:261 '71/'72; Melody Maker 46:40 O 16 '71; Music Journal 30:82 Mr '72; Library Journal 97:200 Ja 15 '72; Listener 86:909 D 30 '71; New Statesman 83:117 Ja 28 '72; National Review 24:601 My 26 '72; Observer (London) p32 O 10 '71; Orkester

Louis Armstrong

Journalen 40:2 Ja '72;   Punch 261:542 O 20 '71;
Second Line 24:17 Summer '72

McCarthy,   Albert. Louis   Armstrong. Kings   of   Jazz. New
York: A. S. Barnes, 1961. 81 pp. photographs. discography.

This   is   a   brief   review   and   outline   of   the
trumpeter's career, with emphasis on the post-1922
years. Focusing on selected recorded performances
and developmental stages in Armstrong's career, the
author   touches   on   key   milestones: the   first
recorded   vocal by the trumpeter in February,   1925
("Everybody   Loves   My   Baby" on   the   Regal   label);
Armstrong's appearance in the revue Hot   Chocolates
in 1929, after which he became "a   stage   and   show
personality in his own right" (p. 32); his   logical
building   of   his   upper-register   endings;   his
"maximum influence on other musicians" during   the
1930s (p. 42); his   shift in 1935 from "the   pure
virtuoso   phase" to   a   "direction   of   greater
simplicity" (p. 46); his conscious   effort,   from
1937 on, to appeal to   a   wider   public; and   the
period of   the   Louis   Armstrong   All-Stars,   which
"brought   the   greatest   commercial   success   to
Armstrong and has made him the best known jazz
musician in the world" (p. 65).

Meryman, Richard. Louis Armstrong--A Self-Portrait. paperback. New York: Eakins Press, 1966. 59 pp. photographs.

This interview appeared originally in Life magazine
and is given here in Armstrong's own words. It
begins with Armstrong's childhood: "When   I   was
about 4 or 5, still wearing dresses, I lived with
my mother in Jane's Alley in a place called Brick
Row--a lot of cement, rented rooms sort of like a
motel. And   right in the middle of that on Perdido
Street was the   Funky   Butt   Hall--old, beat up, big
cracks   in   the   wall" (p. 7). He   describes   the
activities that surrounded funerals in New Orleans
and the music created by bands, including those of
King Joe Oliver, Kid   Ory, and John Robichaux; and
he tells of the events of the New Year's Eve that
ended with his stay in the Waif's Home, where he
learned to play cornet (p. 11). After his release
from   the   Home, Armstrong   began   to   play
professionally in   the   local   honky-tonks   and
eventually "with Fate Marable's band   on   the
riverboat Sidney" (p. 25).

Louis Armstrong

In 1922 Joe Oliver sent for Armstrong to come to
Chicago and join his band, which was playing in the
Lincoln Gardens. After a short stint in New York
with the Fletcher Henderson band, he returned to
Chicago, where he made the famous Hot Five and Hot
Seven recordings that changed the course of jazz.
He speaks about his managers, Joe Glaser and Johnny
Collins, and about financial problems caused by the
latter; about his heart attack in Spoleto, Italy;
and about his world travels. He sums up his life's
work and attitudes: "All those years that trumpet
comes before everything--even before my wife
Lucille. Had to be that way. I mean, I love her
because she understand that. So I'm entitled now
to spend a few years hearing some other cats--maybe
bring back those old eras for myself" (p. 47).

Reviews: AB Bookman's Weekly 48:1238 O 25 '71;
Choice 9:377 My '72; Library Journal 96:3749 N
15 '71

Panassie, Hughes. Louis Armstrong. Photograph collection
by Jack Bradley. New York: Charles Scribner's Sons, 1971.
148 pp. photographs. discography.

Divided into three main sections, this book treats
"The Man," "The Style," and "The Music of Louis
Armstrong on Records." The first section gives
attention to his life and career; the second is an
insightful and provocative discussion of the
trumpeter's musical and technical contributions;
and the third is a brief survey and description of
Armstrong's recorded output. While it appears to
be a condensation and summary of the information
found in previous books and articles on Armstrong,
some of the information in this succinct volume
differs from that in others, and some of it
illuminates certain points and events found in
preceding biographies. This brief overview of
Armstrong's life and achievements begins with the
1913 New Year's Eve incident that led to his
detention, at twelve, in a reformatory for a year
and a half, then goes on to mention Armstrong's
riverboat-band experience; his joining the Kid Ory
band at seventeen; his move to Chicago, at
twenty-two, to join King Oliver's band; his sojourn
and triumphs in New York in 1924 and later; his
marriages to Irene, to Daisy in 1917, to Lil in
1924, and to Lucille in 1942; his trips to Europe
in 1932, 1933, 1948, 1950, 1952, 1955, 1957, 1959,
several times in the 1960s, and his tour of Africa
in 1960; his many trips to California, where he

played and acted in such films as <u>Pennies from Heaven</u>, <u>Every Day's A Holiday</u>, <u>Artists and Models</u>, <u>Doctor Rhythm</u>, <u>Goin' Places</u>, <u>Jam Session</u>, <u>Atlantic City</u>, <u>Cabin in the Sky</u>, <u>A Song is Born</u>, and <u>The Beat Generation</u>.

Of Armstrong's Chicago years, Panassie writes:

> Although he was loaded with work--recordings in the morning, afternoon and evening, engagements at the Vendome Theater, and afterward at the Sunset--Louis Armstrong had such endurance and loved playing so much that when his work at the Sunset was finished he would go to other clubs with a groups of musicians and play for hours, improvising ten, fifteen, twenty choruses in a row, surrounded by enthusiasts shouting with joy or crying with emotion. Some, after hearing Louis play, could not or did not want to speak for several days--the experience had been so moving. Louis did not go to bed until late each morning, if he had time, which was not always the case (p. 16).

Also given attention are his personal relationships with and behavior toward others; his preferences in women; and his orientation on matters of racism and race relations. Of Armstrong as a celebrity, the author points out that Armstrong reached the pinnacle of his fame in 1948-1949 when "even in New York he could no longer walk about without immediately being recognized and causing a crowd to gather" and when "he was named an honorary citizen of New Orleans" (pp. 28, 29). The author characterizes Armstrong as one who gave "an impression of strength, of command, of spontaneity, of triumphant power and a love of life wherever it may be. Louis Armstrong's presence in all circumstances radiates dynamic enthusiasm" (p. 13). The discography lists "The Best of Louis Armstrong On LP Available" and "Important Records by Louis Armstrong Which Are Available."

Reviews: AB Bookman's Weekly 49:589 F 21 '72; America 125:324 O 23 '71; Best Sellers 31:346 N 1 '71; Best Sellers 34:23 Ap 1 '74; Choice 9:377 My '72; Down Beat 39:37 Ap '72; Instrumentalist 26:21 N '71; Jazz Digest 1:26 Ja/F '72; Kirkus Reviews 39:921 Au 15 '71; Notes 29:454-455 n3

'73; Music Journal 29:67 N '71; Orkester
Journalen 41:10 My '73; Publishers Weekly 200:66
S 13 '71; Second Line 25:28-29 Fall '71

SELECTIVE DISCOGRAPHY

The Best of Louis Armstrong. MCA MCA2-4035.
Louis Armstrong and Earl Hines. Smithsonian Collection
   R-002, 1928.
Louis Armstrong and His Hot Five. Columbia CL-851.
Louis Armstrong and His Hot Seven. Columbia CL-852.
Louis Armstrong and His Orchestra. Fontana TFR-17073/
   17106, 1920-1930.
Louis Armstrong, Jazz Masterpieces. Franklin Mint Record
   Society FM-001, 1925-1965.
Louis Armstrong, July 4, 1900/July 6, 1971. RCA VPM-6044.
The Louis Armstrong Story. 12 vols. Columbia CL-851,
   1925-1927.
Satchmo--Autobiography. 4 vols. MCA MCA-10006.
Satchmo Collector's Items. Decca DL-8327.

Pearl Bailey

Bailey, Pearl. <u>The Raw Pearl</u>. New York: Pocket Books, 1969. 189 pp. photographs.

This autobiography begins with the singer's telling of her being a product of a broken home and a somewhat unsettled childhood in Washington, D.C., her winning of amateur contests in Philadelphia and at New York's Apollo Theater while still a teenager, and her job away from home as an entertainer in a Pennsylvania mining town. As a young professional, Bailey joined the Edgar Hayes Orchestra following her stint in the mining town, singing with the band at New York's Savoy Ballroom and Apollo Theater. Then came her association with the Royal Band at Baltimore's Royal Theater, followed by appearances at other locations as a single. The latter were interrupted by World War II, during which she made U.S.O. tours. Later she joined the Cootie Williams Band. By the mid-forties Bailey was getting star billing, performing at choice venues and with major bands such as Cab Calloway's. In 1946 she made her first dramatic appearance with a small part in <u>St. Louis Woman</u>, for which she won the Donaldson Award. Bailey's first movie was <u>Variety Girl</u>; others followed: <u>That Certain Feeling</u>, <u>St. Louis Blues</u>, <u>Fine Young Cannibals</u>, <u>Porgy and Bess</u>, <u>Carmen Jones</u>. In 1954 Bailey and her husband, Louis Bellson, bought a ranch in California and enjoyed country living for nine years before moving back to the city. As she tells her story, Bailey also touches on the high and low points of her personal life; her relationships with other black and white show-business personalities, such as Bob Hope, Frank Sinatra, Tony Bennett, Sophie Tucker, Sammy Davis, Jr., Duke Ellington, Nat King Cole, Ella Fitzgerald, and Humphrey Bogart, as well as a President of the United States--Dwight D. Eisenhower; her marriages; her children; her views on life, interpersonal relationships, and childrearing; and details of her illness and the resulting spiritual growth in 1964.

Reviews: Best Sellers 28:242 S 15 '68; Best Sellers 31:495 F 1 '72; Books & Bookmen 18:88 D '72; Library Journal 93:2648 Jy '68; Library Journal 93:4429 N 15 '68; Kirkus Reviews 36:724 Jy 1 '68; National Observer 7:21 O 28 '68; Negro Digest 18:85 Ap '69; Reference Services Review 11:10 Spring '83; Saturday Review 52:47 F 22 '69; Travel-Holiday 44:39 O '68

SELECTIVE DISCOGRAPHY

Back on Broadway. Roulette 42002.
Echoes of an Era: The Pearl Bailey Years. Roulette RE-101.
Pearl Bailey Sings the Cole Porter Songbook. Roulette 42004.
Songs of the Bad Old Days. Roulette 5004.

Josephine Baker

Baker, Josephine, and Jo Bouillon. <u>Josephine</u>. Translated by Mariana Fitzpatrick. New York: Harper & Row, 1977. xiii, 302 pp. photographs, drawings. index.

This book is Josephine Baker's autobiography, completed after her death by her husband. Written in a conversational style, the material written by Baker herself is supplemented with statements by her friends and co-workers. In the book, we learn of her poor childhood in St. Louis; her tenure in the casts of <u>Shuffle Along</u> and <u>Chocolate Dandies</u>; her performance at The Plantation Club, where she stood in for Ethel Waters when the star was ill and where she gained the attention that allowed her later development; her appearance in Paris in the <u>Revue Nègre</u>; her starring role in the <u>Folies-Bergère</u>; appearances in Offenbach's <u>La Creole</u>; her worldwide tours; her return to New York to appear in The Ziegfeld Follies and the less-than-enthusiastic reception she experienced; and her several "farewell" and "comeback" appearances, including the final smashing success at the Bobino in Paris when she was in her late sixties. Baker tells of her relationship with Count Pepito Abatino, who became her manager; her short-lived marriage to Jean Leon; and her marriage to Jo Bouillon and its dissolution. Also included in the book are accounts of her humanitarian efforts, including her contributions as a performer and intelligence gatherer for France during World War II; the adoption of her "Rainbow Tribe"--twelve children of various races and nationalities--

gathered with the intention of proving to the world that people of all races can live together without rancor; her long-standing struggles for racial equality in the United States and in the world; and her dreams of founding a "College of Brotherhood." Woven through the narrative are accounts of her early increase in wealth and stature, crowned by the purchase and renovation of her estate, Les Milandes, and the financial difficulties that resulted from, among other things, her commitment to her Rainbow Tribe and humanitarian efforts.

Reviews: Best Sellers 37:273 D '77; Book World pE8 D 10 '78; Booklist 74:122 S 15 '77; Kirkus Reviews 45:887 Au 15 '77; Library Journal 102:2054 O 1 '77; New York Times Book Review p26 N 6 '77; New Yorker 53:70+ D 26 '77; Newsweek 90:106 O 31 '77; Publishers Weekly 212:361 Au 29 '77; Times Literary Supplement p904 Au 11 '78; Variety 288:6 O 26 '77

Haney, Lynn. Naked at the Feast: A Biography of Josephine Baker. New York: Dodd, Mead, 1981. xiii, 338 pp. photographs. bibliography. index.

An extremely informative work, this book is a portrait and life story of an Afro-American singer/dancer/entertainer who took Paris by storm in the 1920s and finished her career in her adopted country in 1975, singing and dancing in a production--Josephine--that was a tribute to her more than fifty years in show business. Baker was a "deity of the Folies-Bergère," "an international symbol of Parisian wickedness," and, as a singer and dancer, "a down-home shouter, a yeller, a hollerer" (pp. xii, xii, xiii). Haney informs us that Baker was born in 1906 and spent her early years in St. Louis, Missouri, in dire poverty; was street smart at six; was "filled with rebellion" and waiting tables in a night club when on the threshold of adolescence (p. 23); and joined the Jones Family Band as a singer and dancer while still a child, touring the Theater Owners' Booking Association (T.O.B.A.) circuit, first with the Joneses and later with the Dixie Steppers, seeing, hearing, and meeting such stars as singers Ethel Waters and Clara Smith and pianist Eubie Blake. At fifteen she joined the cast of Shuffle Along and later the company of Chocolate Dandies.

In 1925 Baker left the United States for Paris, traveling with a new show titled La Revue Nègre,

performing to musical accompaniments by the Claude
Hopkins band, which then included Sidney Bechet,
Clarence Williams, and other well-known black
musicians. In her Paris debut, she conquered the
city; and she remained there for the rest of her
life, leaving only to tour and to visit other
countries. Living in Paris as a celebrity
entertainer and as a "notorious character," she
also posed for Picasso, knew Hemingway, Colette,
and other artists and socialites, was advised by
Bricktop, and became immersed in haute couture and
the Paris fashion world (p. 90). In 1926 she joined
the Folies-Bergere and established her night club,
Chez Josephine, in Montparnasse; and she was then
only "twenty years old, basking in the comforting
glow of money, rapturous attention, fame and young
success" (p. 124). As a singer she was not
immediately successful, but she did later grow into
an effective stylist.

During 1928-1929, we learn, she made her first
world tour, encountering acclaim as well as strong
racial prejudice and rejection in some countries.
It was in 1928 that she acquired her theme song,
"J'ai deux amours" ("Two Loves Have I"), "which she
sang at every performance she gave for the rest of
her life" (p. 162). She made other tours in 1927
and 1933 and, between 1931 and 1935, cut over a
dozen records, with "J'ai deux amours" selling more
than 300,000 copies. In 1935 she made her first
visit to the United States, where she played in the
Ziegfeld Follies, attended the premiere of Porgy
and Bess, and traveled to Chicago and St. Louis to
visit her relatives. When war was imminent in
Europe in 1940, she became an undercover agent for
the French Military Secret Police and also joined
the French Resistance; the author tells of Baker's
adventures in her role as an undercover soldier and
of her being awarded the French Lègion d'Honneur
and the Mèdaille de la Resistance.

Following the war Baker returned to her career,
touring Europe and the Americas and emerging as "a
woman of substance" (p. 246): fighting racial
discrimination while traveling in the United States
in 1948 and 1951, integrating audiences, receiving
unprecedented accolades and tributes for her
appearances, winning the NAACP's Most Outstanding
Woman of the Year Award of 1951, being rejected by
many white and black Americans for her
extraordinary views on race and politics, and
returning to France to establish her own small

fiefdom on her second estate, Les Milandes. In 1973 she returned again to the United States to participate in the March on Washington and gave a triumphant benefit for SNCC, CORE, and NAACP.

In 1969, at sixty-two, she lost her entire estate and was virtually penniless. Back in the United States in 1963, almost seventy years old, she made a comeback with a Carnegie Hall appearance that proved to be "one of the high spots of her career" (p. 303). In 1974 Baker appeared in Josephine, a musical based on her life; it was a final, triumphant, smash hit. In 1975 she died in her sleep, "of joy," during the show's run (p. 324). In telling this fascinating story, the author also tells of Baker's extravagance and self-indulgence; her thirty-two-room mansion at Le Vèsinet; her lovers and her husbands; her appearance in Offenbach's operetta La Crèole; her relationships with internationally known entertainers, musicians, socialites, and world leaders; and her adoption of twelve children of different races and creeds in order "to prove to the world that everybody can live together in harmony" (p. 269).

Reviews: Black Books Bulletin 7:56 n3 '81; Booklist 77:377 N 1 '80; Jazz Journal International 34:21 O '81; Kirkus Reviews 48:1609 D 15 '80; Library Journal 106:71 Ja 1 '81; New York Times Book Review 86:13 Mr 29 '81; Observer p33 Ju 28 '81; Publishers Weekly 218:44 D 19 '80; Reference Services Review 11:10 Spring '83; Time 117:92 My 25 '81; Times Literary Supplement p750 Jy 3 '81; Wilson Library Bulletin 55:705 My '81

Papich, Stephen. Remembering Josephine. Indianapolis: Bobbs-Merrill, 1976. xviii, 237 pp. photographs. index.

Written by a man who served as Josephine's musical director at the close of her career, this book concentrates not on the biographical details of dates and figures but on a picture of Josephine the person. As the author states, "When speaking or writing about a famous personality of the theatre, it is difficult to separate fact from illusion. If you pursue 'facts' as diligently as I suppose one should, then you invariably lose something of the aura that surrounds the great stars. For it is just this illusion, this aura, that made them great" (p. xviii). Written in conversational, anecdotal style and using frequent flashbacks, the author's reminiscences are supplemented by Baker's story-telling and correspondence about events in her early life. Included are accounts of the St. Louis race riot that occurred in her youth; her first professional experiences with Bessie Smith, in the chorus line at the Cotton Club, in the casts of <u>Shuffle Along</u> and other Broadway shows; and her Paris appearances in the <u>Revue Nègre</u> and the <u>Folies-Bergère</u>. The reader learns of her love affair with Gustav VI, Adolf, Crown Prince of Sweden; the circumstances of the writing of her theme song, "J'ai deux amours"; the first of her world tours; her disastrous appearance in the Ziegfeld Follies in 1936 and the racial slights that accompanied it; her short film career; and the establishment of her several <u>Chez Josephine</u> cabarets.

Treating Baker's experiences and contributions during World War II, the author relates the incident of her moving her valuable possessions out of France before the Nazi invasion, thereby saving her fortune. During the war, she was a member of the Maquis, the leaders of the French Resistance. We learn of her lengthy illness after Herman Göring tried to poison her (Göring had commandeered her home upon his entry into Paris). The years following the war were focused on her humanitarian dream of establishing a home for her multiracial, multinational adopted children, an effort to prove to the world the practicality of brotherly love; the purchase of her estate, Les Milandes and her eventual bankruptcy caused by her effort to sustain and improve it. The last years of her life saw her spectacular comeback in the United States and in Paris, begun at Carnegie Hall and concluded at the Bobino Music Hall only two days before her death.

Reviews: BooksWest 1:26 Ap '77; Library Journal 101:2365 N 15 '76; New York Times Book Review p5 D 12 '76; Publishers Weekly 210:93 S 13 '76; Variety 285:82 Ja 26 '77; West Coast Review of Books 3:30 Mr '77

SELECTIVE DISCOGRAPHY

"Dangerous Blues"/"I Want Some Loving Blues." Phantasie 17201.

Count Basie

Horricks, Raymond. <u>Count Basie and His Orchestra: Its Music and Musicians</u>. Discography by Alun Morgan. New York: Citadel Press, 1957. 320 pp. photographs. discography.

This work is intended as "a survey of the Count Basie Orchestra's twenty years or more of existence, examining not only the personal fortunes of the leader but also something of the band's highly-individual style of playing and of the important musicians who have passed through its ranks and aided the Count in making such a style of expression possible" (p. 6). In this regard the author points out that "to hear the band play is to sense Basie himself feeling and thinking and speaking, shaping its overall style according to his own nature, giving its policy his own ideals" (p. 17). As far as Basie's life and work are concerned, the author treats such topics as "Basie the Leader," "The Kansas City Melting Pot," and "Basie the Pianist." Throughout these chapters, Basie's personality, character, and leadership qualities are illuminated with quotes from Ernie Wilkins, Basie's arranger before and at the time this book was written. Wilkins gives anecdotes relating to events and incidents in the life of the Basie band; they are revealing and add spice to the book. The author himself observes that Basie "incites friendship with his ready humour and warm sympathy. . . . He has a warm wit . . . and it is noticeable that people laugh with him" (p. 19). Comments are made about Basie's appetite for food, his being "awarded the 'title' of Count in 1936 by

a Kansas City radio personality," Kansas City jam
sessions, Basie's all-star septet of 1950-1951, his
study with Fats Waller, and problems with Jim Crow.

The author emphasizes that, with the Basie band,
"an enormous smelting process took place, and the
music which ultimately emerged was without
precedent in jazz," a music which had the blues as
its most important component and which ultimately
became responsible for the emergence of the swing
era (p. 36). The remaining chapters are devoted to
short biographical sketches of fifty-five of the
sidemen who played with the Basie band between 1935
and 1957, including Buck Clayton, Lester Young,
Clark Terry, Wardell Gray, Thad Jones, Marshall
Royal, Joe Williams, and Benny Powell.

Reviews: Gramophone 35:81 Jy '57; High Fidelity
8:16 Jy '58; Jazz Journal 10:10 Jy '57; Jazz
Review 1:44 D '58; Library Journal 83:773 Mr 1
'58; Melody Maker 32:3 My 18 '57; New Statesman
54:155 Au 3 '57; New York Times p16 F 23 '58;
Orkester Journalen 25:13 O '57; San Francisco
Chronicle p23 F 23 '58

SELECTIVE DISCOGRAPHY

Afrique. Doctor Jazz FW-39520.
At the Savoy. Archives FS-318.
Basie Big Band. Pablo 2310-756.
Benny Moten's Great Band of 1930-32. RCA LPV-514,
   1929-1932.
The Best of Count Basie. MCA MCA2-4050, 1937-1939.
Count Basie and the Kansas City Seven. Impulse AS-15.
The Count at the Chatterbox. Jazz Archives JA-16, 1974.
Count Basie Swings/Joe Williams Sings. Verve V-68488.
Count Basie Swings, Joe Williams Sings. Verve 825770-1.
The Count Basie Years. Roulette RE-102, c1960.
Good Morning Blues. MCA MCA2-4102, 1937-1939.
Kansas City Suite. Roulette RE-124.
On the Road. Pablo GS-2048.
One O'Clock Jump. Columbia JCL-997.
Retrospective Sessions: Dedication Series, XI. Impulse
   IA-9351/2, 1962, 1969.
Sixteen Men Swinging. Verve V-2-2517, 1953-1954.
Super Chief. Columbia CG-31224.

Sidney Bechet

Bechet, Sidney. <u>Treat It Gentle</u>. Foreword by Desmond Flower. New York: Hill and Wang, 1960. vi, 245 pp. photographs. discography. index.

Put into book form by Desmond Flower, all the material in the pages of this work was dictated by Bechet and recorded on tape by Joan Reid. The autobiography discusses the career of this jazz clarinetist/soprano saxophonist, from his grand-parents' experiences in slavery to his contentment in old age, when he was dedicated to the perpetuation of the art form that had brought him a good life. He treats of bucking contests, funerals, and the second line in New Orleans; his brief studies, in his formative years, with George Baquet, Big Eye Louis Nelson, and Lorenzo Tio; his residencies with the Young Olympia Band, John Robichaux's Orchestra, and the Eagle Orchestra; performing, around 1913, with Bunk Johnson, Louis Armstrong, and Joe Oliver; influencing Johnny Dodds, Jimmy Noone, Albert Nicholas, Larry Shields, and others; hearing Freddie Keppard in his best years; and his move to Chicago in 1917.

The book also contains information on and about Bechet's encounters with other black musicians of the period, such as Clarence Williams, Armand J. Piron, Will Marion Cook, the Swiss conductor Ernest Ansermet, and Perry Bradford; his introduction to Europe as a member of Cook's Southern Syncopated Orchestra in 1918 or 1919; his tours with Bessie Smith in the show <u>How Come</u>; his performance stints

with James P. Johnson, Duke Ellington, Louis Armstrong, Noble Sissle, and Lorenzo Tio; and the
formation of his own band, with Tommy Ladnier, in
1932. Bechet also talks candidly about his
deportation from England, his participation in Revue
Negre during 1925 in Paris, Brussels, and Berlin; and
of events surrounding his eleven-month prison
sentence in 1928 in Paris. Bechet offers a different
version of the Bunk Johnson "rediscovery" story as
told in Bethell and Fairbairn (see pp. 196 and 197,
respectively); and tells of his permanent move to
Paris in 1949 and his subsequent occasional visits to
the United States.

In discussing performer/performer and performer/
audience relations, Bechet remembers New Orleans as
"a place where the music was natural as the air. The
people were ready for it like it was sun and rain. A
musicianer, when he played in New Orleans, was home;
and the music, when he played it, would go right to
where he sent it. The people there were waiting for
it, they were wanting it" (p. 215). He sums up his
aesthetic philosophy as follows:

> All the beauty that there's ever been,
> it's moving inside that music. Omar's
> voice, that's there, and the girl's voice,
> and the voice the wind had in Africa, and
> the cries from Congo Square, and the fine
> shouting that came up from Free Day. The
> blues, and the spirituals, and the
> remembering, and the waiting, and the
> suffering, and the looking at the sky
> watching the dark come down--that's all
> inside the music. And somehow when the
> music is played right it does an explaining
> of all those things. Me, I want to explain
> myself so bad. I want to have myself
> understood. And the music, it can do
> that. The music, it's my whole story"
> (p. 218).

Reviews: Booklist 57:178 N 15 '60; Chicago Sunday
Tribune p9 D 11 '60; Down Beat 28:46 F 16 '61;
Guardian Weekly p15 Ap 8 '60; Jazz Journal 13:15 Jy
'60; Jazz Monthly 6:25-26 Ju '60; Jazz Monthly 8:24
S '62; Kirkus Reviews 28:712 Au 15 '60; Library
Journal 85:3977 N 1 '60; Melody Maker 35:5 Ap 23
'60; Metronome 78:30-31 Mr '61; New York Herald
Tribune Lively Arts p26 Ja 1 '61; New York Times

Sidney Bechet

Book Review 110:3 D 18 '60; Times Literary Supplement p252 Ap 22 '60

SELECTIVE DISCOGRAPHY

Bechet. GNP Crescendo GNP-9012.
Bechet of New Orleans. RCA LPV-510, 1932-1941.
The Blue Bechet. RCA LPV-535, 1932-1941.
The Fabulous Sidney Bechet. Blue Note BLP-7026.
The Greatest Jazz Recordings of All Time: Kings of New Orleans Jazz/Jelly Roll Morton, King Oliver, and Sidney Bechet. Franklin Mint Record Society Tapes 17-20, 1983.
Really the Blues. Vogue LAE-12017, 1945-1947.
Sidney Bechet. 2 vols. Everest FS-228/FS-323.
Sidney Bechet: In Memoriam. Riverside RLP12-138, 1940.
Sidney Bechet: Master Musician, 1938-1941. Bluebird AXM2-5516.
Sidney Bechet and His Blue Note Jazzmen. 10 vols. Vogue LDE-025, 1946-1950.
Sidney Bechet and His Feet Warmers. Esquire 20-058, 1949.
Sidney Bechet at Storyville. 10 vols. Vogue LDE-132, 1953.
Sidney Bechet Has Young Ideas. Inner City 7008, 1957.
Sidney Bechet Jazz Classics. 2 vols. Blue Note BLP-1201/2, 1939-1951.
Sidney Bechet Memorial. Fontana TFL-5087, 1923-1925.
The Sidney Bechet Story. Brunswick BL-54048, 1938-1956.

Harry Belafonte

Shaw, Arnold. Belafonte: An Unauthorized Biography. Philadelphia: Chilton, 1960. xiv, 338 pp. photographs. discography. index.

This is the story of a man who "made exciting theater of the folk ballad and became the first folk singer in entertainment history to command giant audiences," a sensitive man who rose from an underpriviliged childhood to become "the King of Calypso and the first Negro matinee idol" (p. 1, 6). Belafonte grew up in New York's Harlem and in Jamaica. In 1944 he joined the Navy; after his discharge he enrolled in a dramatic workshop with the intention of becoming an actor. He remained in the workshop two years, exploring "the exciting world of the theater . . . and the provocative world of books, of music, of culture" (p. 43). In 1948 he was married to his first wife, Margurite, a school teacher who continued to work while Belafonte struggled, to no avail, to make a place for himself in the dramatic world: "It was impossible . . . for me to get work in the theater. The closest I ever got to the Broadway stage was when I got an Equity card for a theater guild tryout in Westport, Connecticut. The show ran for three weeks but never got to Broadway" (p. 54). In 1949 he made his debut as a jazz singer at New York's Royal Roost (a jazz club where his appearance lasted for twenty weeks), made his first Carnegie Hall appearance, and cut his first commercial record. Gradually he moved from jazz singing to pop singing, then on to folk singing by 1950.

Living and working in Greenwich Village, "Harry occupied himself buying every folk record he could find. Weekends he would hop down to Washington and dig through the archives of the Library of Congress" (p. 78). In the Village, in his newly acquired coffee shop, he "found himself . . . with the help of the many characters who dropped in; under the stimulus of the nightly song fests; through his research in the folk song field" (p. 82). By late 1952 he had been accepted by his Village crowd and at Uptown's Blue Angel night club, and he had made a movie. He was also feeling his oats: "He was pedantic and almost babylike in the way he carried on about 'culture.' There was always the question, of what you were talking about meant 'ethically.' And each problem, no matter how minor, was approached with an intensity as if it were of earth-shaking import. He never really came off-stage" (p. 115).

By 1954 Belafonte had arrived as a professional singer, he "made his first starring movie, was featured in two theatrical productions, became a father for the first time, 'met' his wife-to-be, broke with his dedicated manager, and faced a crisis in his relationship with Margurite" (p. 130). In 1957 he was divorced, remarried, and also arrived as an international singing star. In the next year he made his first tour of Europe. In addition to telling of Belafonte's life through 1959, the author also treats his making of films such as The Bright Road, Carmen Jones, Island in the Sun, The World, the Flesh, and the Devil, and Odds Against Tomorrow; his activities as a producer; and his relationship to his children, his friends, and his business associates.

Reviews: Booklist 56:568 My 15 '60; Chicago Sunday Tribune p10 Ap 24 '60; Jazz Review 3:36 Jy '60; Kirkus Reviews 28:168 F 15 '60; Library Journal 85:1108 Mr 15 '60; Notes 17:408 n3 '60; New York Times Book Review p30 Ap 10 '60; San Francisco Chronicle p20 Ap 3 '60; Springfield Republican p40 Ap 17 '60; Theatre Arts 44:70 Ju '60; Variety 218:43 Mr 23 '60

SELECTIVE DISCOGRAPHY

An Evening with Belafonte. RCA Victor LPM-1402.
Harry Belafonte: Calypso. RCA Victor LPM-1248, 1956.
My Lord What a Mornin'. RCA LPM-2022, LSP-2022.
Porgy and Bess. RCA LOP-1507, LSO-1507.
To Wish You a Merry Christmas. RCA Victor LPM-1887,
    LSP-1887.

Chuck Berry

Reese, Krista. <u>Chuck Berry: Mr. Rock N' Roll</u>. London and
New York: Proteus Books, 1982. 127 pp. photographs.
discography.

> At Sumner High School in the 40s, Chuck
> Berry met an age he loved so much he
> would never leave it. It was while he
> was in his teens that he bought a used
> Spanish 6-string guitar for $4.00. He
> also taught himself piano and sax and met
> the woman he would later say was his
> first, biggest influence--his music
> teacher at Sumner, Julia Davis, who had
> helped him learn guitar. And when he was
> a junior, he started his All Men's
> Musical Review audience with a version of
> Joe Turner's "Confessin' the Blues"
> (p. 17).

It is against this background that Reese chronicles
the career of singer-guitarist Charles Edward
Anderson Berry, tracing his growth and development
from his birth in San Jose, California, in the
midst of the "Jazz Age" to his arrival as a rock &
roll star extraordinaire. Mention is made of
Berry's family's participation in the musical
activities of their church and of Berry's early
musical exposure and participation there; his early
exposure to and appreciation of rhymes--the basis
for his songwriting; his "stringent business
policies" (p. 41); his sometimes bizarre personal
behavior; and his reform-school or prison terms.

Chuck Berry

We learn that Berry studied cosmetology and
moonlighted as a hairdresser while working at an
automobile plant; that he joined the Johnny Johnson
Trio in the early 1950s and later took charge of
that band as his own; and that he followed the
routine of: "Write a song, tour with it, push it
till you get a hit, write another, tour with
it. . . ." (p. 24). Also discussed are the roles
played by talent scouts, major and independent
labels, and disk jockeys in the rise of rock &
roll; the public's reaction to it; rock in the
movies and the effects of film production
techniques on record production; 1950s "schlock
rock" (p. 54); and 1980s rock music manifestations. All of this is treated within the context
of the social, cultural, and technological
developments of the time and from the perspective
of Berry's hit-song output.

SELECTIVE DISCOGRAPHY

<u>After School Session</u>. Chess 1426, 1958.
<u>Bio</u>. Chess 50043, 1973.
<u>Chuck Berry's Greatest Hits</u>. Chess 1485, 1964.
<u>St. Louis to Frisco to Memphis</u>. Mercury SMR-2, 1972.
<u>Sweet Little Rock & Roller</u>. Pickwick 3345, 1967.

Eubie Blake

Carter, Lawrence T. <u>Eubie Blake: Keys of Memory</u>. Detroit:
Balamp Publishing, 1979. 116 pp. index.

This book consists of an undocumented series of
anecdotes about events that Blake took part in and
people whom he encountered between his birth in
1883 and 1946. Among the childhood stories
recounted are: Blake's attempt to play a pump organ
in a Baltimore market and the resulting purchase of
that instrument; early piano lessons from a
neighbor and from "Lewellen Wilson, a black
orchestra leader" (p. 26); early jobs at Aggie
Shelton's bordello, in Doc Frisbee's medicine show,
in a show called "In Old Kentucky," and at
Baltimore's Goldfield Hotel; employment at Barron
Wilkins's Little Savoy in New York and at parties
in Saratoga, New York; the production of <u>Shuffle
Along</u>; Blake's first European tour; and his
performances with Noble Sissle on the Keith Circuit
vaudeville tour. Among those whose relationships
with Blake are treated in the book are: Blake's
father and mother; his first wife Avis Lee; Joe
Gans; Madison Reed, Blake's first partner; Irving
Berlin and George M. Cohan; Willie the Lion Smith;
Luckey Roberts; James P. Johnson; Fats Waller;
James Reese Europe; Will Marion Cook; Noble Sissle;
Harry T. Burleigh; and Anton Dvořák.

Reviews: Cadence 6:15 S '80; Choice 17:397 My
'80; Orkester Journalen 49:2 F '81

Kimball, Robert, and William Bolcom. <u>Reminiscing with Sissle and Blake</u>. New York: Viking Press, 1973. 256 pp. photographs, music facsimiles, posters, charts. appendixes.

> This is a "story of great musical theater" as told by ·Noble Sissle and Eubie Blake and as elaborated on by the authors. The work chronicles the activities of Sissle and Blake from their first meeting in 1915 to the year 1973, when the book was published. It begins with a brief sketch of the history of black musical theater and progresses through Sissle and Blake's relationships with James Reese Europe, the team of Flournoy Miller and Aubry Lyles, and other black show-business personalities. It treats Sissle and Blake's development from a two-man vaudeville act into Broadway showmen and composers; James Reese Europe's influence on their careers; matters pertaining to <u>Shuffle Along</u>—its plot, its music, its initial tour, its success on Broadway, etc.; and information about the development and plots of other black musicals of the period, such as <u>In Bamville</u> (later to be named <u>Chocolate Dandies</u>), <u>Lew Leslie's Blackbirds of 1930</u>, <u>Shuffle Along of 1933</u>, and <u>Tan Manhattan</u>. The reader senses the "<u>zany</u> comedians, <u>beautiful</u> showgirls, <u>lavish</u> costumes, and many wonderful singers and dancers" of the Broadway of the 1920s (p. 6). Also highlighted are the musical contributions of James Reese Europe and his relationship to the white dance team of Irene and Vernon Castle. Mention is made of such show-business personalities as Josephine Baker, Florence Mills, Katherine Yarborough, Andy Razaf, and others. Included are reprints of letters and news clippings; large and striking photographs of significant events, groups, and individuals; and an appendix which includes lists of compositions, productions and films, a rollography, and a discography.

> Reviews: Best Sellers 33:113 Ju 1 '73; Jazz Journal 26:16 My '73; Jazz Report 8:32 n4 '73; Kirkus Reviews 41:378 Mr 15 '73; Library Journal 98:1822 Ju 1 '73; Music Journal 31:10 Annual '73; Newsweek 81:81 Ap 30 '73; Publishers Weekly 203:56 Mr 12 '73; Variety 271:43-44 Au 8 '73

Rose, Al. <u>Eubie Blake</u>. Foreword by Eubie Blake. New York: Schirmer Books, 1979. xvi, 214 pp. photographs. list of compositions. discography. piano rollography. filmography. index.

"By artistic effort, determination, and awesome talent, Eubie Blake became one of the small group of black performing artists who paved the way for blacks to demand and win acceptance and equality in the American entertainment industry, not only in billing and the right to perform in other than racially stereotyped roles but also in payment according to the standards of white artists. This book sets these accomplishments and the rest of Eubie's life in the perspective of the times he has lived through" (pp. xiii-xiv).

Much of the book is in Blake's own words, gleaned by Rose from many hours of tape-recorded interviews. The book begins with Blake's birth in 1883 in Baltimore, Maryland. His early musical influences included the music in his mother's church and the playing of local ragtime pianists, such as Jack the Bear Wilson and Jesse Pickett. Early in his life, Blake sang in a quartet that performed in the streets of Baltimore, played cornet for a time at twelve, and was well known in the area as a buck dancer. He began playing piano in a bordello at fifteen, sneaking out of his mother's strictly religious home to do so. The year 1899 saw the composition of Blake's "The Charleston Rag," "a piece that would establish a basis for the Eastern 'stride' style of piano playing" (p. 26). During Blake's early career he did short stints with a medicine show and with a traveling show titled "In Old Kentucky"; played in various venues in Baltimore, Atlantic City, and New York City; and performed regularly during 1907-1910 in Baltimore's Goldfield Hotel, owned by world lightweight boxing champion Joe Gans.

In 1915 Blake met Noble Sissle, with whom he formed a song-writing partnership, Blake composing the music and Sissle, the lyrics. This partnership was to last more than a decade and result in many songs that were to become famous and appear in several Broadway musicals whose casts consisted completely of black performers. Soon after the beginning of the partnership, Sissle and Blake joined the James Reese Europe orchestra, Blake becoming assistant conductor as well as pianist. During this time, William Grant Still played oboe with the Europe group. In 1919 the partners performed on the Keith vaudeville circuit as the Dixie Duo; they "were the first Negro act in history to succeed in show business, playing to white audiences, without cork. Before them the white public would never take seriously colored actors pretending to the same creativity and the same emotional capacities as whites" (p. 68).

The following year Sissle and Blake met Miller and Lyles--another famous vaudeville team--and the idea for Shuffle Along was born. This musical was produced in 1921 and included such songs as "I'm Just Wild About Harry" and "Love Will Find a Way"--the first serious love song sung by black performers on the Broadway stage. After leaving Broadway, the cast of Shuffle Along formed several touring companies that performed across the country. During the years when Shuffle Along was being performed on Broadway and on tour, the stars of the show included Florence Mills, Paul Robeson, Josephine Baker, Adelaide Hall, Eva Taylor, and Lucille Hegamin.

During the 1920s and 1930s Blake performed both in the United States and in Europe. The early 1930s saw him appearing in several of the early "talkies," one of which was the first musical act to be filmed. In the mid-1940s, Blake studied the Schillinger method of composition at New York University under the tutelage of Rudolph Schramm, a Schillinger protege. The year 1952 saw the reunion of the Sissle-Blake team for the revival of Shuffle Along, which unfortunately was unsuccessful. In 1967, at eighty-four, Blake appeared in his first concert performance at the St. Louis Ragfest.

During the last decade of his life, Blake appeared at such prestigious venues as the Newport Jazz Festival, Alice Tully Hall, Town Hall, Carnegie Hall, Princeton University, New York University, the Nice Jazz Festival, and the White House; he performed with the New York Philharmonic Orchestra, the Boston Pops, and other such groups. He appeared on many television talk shows including the Tonight Show, the Mike Douglas Show, and Bookbeat. He was awarded honorary degrees from Brooklyn College, Rutgers University, the New England Conservatory of Music, and Dartmouth College. The cap on his long and illustrious career was the 1978 production on Broadway of Eubie!, a "program of the music of Eubie Blake" (p. 166). During his lifetime, Blake had many friends of note, including Bert Willimas, Victor Herbert, Willie the Lion Smith, Luckey Roberts, James P. Johnson, Will Marion Cook, Alberta Hunter, James Bland, Irving Berlin, Perry Bradford, Will Vodery, Ford Dabney, J. W. and J. R. Johnson, Cole Porter, lyricists Henry Creamer and Andy Razaf, Ethel Waters, the comedy team of Buck and Bubbles, Fats Waller, Art Tatum, and Jelly Roll Morton. Rose's book concludes with a chapter on "Musical Matters" that presents Blake's views on the talents of various pianists, past and present; on making piano rolls; on ragtime piano technique; and an overview of the range of Blake's compositions.

Reviews: Booklist 76:647 Ja 1 '80; Booklist 80:1621 Au '84; Choice 16:1593 F '80; Kirkus Reviews 47:1126 S 15 '79; Library Journal 104:2465 N 15 '79; Publishers Weekly 216:136 S 17 '79; Radio Free Jazz 21:13 My '80

SELECTIVE DISCOGRAPHY

The Eighty-Six Years of Eubie Blake. Columbia C2L-847.
Eubie Blake, Volume I: Blues and Rags. Biograph BLP-1011Q, 1973.
Eubie Blake, Volume II: 1921. Biograph BLP-1012, 1973.
Sissle and Blake: Early Rare Recordings. 2 vols. Eubie Blake Music EBM-4/7.
Sissle and Blake's "Shuffle Along." New World Records NW-260, 1976.
Songs from "Shuffle Along." RCA Victor LPM-3514, EPA-482.
Wild About Eubie. Columbia 34504.
The Wizard of the Ragtime Piano. Twentieth Century-Fox 3003.

James A. Bland

Daly, John Jay. <u>A Song in His Heart</u>. Introduction by Harry F. Byrd. Illustrated by Marian Larer. Philadelphia and Toronto: John C. Winston, 1951. ix, 102 pp. drawings, photographs, musical examples.

Known as "one of the greatest troubadours of his day," James A. Bland, "composer, lyricist, jokester, skit writer and banjoist" composed more than 700 songs, including the world famous "Carry Me Back to Old Virginny" and "Oh, Dem Golden Slippers" (p. 3, 63). This book tells of his early fascination with the banjo and his teaching himself to play and to sing; his later studies, during his college days, in music reading and writing with an impoverished "professor White"; his days at Howard University in the preparatory and college departments; his visit to Virginia, also during his college days, where he was inspired to write "Carry Me Back to Old Virginny"; and how the latter song entered the white minstrel repertoire. Performing at fashionable dining rooms in Washington, D.C., and at "private dinners . . . and weddings among his own people as well as at affairs staged by the white population," Bland "turned out his songs so fast that many were not copyrighted, and in some cases they appeared under the name of another composer" (p. 58).

We learn that Bland entered show business as a professional when he joined Haverly's Colored Minstrels at twenty; and that by 1881 "his salary had reached the then princely sum of ten thousand

James A. Bland

dollars for a single season" (p. 64). We learn of
his trip to England with Haverly's troupe, where he
himself "was an immediate hit," and of his decision
to remain there when the tour was completed; and of
his status as a fashionably dressed "Idol of the
Music Halls," from which he toured the European
continent as an solo stage performer (pp. 64, 65).
Bland returned to America in the 1900s "absolutely
penniless," and he became destitute following the
decline of minstrelsy in favor of vaudeville
(p. 69). He died in 1911 "unwept, unhonored, and
forgotten" (p. 70). The book contains full reprints
of eight of Bland's songs: "Carry Me Back to Old
Virginny," "You Could Have Been True," "In the
Evening by the Moonlight," "Dancing on de Kitchen
Floor," "Gabriel's Band," "Oh, Lucinda," "Oh, Dem
Golden Slippers," and "The Old Fashioned Cottage."

Reviews: Etude 69:7 O '51; Newsweek 38:88 S 17
'51

SELECTIVE DISCOGRAPHY

"Don't Give the Name a Bad Place"/"De Golden Wedding." New
World Records NW-265, 1978.

Blind Boone

Fuell, Melissa. Blind Boone: His Early Life and His Achievements. Kansas City, Mo.: Burton, 1915. 256 pp. photographs, musical examples.

Written by one who knew the composer and pianist John William Boone from her "earliest childhood days," this work traces Boone's life from his birth at the close of the Civil War to his arrival, a few short decades later, as "the successor of the celebrated Gottschalk" (p. 165). The author provides information about and related to Boone's loss of his eyes at the age of six months; his childhood in Warrenburg, Missouri; and his precocious musicality and leadership of a children's "tin whistle" band at the tender age of seven. In 1873 he moved to St. Louis, where he enrolled in a school for the blind and studied music at that school. At an early age he evidenced a talent for mastering a piece "by ear" after hearing it only a few times. When he matured as a performer, he could reproduce compositions after only one hearing. We learn about his running away from home to hustle for a living by performing music and his subsequent settling down in a minister's home, from which he toured the church circuit as a musician; his encounter with Blind Tom in 1880; and the subsequent formation of The Blind Boone Concert Company with its early struggles and later immense successes of many years' duration.

Also treated are Boone's marriage; his phenomenal memory; how he learned his repertoire by way of the

player piano; his participation in social, civic,
and charitable affairs; and how he could "play the
classics and ragtime with equal pleasure," with his
repertoire ranging from Beethoven, Liszt, and
Mozart to Afro-American folk songs and his own
original compositions (p. 148). In a chapter titled
"What Others Think," critical reviews of the
pianist-composer's work are reproduced. Chapter
Ten contains a collection of some of Boone's song
texts; Chapter Eleven is a collection of some of
his "Instrumental Selections."

SELECTIVE DISCOGRAPHY

"Woodland Murmurs" (piano roll). QRS, 1912.
"Sparkling Spring" (piano roll). QRS, 1912.
"Rag Medley No. 1" (piano roll). QRS, 1912.
"Blind Boone's Southern Rag Medley No. 2" (piano roll).
  QRS, 1912.

Blind Tom

Southall, Geneva H. Blind Tom: The Post-Civil War Reen-
slavement of a Black Musical Genius. Introduction by
Samuel A. Floyd, Jr. Minneapolis: Challenge Productions,
1979. xx, 108 pp. appendixes. bibliographical notes.

_____. The Continuing Enslavement of Blind Tom,
the Black Pianist-Composer (1865-1887). Introduction by
T. J. Anderson. Minneapolis: Challenge Productions, 1983.
xiii, 318 pp. bibliography. index.

This two-volume set chronicles the musical activities and public life of Thomas Green Bethune and
documents developments related to his legal status
from his birth in 1849 to 1887. The meticulously
documented volumes provide details about the
subject's repertoire, performance procedures,
talents, tribulations, and relationships with
others. They also show how Bethune, this
"inexplicable phenomenon," was viewed by the
musical, medical, and legal communities, as well as
by the general public, during his lifetime (p. 56).
In tracing Bethune's life and career, the author
follows Blind Tom's tour schedule from city to city
in the United States and abroad, revealing the
perceptions of audiences, the press, the public,
and musicians regarding his talents, precocity, and
behavior; the numerous musical "tests" he
underwent; the resulting testimonials to his
abilities; and the guardianship trials in which
individuals vied for his custody with the intention
of exploiting his talent for financial gain. All
this information is presented within the context of

the musical, historical, and political climates of
the time.

Reviews: <u>Blind Tom</u>: Black Perspective in Music
8:128-129 nl '80; Music Educators Journal 67:27
N '80. <u>The Continuing Enslavement</u>: Black Perspective in Music 13:119-121 nl '85

SELECTIVE DISCOGRAPHY

<u>Geneva Southall--Pianist--Plays Music of Blind Tom</u>. CP-
   8206, 1982.
"Oliver Galop." Opus One 39, 1978.

Buddy Bolden

Marquis, Donald M. In Search of Buddy Bolden: First Man of Jazz. Baton Rouge: Louisiana State University Press, 1978. xix, 176 pp. photographs, maps, drawings, facsimiles. bibliography. appendixes. index.

This well-documented study of legendary New Orleans jazz trumpeter Buddy Bolden is the first serious study of its subject. Among the many things we learn from this work are, for example, the facts: that "Bolden's earliest documented musical liaisons were with Manuel Hall around 1894 and a little later with Charlie Galloway" (p. 40); that "by 1897 the style and membership of [Bolden's] band was taking a definite shape" (p. 43); that around this same time, "Buddy . . . was becoming a ladies' man, enjoying a taste of the music idol worship that would blossom more fully with Frank Sinatra in the 1940s and later with Elvis Presley, the Beatles, and other rock stars" (p. 45); that "Bolden began to attain city-wide fame around the turn of the century and most people who heard him mention seeing him between 1900 and 1905" (p. 47); and that "Buddy Bolden played all over town for different stratas of black society and for every conceivable function. The people who remembered his playing often associated him with Lincoln and Johnson Parks and the Odd Fellows and Funky Butt Halls, but their recollections also place him on advertising wagons, at picnic excursions, and parties" (p. 56). Among the points that this work refutes are those claiming that Bolden was a barber, that he was editor of a scandal sheet called The Cricket, and that Bunk Johnson played with Bolden.

The author clearly establishes that there were two Storyvilles--one black and one white--and lists the bars in black Storyville that were frequented by musicians and dance-hall patrons between 1895 and 1910. He discusses the halls and the parks in which Bolden played; lists "Bolden's Sidemen and Contemporaries"; discusses the differences between uptown "blacks" and downtown creoles; shows how the 1894 Black Code amendment affected black musicians in New Orleans; compares the styles, popularity, and activities of the John Robichaux and Buddy Bolden bands of the turn of the century; and discusses cutting contests between these two groups--the most outstanding in New Orleans at the time (although the author claims that Bolden's group was the most famous band in the city between 1900 and 1906). Additionally, the author discusses Bolden's friend-ships with Willie Cornish and Louis Jones; lists all the black musicians whose names appear in New Orleans city directories between 1800 and 1915; and discusses Bolden's "Personality and Family Life," "How and What He Played," his "Demise as a Musician," and his "Institutionalization and Death."

Reviews: Booklist 12:81 Mr '81; Cadence 4:44 Au '78; Choice 15:1229 N '78; Jazz Podium 27:42 O '78; Library Journal 103:874 Ap 15 '78; Melody Maker 53:27 S 23 '78; Music Journal 36:40 N '78; Orkester Journalen 46:2 O '78; Publishers Weekly 213:110 F 20 '78; Reprint Bulletin--Book Reviews 25:17 n4 '80; Southern Living 13:203 Jy '78

Perry Bradford

Bradford, Perry. <u>Born with the Blues: Perry Bradford's Own Story</u>. New York: Oak Publications, 1965. 175 pp. photographs, sheet music reproductions. index.

These memoirs of pianist/singer/songwriter Perry Bradford are entertaining, lively, and informative. They are sometimes also circuitous, condescending, patronizing, and accusatory toward many of the publishers, record company executives, and musicians who were his contemporaries. The book is, in essence, an appeal by Bradford for recognition as a "first" and as an important pioneer in the field of jazz. According to Bradford, he was born in Atlanta in 1895 and spent the first years of his career there, using his home city as a base from which to tour the South. Later he lived briefly in Chicago and moved to New York in 1910. In both cities he developed friendships and musical relationships with a number of black musicians, including Jelly Roll Morton, Wilbur Sweatman, Bert Williams, Bill Robinson, Will Vodery, Will Marion Cook, Fats Waller, Shelton Brooks, James P. Johnson, and W. C. Handy. With his origins and early career as a brief and sketchy backdrop, Bradford addresses his main points: his difficult quest to record a black female singer, the success of which eventually resulted in the making of the first recording of a blues song--Mamie Smith's rendition of "Crazy Blues" in 1920; and his ostensible artistic and financial exploitation by music-business executives, resulting in his financial ruin. In the process

the author tells of the establishment and operation
of his publishing company in New York's Tin Pan
Alley; his role in the production of the musical
show __Put and Take__; the origin and development of
the night-club phenomenon in the 1880s and the
succeeding years in New York's black community
(Greenwich Village); and other matters. Ten of
Bradford's songs and a wealth of photographs add to
the book's interest.

Reviews: AB Bookman's Weekly 36:124 Jy 19 '65;
AB Bookman's Weekly 39:2106 My 22 '67; Down Beat
32:39-40 Au 26 '65; Ethnomusicology 10:343-345
n3 '66; Inter-American Institute for Musical
Research Yearbook 2:183-186 '66; Jazz 4:30-31 n7
'65; Jazz Journal 18:13 Au '65; Jazz Report 4:6
n4 '65; Library Journal 90:2857 Ju 15 '65;
Orkester Journalen 34:14 Ap '66; Sing Out! 15:75
n4 '65

SELECTIVE DISCOGRAPHY

"Daybreak Blues." Columbia 81022.
"Everybody Mess Aroun'." Harmony 142512, 1926.
"Fade Away Blues." Columbia 81021.
"Georgia Grind." Harmony 142513, 1926.
"Hallelujah Blues." Columbia A3839, 1923.
"I Ain't Gonna Play No Second Fiddle"/"Steppin' on the
  Gas." New World Records NW-269, 1977.
"Kansas City Blues." Okeh 74429.
"Original Black Bottom Dance". Okeh 74428.

Bricktop

Bricktop, with James Haskins. <u>Bricktop</u>. New York: Atheneum, 1983. xviii, 300 pp. index.

She was a saloon singer in Chicago during the rough and tumble days of Jack Johnson, Florence Mills, Bill Robinson, and Legs Diamond. In Prohibition Harlem she gave Duke Ellington his first big New York break. In café-society Paris she took a young Josephine Baker under her wing and worked with a busboy named Langston Hughes. Cole Porter had breakfast in her first Paris <u>bôite</u> one morning, heard her singing one of his songs, and started bringing his friends; soon Noel Coward, Tallulah Bankhead, and all the great and glittering names of Europe between the wars had made Bricktop's their own private enclave. Later Porter wrote "Miss Otis Regrets" with her voice in mind, and took it to her to sing. F. Scott Fitzgerald, during his carefree Paris days, did not consider a night complete without a visit to Bricktop's; Ernest Hemingway incurred her wrath; T. S. Elliot put her in a poem; Cole Porter asked her to give dance lessons at his parties; and the Duke of Windsor spent many early mornings on the floor by the piano in her clubs, listening to the music of Bricktop's. When Hitler's soldiers advanced on Paris, the Duchess of Windsor, in concert with Elsie de Wolfe, Lady Mendl, aided her escape. Relocating in Mexico City, Bricktop became friends with Cantinflas. Back in Paris after the war, she comforted the people who had made their way back to Bricktop's in search of an era that would never exist again. In Rome the movie celebrities flocked to her club. She watched the marriage of Frank Sinatra and Ava Gardner break up, played mother hen to the likes of Anna Magnani and Shirley MacLaine, and unwittingly presided over the first appearances together in public of Elizabeth Taylor and Richard Burton. Martin Luther King, Jr., in Europe to accept the Nobel Prize for Peace, phoned to ask if he could meet <u>her</u>. In Bricktop's story there is such an array of famous names and places that the mind short-circuits (pp. xiii-xiv).

Thus does the co-author summarize the story of Ada Smith Ducongé, better known as Bricktop. In this chatty book Bricktop tells her own story, and Haskins skillfully and unobtrusively weaves in important supplementary information. The reader learns that Bricktop, born in 1894 in Alderson, West Virginia, growing up on Chicago's South Side, was stagestruck when she was in her mid-teens. She joined the chorus of a Miller and Lyles vaudeville show at sixteen, later joined McCabe's Georgia troubadours, and then became a member of the Oma Crosby Trio, playing the vaudeville circuit where she suffered "long hours, food on the run, tiny dressing rooms, running for trains, subways, and trolley cars" (p. 34). At seventeen, she joined the Ten Georgia Campers, touring to the West Coast and back. Then she became part of the the Kinky-doo Trio. While still seventeen she began her "career as a saloon singer that lasted sixty years," holding jobs in those early years at Chicago venues such as Roy Jones's Saloon, world heavyweight boxing champion Jack Johnson's Cafè Champ, and saloons in other Midwestern, West Coast, and East Coast cities, and also in Canada (p. 39).

In 1922 Bricktop landed in Harlem and worked at Barron's Exclusive Club and at Connie's Inn. In 1924 she headed for Paris to headline at Le Grand Duc, where she was slow to attract attention. But by 1926, in the midst of <u>Le Tumulte Noir</u>, the Paris counterpart of the Harlem Renaissance, she had opened her own place, christening it "Bricktop's," entertaining a select, monied, artistic, and artistically inclined clientele.

Proceeding with her story, Bricktop tells of: her opening in 1932 of a Bricktop's in Biarritz for its summer seasons; the effect of the depression on Paris night life in general and on Bricktop's in particular; her loss of Bricktop's for a period; her radio programs during the late 1930s for the French government network, on which she sang requests sent in by listeners; her return in 1939 to New York, where she had "a hard time making it," because of the outbreak of World War II (p. 216); and her leaving New York in 1943 to open successful Bricktop's clubs in Mexico City (1943-1949), Paris again (1950-1951), and Rome (1951-1964). In 1970 Bricktop returned to the United States for good, performing occasionally at clubs in New York and Chicago through 1979. During her sixty-year career as an entertainer, Bricktop had as friends, acquaintances, and colleagues black celebrities such as Duke Ellington, Jelly Roll Morton, Josephine Baker, Florence Mills, Paul Robeson, Bobby Short, Ethel Waters, Mabel Mercer, Will Vodery, Alberta Hunter, Louis Armstrong, and many others.

Reviews: Best Sellers 43:292 N '83; Booklist 79:1379 Jy '83; Christian Science Monitor 75:B8 S 2 '83; Jazz Times p12 Ja '84; Kirkus Reviews 51:643 Ju 1 '83; Library Journal 108:1378 Jy '83; New York Times Book Review 89:23 Mr 4 '84; Publishers Weekly 223:68 Ju 3 '83

SELECTIVE DISCOGRAPHY

"So Long, Baby" (with Cy Coleman). 1970.

Big Bill Broonzy

Broonzy, William, as told to Yannick Bruynoghe. <u>Big Bill Blues: William Broonzy's Story</u>. Foreword by Stanley Dance. London: Cassell & Co., 1955. viii, 139 pp. photographs. discography. index.

This book is a discourse on the virtues and vices of the blues life as presented through the lyrics of Broonzy's songs and his commentary on them. It is also a truncated and casual review of his life as it is revealed in these presentations. The song texts and Broonzy's commentary show his perceptions of and responses to racism, plantation life, romantic liaisons, and rural and urban sociology. Born in Mississippi, raised and acculturated there and in Arkansas, Broonzy tells his story in his own homespun manner, beginning with his origins and early life and detailing incidents, behaviors, and events such as making homemade stringed instruments out of cigar boxes, broomsticks, tubs, and other such items; drinking bouts; hopes and aspirations; matters pertaining to the religious and the secular; the development of bluesmen; getting along in Chicago; and his interactions and friendships with other blues singers such as Sleepy John Estes, Tampa Red, Sonny Boy Williamson, Memphis Slim, Memphis Minnie, and Washboard Sam. Broonzy made his first records in 1923 or 1925--"Big Big Blues" and "Gonna Tear it Down" among them. "Big Bill was a well-known blues singer and player and has recorded 260 blues songs from 1925 up till 1952; he was a happy man when he was drunk and playing with women" (p. 117).

Reviews: Library Journal 90:633 '65; Library Journal 82:1246 '57; New York Times p6 N 4 '56; San Francisco Chronicle p10 N 25 '56; Times Literary Supplement p64 F 3 '56

SELECTIVE DISCOGRAPHY

Big Bill Broonzy. Columbia 30-153.
Big Bill Broonzy Sings Country Blues. Folkways/Scholastic 31005.
Big Bill Broonzy Sings Folk Songs. Folkways/Scholastic 2328.
The Big Bill Broonzy Story. Verve MG-V-3000-5.
The Young Bill Broonzy. Yazoo L-1011.

Cab Calloway

Calloway, Cab, and Bryant Rollins. <u>Of Minnie the Moocher and Me</u>. New York: Thomas Y. Crowell, 1976. 282 pp. photographs. music bibliography. appendixes.

Born in Rochester, New York, in 1907 and growing up in Baltimore, Cab Calloway, singer/bandleader/ entertainer, as a child "played hooky, hung out in the streets, hustled to make money, and was always in and out of trouble" (p. 7). At thirteen or fourteen he was sent by his parents to Philadelphia to an "industrial school" for a year. Upon his return to Baltimore he became involved in athletics, studied hard, and graduated first in his junior high-school class. Through high school he played drums, did vaudeville, took serious voice lessons, and sang in his church choir and in local night clubs. By his senior year he was "a big basketball star, a handsome, successful singer and drummer, and a guy with quite an ego," playing semi-professional basketball and playing in Johnny Jones's Arabian Tent Orchestra (p. 47). At about eighteen he graduated from high school and joined the revue <u>Plantation Days</u>, traveling the Theater Owners' Booking Association (T.O.B.A.) circuit. He settled for a while in Chicago, where he attended college, met and performed with Louis Armstrong, and was influenced by the latter's scat singing.

In 1929 Calloway married, acquired his own band, moved to New York, and was introduced to big-time show business when he landed a role in the Broadway hit revue <u>Hot Chocolates</u>. Shortly thereafter, we

learn, Calloway assumed leadership of a band called
The Missourians, which followed the Ellington band
into the Cotton Club in 1930 and which later became
known as Cab Calloway's Cotton Club Orchestra. By
1931 Calloway was making "more than $50,000 a year
in the middle of the Great Depression," broadcasting live over nationwide radio and spreading
the sound of New York jazz across the country
(p. 110). Through 1935 the band also toured the
Northeast, the Midwest, the South, and Europe.
Including at various times Doc Cheatham, Milt
Hinton, Benny Payne, Chu Berry, Dizzy Gillespie,
Jonah Jones, Cozy Cole, and other celebrated
instrumentalists, the band had "a clear, sharp,
crisp sound with strong musicianship . . . a rhythm
section that rocks, a brass section that always
hits when it's supposed to hit, a reed section that
is all over the place, just beautifully toned"
(p. 175). But by 1947 the band could not find
bookings. The big-band era had come to an end, and
the group disbanded.

In 1950 Calloway moved to the Broadway stage.
Over the next two decades he played Sportin' Life
in _Porgy and Bess_, Heinze in _Pajama Game_, and
Horace Vandergelder in _Hello Dolly!_ In the course
of his career Calloway also made about ten films,
including _The Singing Kid_ with Al Jolson, _Stormy
Weather_, and _St. Louis Blues_. As this story of Cab
Calloway's life and career unfolds, is also
portrays his relationships with Fletcher Henderson,
Louis Armstrong, black cartoonist E. Simms
Campbell, and others; his songwriting; his writing
of _The Cab Calloway Hepster's Dictionary_ and
Professor Cab Calloway's Swingformation Bureau;
racial incidents during tours of the South;
organized crime and its relationship to the
entertainment business and to jazz; and narrative
portraits of Calloway by former members of his band
and by his wife and daughters.

Reviews: AB Bookman's Weekly 59:18 Ja 3 '77;
Booklist 72:1381 Ju 1 '76; Booklist 72:1398 Ju 1
'76; Coda n161:14 Ju 1 '78; Kirkus Reviews
44:431 Ap 1 '76; Library Journal 101:1214 My 15
'76; Music Journal 34:43 O '76; National
Observer 15:24 N 20 '76; New York Times 125:C21
Au 13 '76; New York Times Book Review p8 S 12
'76; Publishers Weekly 209:52 Ap 26 '76; Second
Line 29:34-35 Fall '77

Cab Calloway

SELECTIVE DISCOGRAPHY

Blues. Vocalion 78320.
Cab Calloway and His Orchestra. Smithsonian Collection
   R-004, P-13456, 1940.
Club Zanzibar Broadcasts, July 0 and 10, 1945. Unique Jazz
   UJ-006, 1978.
"History Repeats Itself." Boom 60.006, 1966.
"Little Child." ABC-Paramount 9671, 1956.
"Minnie the Moocher." Brunswick 80015.
"Pickin' the Cabbage." New World Records NW-217.
St. James Infirmary. Epic LN-3265.
Sixteen Cab Calloway Classics. Epic LN-3265, 1939-1941.
Stars of the Apollo. Columbia KG-30788.

Benny Carter

Berger, Morroe, Edward Berger, and James Patrick. Benny
Carter: A Life in American Music. Volume I. Foreword by
Benny Carter. Introduction by Dan Morgenstern. Metuchen,
N.J., and London: Scarecrow Press and the Institute of
Jazz Studies, Rutgers University, 1982. xiii, 422 pp.
photo- graphs, musical examples, charts. index.

In this work, the career of a multi-instrumental-
ist/bandleader/composer/arranger is discussed in
the context of social, musical, and cultural
developments that occurred over the more than
seventy years of the subject's life. Born in New
York City in 1907, Bennett Lester Carter began his
career around 1923. A member of a musical family,
he began playing the saxophone at thirteen, and
although "jazz was never heard in his own home when
Carter was in his early teens . . . he used to hear
it frequently in the home of his neighbors"
(p. 14). "In his early teens Carter spent all his
time practicing, reading, sitting in with musicians
who let him gain experience and share the kitty,
and in other jobs to earn money" (p. 16).

By 1928 Carter had played in the bands of Duke
Ellington, Charlie Johnson, Fletcher Henderson, and
Earl Hines and was leading his own band at Harlem's
Savoy Ballroom. He had also "started arranging
music, was a star alto saxophone soloist, a budding
composer, and had been recorded on wax" (p. 38). In
1932, after having led the Wilberforce Collegians
and McKinney's Cotton Pickers, Carter formed his
own big band, which played a variety of venues in

Benny Carter

New York (including the Harlem Club, Apollo
Theater, and Empire Ballroom) and toured the East
Coast, Europe, and California. In 1935, we learn,
Carter left for Europe and stayed three years,
traveling to France, England, Holland, and other
countries and winning acclaim throughout Europe.
Returning to the United States in 1938, he formed a
big band and began to perform on New York's 52nd
Street, from which he also toured.

In 1942 he moved with his band to Los Angeles
where he settled, touring and making records. In
the next year he wrote and performed some of the
music for his first film--Stormy Weather. Later
that year he did arrangements for the films
Jitterbug, Wintertime, The Gang's All Here, and
This Is the Army. Also in 1943, Duke "Ellington
placed Carter among the greatest arrangers, Benny
Goodman listed Carter and Hodges as his favorite
altos, and Roy Eldridge called attention to
Carter's ability on trumpet" (p. 223). In 1944 he
arranged for Here Come the Waves, Thousands Cheer,
Young Ideas, and Canterville Ghost. Between 1942
and 1946 "Carter and his band played about fifty
engagements at Military Camps and hospitals across
the country" (p. 221). In 1944 he disbanded, and
between 1947 and 1957 his professional life
consisted of "mainly writing for films and playing
on soundtracks and studio recordings of various
types. He intermittently put together small bands
for special engagements and played with some bands
assembled by other leaders and promoters" (p. 258).

In the late 1940s Carter began writing again for
films and performing in them. A Song Is Born and
Portrait of Jenny of 1948 contained Carter
arrangements; in 1950 he wrote arrangements for
Love Happy, Panic in the Streets, My Blue Heaven,
and three other films. The authors inform us that
between 1951 and 1957 Carter composed, arranged,
and performed music for eight films, including An
American in Paris, That's Entertainment, The Snows
of Kilimanjaro, The View from Pompey's Head, and
The Sun Also Rises. Between 1950 and 1959 Carter
added television music-writing to his professional
activities, led a big band and a quintet for short
periods, and performed abroad on ten different
occasions. Also in the 1950s Carter played a
leading role in the "amalgamation of the black and
white union locals in Los Angeles, served as
chairman of the committee on arranging of local 47,
on the board and executive committee of the

National Academy of Recording Arts and Sciences and a member of the executive board of the Composers and Lyricists Guild of America" (p. 264). He also wrote compositions and made studio recordings for a variety of singers. His television composition credits include M Squad, Bob Hope Chrysler Theater, Ironside, and The Name of the Game.

Through the 1960s Carter engaged in music-related business ventures, played a number of festivals and concerts, and engaged in jazz education. In the 1970s, as an "elder statesman," Carter was "rediscovered," and "the rediscovery process led Carter to resume activities, such as night club dates, in which he had not regularly engaged for some years. The decade also saw him assume new roles: as an educator, advisor to his country's government on arts policy, and a representative of that government abroad" (p. 348). During this period he played and spoke at a number of colleges and universities, including five engagements at Princeton, where, in Carter's own words, he liked "the scholarly atmosphere, the civilized tranquility, the chance to get to know students and faculty members. I think of the 1970s as my academic decade, with experiences and memories I cherish" (p. 366). In the 1970s and into the 1980s he also played more frequently at "Clubs, Festivals, and Tours Abroad," wrote music for films and television shows, and received numerous honors, awards, and tributes (p. 367).

In the process of relating these and other aspects of Carter's career, the authors also present short biographical sketches of Will Marion Cook, J. Rosamond Johnson, and Will Vodery; mention Carter's professional relationships with Willie the Lion Smith, Bill "Bojangles" Robinson, Irving Mills, John Hammond, Miles Davis, Dizzy Gillespie, and others; discuss those musicians who influenced Carter and whom he influenced, "Pre-jazz black music," "Harlem in the 1920s," Carter on 52nd Street, his writing for the "Hit Parade" radio series, and "Race, Politics and Music in Wartime" (p. 225).

Reviews: American Libraries 14:249 Ap '83; American Reference Books Annual 15:452 '84; Billboard 94:32 N 6 '82; Booklist 80:611 D 15 '83; Choice 20:1147 Ap '83; Coda n191:10 Au 1 '83; Down Beat 50:62 Ap '83; Jazz Podium 31:58 D '82; Jazz Times p12 Mr '83; Orkester Journalen

Benny Carter

51:45 O '83; Popular Music and Society 9:88 n2
'83; Village Voice 28:76+ Ju 28 '83

SELECTIVE DISCOGRAPHY

Art Tatum--Benny Carter Trio. 2 vols. Pablo 2310-732/3,
   1954.
Benny Carter: Holland, 1937. Decca (France) 154.052, 1937.
Benny Carter and His Orchestra 1940-1941. RCA (France)
   741.073, 1940-1941.
Benny Carter: 1938 and 1946. Swing SW-8403.
Benny Carter: 1944: Live at the Trianon Ballroom, South-
   gate, California. Hindsight HSR-218.
Concert in Sweden, 1972. Unique Jazz UJ-002, 1978.
Further Definitions. Impulse S-12, 1961.
A Gentleman and His Music. Concord Jazz CJ-285.
Louis Armstrong, Jazz Masterpieces. Franklin Mint Record
   Society FM-001, 1982.
Swinging at Maida Vale. Jasmine JASM-2010, 1936-1937.

Ray Charles

Charles, Ray, and David Ritz. <u>Brother Ray: Ray Charles' Own Story</u>. New York: Dial Press, 1978. xii, 340 pp. photographs. discography.

This wide-ranging memoir of a master of "jazz or pop, country or soul" (p. 315), tells Ray Charles's life story from its beginning in the poverty of his north Florida home to his success as a musician and businessman in the 1970s, discussing or touching on such matters as: his childhood influences; his early and precocious attraction to boogie woogie and its influence on his early musical development; his education and training in a school for the blind; his musical training by way of scores in braille; his formal instruction on the piano and clarinet; his performing on the saxophone, which he taught himself to play; his approach to arranging and composition; the performers who were his idols and influences; extra-musical events that helped shape his life; the struggles and fulfillments in his personal and professional lives; his development as a professional musician and his life on the road; his addiction to heroin and his overcoming it; his method of operation as a bandleader; his motivations and religious philosophy; his love life and his family life; his cosmopolitan musical tastes; his stint with an otherwise all-white country and western band in the 1940s; his observation of the rock & roll scene of the 1950s; and his perception and support of the civil rights movement of the 1960s. This story is an example of music as a means of survival. David

Ritz's afterword provides insight into Charles's personality, his moods, and his behavior, and explains the method of collaboration. Explanatory notes accompany the discography.

Reviews: Best Sellers 38:350 F '79; Billboard 90:50 D 2 '78; Booklist 75:269 O 1 '78; Cadence 4:23 N '78; Choice 15:1674 F '79; Coda n172:29 Ap 1 '80; Jazz Magazine (US) 3:54 N 2 '79; Kirkus Reviews 46:843 Au 1 '78; Library Journal 103:1751 S 15 '78; Melody Maker 54:36 S 22 '79; Notes 36:364 n2 D '79; Orkester Journalen 48:2 F '80; Publishers Weekly 214:160 Jy 17 '78; Publishers Weekly 216:144 S 17 '79; Radio Free Jazz 20:26 O '79; Second Line 31:23 Fall '79; Variety 293:74 N 15 '78

SELECTIVE DISCOGRAPHY

The Best of Ray Charles. Atlantic SD-1543.
Doing His Thing. Tangerine/ABC Records ABC-S-695.
Friendship. Columbia FC-39415.
Greatest Hits. ABC 415, 1962.
The Greatest Hits of Ray Charles. Atlantic 7101.
Hallelujah I Love Her So. Atlantic 8006.
Modern Sounds in Country Music. ABC 410, 1962.
The Ray Charles Story. 4 vols. Atlantic 8063/8064/8083/
    8094, 1962-64.
What'd I Say. Atlantic 8029.
Wish You Were Here Tonight. Columbia FC-38293.

Nat King Cole

Cole, Maria, with Louis Robinson. <u>Nat King Cole: An Intimate Biography</u>. New York: William Morrow, 1971. 184 pp. photographs. discography.

The author of this book, Cole's second wife--who was a big-band singer in the 1940s--has "attempted . . . to do but one thing: to let those who were his admirers know more about Nat Cole the father, the husband, the man" (p. 160). During the 1950s and early 1960s, Cole had "become one of the foremost entertainers of the American stage, and one of the best-known men in the world. (As a national magazine was to say later at the time of his passing, '. . . he was the most celebrated Negro to die in world history')" (p. 36). He grew up in Chicago as the son of a Baptist minister. Showing early a musical talent, during his high-school years he formed a jazz group called the Royal Dukes. He later joined a group called the Rogues of Rhythm, led by his brother Eddie. This group became part of the cast of the touring <u>Shuffle Along</u>, and Cole traveled with it to California.

The Nat Cole Swingsters were formed to fill an engagement at Bob Lewis's Swanee Inn in Los Angeles. It included Cole (piano), Wesley Prince (bass), and Oscar Moore (guitar) and was shortly renamed the Nat King Cole Trio. In 1942 Carlos Gastel became their manager. A year later they began recording for a new company, Capitol Records. Among the songs recorded by the group were: "Nature

Boy," "Mona Lisa," and "Straighten Up and Fly
Right." "The commercial success of the King Cole
Trio and the increasing demand for the
vocalizations of its leader was not going unnoticed
by the trio's loyal jazz aficionados, however.
Soon some began to express their concern and,
gradually, to look accusingly at Nat" (p. 48). But
his success had come singing pop ballads, and he
would continue providing them for his audience. In
1951 Cole became a solo act and, within three
years, a multimillion dollar seller of records. He
was featured on the Wildroot Cream Oil Show on
radio from 1946 to 1950. In the late 1950s the Nat
King Cole Show had a short run on television.

The years 1962 and 1963 saw the advent of _Sights
and Sounds_, a

> show [which] was pure American. There
> was comedy, dancing and music all
> performed by a cast of a dozen bright and
> pert singers and dancers who did songs
> like "Buttons and Bows," "Lullaby of
> Broadway" and "Precious Lord." Holding it
> all together was Nat King Cole, singing
> the old favorites like "Paper Moon" and
> "Mona Lisa" together with the hits that
> had come twenty years later like
> "Rambling Rose." For the really
> sentimental oldtime Cole fans, he played
> some magnificent piano (p. 131).

Cole died of lung cancer in 1965. The author
gives us a lengthy account of his final illness.
Scattered throughout the book are revelations of
the discrimination to which Cole was subjected
during his life and career. Of Cole himself, she
says, "Nat had one overwhelming weakness, and he
never succeeded in overcoming it: he was as
gullible a man as ever lived. . . . He was a man
who could find some good in everybody" (p. 68).

Reviews: AB Bookman's Weekly 48:1237 O 25 '71;
Best Sellers 31:321 O 15 '71; Booklist 68:448 F
1 '72; Booklist 68:462 F 1 '72; Books & Bookmen
18:88 D '72; Christian Century 88:1175 O 6 '71;
Jazz & Blues 3:11-12 S '73; Jazz Digest 1:1+ Mr
'72; Kirkus Reviews 39:780 Jy 15 '71; Library
Journal 97:200 Ja 15 '72; Publishers Weekly
200:111 Jy 19 '71; Variety 264:67 S 15 '71

Nat King Cole

Haskins, James, with Kathleen Benson. Nat King Cole. New York: Stein and Day, 1984. 204 pp. photographs. discography. index.

This is the story of a much-appreciated singer and a much-unappreciated jazz pianist whose "effortless delivery and words of love masked a profound tension and unhappiness born of frustration and abundance, . . . whose records sold millions of copies," and whose success as a vocalist "overshadowed his talent as a pianist to such an extent that even in his own lifetime most people regarded his piano as little more than a prop" (pp. 9-10). Born in Montgomery, Alabama, in 1919 and raised in Chicago, Cole played "by ear" until adolescence, when he began to study seriously. As a young aspiring pianist, he was influenced by Earl Hines. He organized his first band while still attending high school--"Nat Cole and His Rogues of Rhythm or Royal Dukes, depending on the source" --and the group won a "battle of the bands" against Earl Hines's band at the Savoy Ballroom (p. 19).

In 1936, we learn, Cole's band made its first recording with Decca; in 1937 Cole played in the band of a revived Shuffle Along and was stranded in California, where he "played [solo piano] in every beer joint from San Diego to Bakersfield" (p. 24). Also in 1937 the King Cole Trio, a jazz group, was formed in Los Angeles; it recorded and played on a radio series during 1938-1939. In 1941 the group made its first tour, with extended engagements in Chicago, Philadelphia, Washington, D.C., and New York, where the Trio became immersed in the jazz culture of 52nd Street. In 1943 Cole's Capitol recording of "Straighten Up and Fly Right" became "a major hit in the Negro market and among white jazz fans," bringing the Trio its first national fame (p. 41). In 1946 the Trio secured its own radio show, broadcasting nationally one day a week. By 1948 the King Cole Trio had "won the Metronome best small band designation for the third year in a row" (p. 91). In 1956 Cole got his own television show--NBC's "The Nat King Cole Show" --which, by 1957, had been canceled for lack of sponsorship.

But film opportunities had emerged for Cole, with roles in China Gate, St. Louis Blues (in which he played W. C. Handy), The Night of the Quarter Moon, and Cat Ballou. Cole's biographers, in addition to discussing these aspects of his life and career,

also touch on or detail aspects of: his two
marriages; his relationships with his wives and his
children; the interesting story behind the
recording of his 1948 hit song "Nature Boy"; the
ordeal he experienced in trying to purchase and
move into a home in an all-white neighborhood in
Los Angeles; his troubles with the Internal Revenue
Service, which resulted in his becoming "'more
commercial' in the early 1950s" (p. 115); his
illness in 1953; and his diminishing of the role of
his trio and of his piano playing to emerge
primarily as a vocalist. In 1956 Cole was
physically attacked by white thugs while performing
on stage in Birmingham, Alabama. He was also
attacked, journalistically, by the black and the
white-liberal press, as well as by civil-rights
leaders. But he continued making tours of the
United States, Europe, and Latin America; formed a
partnership with Harry Belafonte (Cole-Belafonte
Enterprises) to produce films and television
specials; and continued to face the inevitable
racial barriers and discriminatory treatment
nationwide as a night-club and theater entertainer
and film and television actor. The authors
conclude with details of his death in 1965 and of
the subsequent activities of his wife and
children.

Review: Jazz Times p16 O '85

SELECTIVE DISCOGRAPHY

The Best of Nat Cole. ST-2944, 1968.
The Best of Nat Cole Trio 2 vols. N-12260/1, 1982.
Nat Cole's Greatest. SKAO-373, 1969.
Nat King Cole at the Piano. H-156, 1950.
Nat King Cole Story. 4 vols. Capitol SWCL-1613, 1961.
The Piano Style of Nat King Cole. DT-689, 1956.
This Is Nat King Cole. DT-870, 1957.

Samuel Coleridge-Taylor

Coleridge-Taylor, Avril. <u>The Heritage of Samuel Cole-ridge-Taylor</u>. Foreword by Sir Thomas Armstrong. London: Dennis Dobson, 1979. 160 pp. photographs, musical examples, plates. appendixes. index.

The daughter of composer Samuel Coleridge-Taylor divides her book into two sections: "My Father," and "My Father's Daughter." The first begins with Samuel Coleridge-Taylor's birth and early life. He was a protégé of Col. Herbert A. Walters, who supported him and sent him to the Royal College of Music. His early compositions, written during his stay at the school, included the <u>Clarinet Quintet</u>, the <u>Symphony in A minor</u>, and <u>Fantasiestücke</u> for string quartet. The composer lived most of his life at Croyden, England, where he taught violin at the Conservatoire of Music during his student days and acted as the conductor of the Rochester Choral Society, the Handel Society (1904-1912), and the Westmorland Festival for three years. He also served often as a festival adjudicator and taught at Trinity College of Music, Crystal Palace School of Art and Music, and Guildhall School of Music.

Coleridge-Taylor's friendship with Paul Lawrence Dunbar began in 1896. At that time he set some of Dunbar's poems to music, and the two collaborated on an "operatic romance" titled <u>Dream Lovers</u>. Coleridge-Taylor became familiar with Afro-American spirituals through his acquaintance with the Fisk Jubilee Singers, who were touring England on their famous quest for funds to support Fisk University.

During his lifetime, Coleridge-Taylor published
many works with Novello--particularly his choral
compositions. We learn of the circumstances of the
composition of the famous Hiawatha trilogy
("Hiawatha's Wedding Feast," "The Death of
Minnehaha," and "Hiawatha's Departure"), the Violin
Sonata in D minor, and the posthumous Hiawatha
Ballet Suite. Coleridge-Taylor made several trips
to the United States to conduct his compositions as
they were performed by the Samuel Coleridge-Taylor
Society in Washington, D.C., and the orchestra and
chorus of the Norfolk Festival. During one of his
American visits, he met Harry T. Burleigh, who sang
the solo parts of Coleridge-Taylor's Hiawatha.

The book contains discussions of several of
Coleridge-Taylor's compositions, including Ballade
in A minor (1898), Symphonic Variations on an
African Air (1906), and The Bamboula (1910). The
second part of the book treats Avril
Coleridge-Taylor's remembrances of her father and
her life after his death in 1912. We learn of her
study at Trinity College, her career as a composer
and conductor, and the circumstances of her living
for several years in South Africa. The appendixes
include a biographical statement by Booker T.
Washington that appeared in Samuel Coleridge-
Taylor's Twenty-four Negro Melodies, Coleridge-
Taylor's foreword to the same publication, and
lists of compositions by both Samuel and Avril
Coleridge-Taylor.

Reviews: British Book News p306 My '80; British
Book News p457 Au '80; Music Teacher 122:31 Ja
'81; Times Literary Supplement p167 F 15 '80

Coleridge-Taylor, Jessie F. A Memory Sketch, or Personal
Reminiscences of My Husband, Genius and Musician, Samuel
Coleridge-Taylor, 1875-1912. London: The author, n.d. 76
pp. photographs. appendix. index.

This intimate little memoir by a wife enlarges upon
and gives details of several events mentioned in
the Sayers biography of the composer and also
shares intimacies of their family life. Such
treatment here provides insight into the composer's
musical and personal motivations and his feelings
about certain events and incidents of his life,
including those pertaining to race. The appendix
is said to be "a complete list of the music of
Coleridge-Taylor, both published and unpublished,

so far as it has been possible to trace it"
(p. 62).

Sayers, W. C. Berwick. <u>Samuel Coleridge-Taylor, Musician:
His Life and Letters</u>. 2nd edition. London: Augener, 1927.
xv, 331 pp. photographs, musical examples. appendixes.
index.

This work presents the life of an Anglo-African
composer of orchestral, choral, and chamber music,
one who had his first music lesson when he was five
and died when he was thirty-seven. The book
discusses Coleridge-Taylor's economically humble
but culturally rich and precocious childhood; his
development into an accomplished violinist and
pianist; and his growth into a prolific composer
and an enormously popular conductor, for which
accomplishments he was showered with accolades and
critical acclaim by the time he was twenty-five.
Effectively treated are such items as: his
enrollment in London's Royal College of Music in
1890; his intense six years at the college, during
which he produced more than thirty compositions;
the publication of his first composition in 1891;
his encounters and relationships in England with
celebrities such as Sir Edward Elgar, Paul Lawrence
Dunbar, the Fisk Jubilee Singers, and others; his
method of composing music; and the the critical
fraternity's perceptions of his music over the
course of his lifetime.

His teaching and leadership experiences are also
given attention, including his professorship at
Trinity College and the methods he employed there
as an "engrossing teacher" (p. 173); his conducting
activities with various orchestras and societies;
and his role in founding Croydon's prestigious
String Players Club. Additionally, the reader is
provided with details of Coleridge-Taylor's
introduction to America and his visits there in
1904, 1906, and 1910; the two-year preparation of
Washington, D.C.'s Samuel Coleridge-Taylor Society
for its performance of the composer's <u>Hiawatha</u>; his
visits to Boston, New York, Baltimore, Philadelphia, Detroit, Chicago, and Norfolk,
Connecticut; and his performances of his music with
American black musicians, such as Harry T.
Burleigh, John Turner Layton, Arthur Freeman,
Clarence Cameron White, Felix Weir, Gerald Tyler,
and others, as well as with white composers and
performers, such as George Chadwick, Horatio
Parker, and Alma Gluck.

Samuel Coleridge-Taylor

Coleridge-Taylor's personal life and his outlook on life and art are also discussed: his happy and contented family life; his exemplary personal habits; "the fluidity of his opinions" (p. 97); his status as "a man unassuming and of great personal magnetism" (p. 159); his race consciousness and racial pride; his responses to race prejudice; and his concern and occupation with the welfare of his race. Spaced throughout the book are discussions of his compositions, including critical analyses of Hiawatha, The Atonement, A Tale of Old Japan, Bamboula, African Suite, Dream Lovers, and the Clarinet Quintet. A product of its day and locale and therefore rather stilted in its prose and, where racial matters are concerned, dated, the work nevertheless is an effective portrait of Coleridge-Taylor as a man and as a great musician who was a vital source of inspiration for black musicians in the United States. The appendix is a complete list of the composer's musical compositions as they were traceable in the year 1912.

Tortolano, William. Samuel Coleridge-Taylor: Anglo-Black Composer, 1875-1912. Metuchen, N.J.: Scarecrow Press, 1977. xiii, 223 pp. photographs, music examples. appendix. bibliography. discography. index.

The purpose of this little volume is "to try to make Coleridge-Taylor known as a significant composer so he can be given his rightful place in history" (p. xii). In spite of its 223 pages, the book is merely a biographical sketch which appears to be a severely condensed reiteration of the information contained in Sayers's book on the composer, together with material from other sources. Treated are the composer's early childhood, his marriage, children, musical influences, and career; his trips to America; and three of Coleridge-Taylor's works: Hiawatha, Twenty-Four Negro Melodies, and the Violin Concerto. These three compositions are rather extensively analyzed and illustrated with lengthy musical examples. In connection with Coleridge-Taylor's trips to America, the author mentions his role as "the prototype for a renaissance of black culture" vis-à-vis the Harlem Renaissance and includes extensive quotes from writings of W. E. B. DuBois and Booker T. Washington (p. 73). A chapter titled "Coleridge-Taylor's Writings" contains five short articles, speeches, and letters written by the composer. The appendixes include listings of

Coleridge-Taylor's entire compositional output.
The discography is quite useful, for it not only
gives discographical information but also provides
a list of available tapes and a list of record
specialists in England where recordings of the
composer's compositions might be acquired.

Reviews: Choice 14:1072 O '77; Library Journal
102:1652 Au '77; Music (AGO) 11:12-13 Jy '77;
Music Educators Journal 65:29 S '78; Music
Teacher 118:821 O '77; NATS Bulletin 34:37-38 nl
'77

SELECTIVE DISCOGRAPHY

"Danse nègre," from African Suite. Columbia
M-32782, 1974.
Eleanore, op. 37, no. 6. L'Oiseau-Lyre SOL-324, 1971.
"The Evening Star." Audio House AHS-30F75, 1975.
Hiawatha's Wedding Feast. His Master's Voice ASD-467,
1962.
"Papillon." Da Camera Magna SM-93144, 1975.
Petite Suite de Concert. Columbia ML-2180, 1950.
Quintet, for clarinet and strings. Spectrum SR-127, 1980.
Sonata in D minor. Columbia CL-1396/7.
Thou Art Risen My Beloved. CFB-3031.
Twenty-Four Negro Melodies. Orion ORS-78305/6, 1978.
Viking Song. ZON G-076.

Lee Collins

Gillis, Frank J., and John W. Miner, eds. <u>Oh, Didn't He Ramble: The Life Story of Lee Collins, as told to Mary Collins</u>. Urbana, Chicago, and London: University of Illinois Press, 1974. xv, 159 pp. photographs. discography. index.

This is the story of "a member of the early generation of musicians who marched in funeral processions and parades, played the clubs and cafes, and contributed to the development and dissemination of the New Orleans style of jazz" (p. 138), one whose name "will go down in jazz history alongside other early trumpet 'Kings' in the lineage--Buddy Bolden, Bunk Johnson, Freddie Keppard, Buddy Petit, Louis Armstrong" (p. 139). Collins has left here details of his childhood activities and relationships; his childhood memories of the music of New Orleans; his knowledge of the night life and vice world of New Orleans; his transition to Chicago's jazz scene; his participation in bands fronted by or including such jazz greats as Zutty Singleton, Jack Carey, Luis Russel, Alphonse Picou, Joe Oliver, Jelly Roll Morton, Danny Barker, Manuel Perez, Albert Ammons, Little Brother Montgomery, and others. He also speaks of New Orleans' Mardi Gras; his recordings and performances with Kid Ory, with blues singers such as Bertha "Chippie" Hill, and with others; his tours and musical performances in Europe; and the cutting-contest tradition in New Orleans.

Lee Collins

Reviews: AB Bookman's Weekly 54:1936 N 4 '74;
Black Perspective in Music 3:109-110 nl '75;
Coda 12:26 n6 '75; Down Beat 41:48 D '74;
Ethnomusicology 19:497 n3 '75; Jazz Report 8:3
n5 '74; Jazz Journal 29:9 Ja '76; Popular Music
and Society 4:52-53 nl '75 Second Line 26:32
Fall '74

SELECTIVE DISCOGRAPHY

"Astoria Strut"/"Duet Stomp." Victor V-38576, 1929.
"Careless Love"/"Charleston Blues." Circle J-1004, 1946.
"Dreaming of You"/"I Can't Last Long." Vocalion 03314,
    1936.
"High Society"/"Fish Tail Blues." Autograph 606, 1924.
"Just a Rank Stud"/"Kansas City Hill." Vocalion 03313,
    1936.
New Orleans. Collectors' Classics CC-45, 1929.
"Swingin' with Lee"/"Woman That I Love." Century 4010,
    1947.
"Weary Blues"/"Tiger Rag." Autograph 607, 1924.

John Coltrane

Cole, Bill. John Coltrane. New York: Schirmer Books; London: Collier Macmillan, 1976. vi, 264 pp. photographs, musical examples. bibliography. discography. indexes.

Written by one who has been close to the contemporary jazz scene, this last-published of the three books on John Coltrane is an attempt to understand the subject from the standpoint of the African cultural heritage as espoused in the provocative philosophical writings of Fela Sowande. In spite of its mystical approach, underdeveloped narrative, and editorial shortcomings, the book provides insights not found in the other books on Coltrane. It treats Coltrane's professional career from the mid-1940s to his death in 1967; individuals who influenced his musical development--Charlie Parker, Jimmy Heath, Miles Davis, Johnny Hodges, Thelonius Monk, Ahmed Malik, Eric Dolphy, and John Gilmore; and mentions his support for other and younger jazz artists such as Archie Shepp. In the process the author discusses Coltrane's "visionary contacts with Charlie Parker . . . ; his breaking [of] the cycle of drugs and alcohol; his constant search into and preoccupation with music; and in 1958, the payoff of hard work manifesting itself through Trane's acknowledgement as the greatest tenor saxophonist alive" (p. 135). The work includes a chronology of "Recording Dates and Personnel" and indexes of "Names and Subjects" and "Music Discussed."

John Coltrane

Reviews: Booklist 73:874 F 15 '77; Cadence
2:28-29 Jy '77; Choice 14:693 Jy '77; Coda
n162:12-13 Au 1 '78; High Fidelity/Musical
America 27:137 Ju '77; Jazz Journal
International 30:24 Au '77; Melody Maker 52:46
Jy 16 '77; Music Journal 36:43 F '78; New
Republic 176:26 F 12 '77; Publishers Weekly
210:65 N 15 '76; West Coast Review of Books 3:31
Mr '77

Simpkins, Cuthbert Ormond. Coltrane: A Biography. Perth
Amboy, N.J., and Philadelphia: Herndon House, 1975. 287
pp. photograph, musical examples. appendixes.

This perceptive and authoritative-appearing work on
the life and music of the great saxophonist strikes
an effective balance between objectivity and
subjectivity, giving a fairly balanced view of its
subject. With information taken from numerous
interviews, writings, and firsthand knowledge, the
author first tells of Coltrane's family background
and his childhood in High Point, North Carolina;
his start in music at twelve, when he joined a new
community beginner's band; and his childhood social
and academic orientations and activities. We learn
that Coltrane enrolled in Philadelphia's Granoff
Studios, following high school, where he studied
the saxophone and musical composition. We learn
that his early musical influences were Lester
Young, Charlie Parker, and Coleman Hawkins and that
his first professional job was as a member of a
Philadelphia "cocktail lounge group in 1945"
(p. 21). Coltrane then performed, successively, in
bands led by Joe Webb, King Kolax, Eddie
"Cleanhead" Vinson, Jimmy Heath, Dizzy Gillespie,
Earl Bostic, Johnny Hodges, Miles Davis, and
Thelonius Monk; his first professional recording
was made with the Gillespie band in 1949. In the
late 1940s Coltrane became addicted to narcotics
and, later, to alcohol. He subsequently conquered
both, adopted rigid health measures, and developed
an extensive practice regimen.

Simpkins includes information and speculation
about how Coltrane may have been motivated to
develop the "high sound" on his instrument, how he
"discovered" the soprano saxophone, and how he
derived his "sheets of sound" concept from sounds
and procedures characteristic of the concert harp.
Coltrane early had difficulties with critics, but
the gap between his music and the critics'
perception of it narrowed gradually. Around 1961

his acceptance by both critics and the public was widespread. Then came a quick return to poor critical notice when his style began to change again, only to lead to new critical acclaim in 1965, when he rose to unprecedented heights of fame.

Coltrane's obsession with his art, his two marriages, his unusual personal and social demeanor, his religious orientation and behavior, and his personality and character are all treated here in the context of his personal and musical desires, strivings, and accomplishments. Professionally and historically, the work chronicles, essentially, the logical development of Coltrane's style from bebop; through his harp-inspired harmonic approach; through modal improvisation, use of ragas, and procedures attendant on all of these; and the formation of his own band in 1960. Intellectually, Coltrane is treated as one who "engaged in an accelerated accumulation of knowledge and understanding" (p. 105), in which he read "books on other cultures, math, art and artists such as Van Gogh, music theory, physics, biology, African history, spirituals, among others" (p. 105). His record collection included music from a variety of cultures. In discussing these matters, Simpkins reveals Coltrane's aesthetic orientation and beliefs; views on the critics and their effect on his career; and use of new and unusual performance techniques and procedures. Mention is made of Coltrane's tours of Europe and Japan and the influence of Duke Ellington on his recording procedure. The author also gives analyses and criticisms of some of Coltrane's recordings and presents brief bio-career sketches of Lester Young, Charlie Parker, Sun Ra, and Ornette Coleman, with mention of Coltrane's relationships with Eric Dolphy, Alvin Ayler, and others.

Reviews: Come-All-Ye 5:10 Fall '84; Coda n146:26+ Ap '76; Jazz Magazine (US) 1:43 nl '76; Kliatt Young Adult Paperback Book Guide 15:40 Fall '81; Melody Maker 52:46 Jy 16 '77; New York Times 124:25 Ju 28 '75; New York Times Book Review p16 Au 10 '75; Orkester Journalen 44:30-33 Ju '76

Thomas, J. C. Chasin' The Trane: The Music and Mystique of John Coltrane. Garden City, N.Y.: Doubleday, 1975. 252 pp. photographs. discography.

John Coltrane

Thomas offers details that are absent from the
other Coltrane biographies and also provides a few
different accounts of the same events. Although
the book is fraught with musical malaproprisms,
misperceptions, and errors of fact and assumption,
it nevertheless is a good source of information on
and insight into the saxophonist's life and
career. Treated are Coltrane's early life,
including his family and school life in High Point,
North Carolina, his childhood friends, and his move
to Philadelphia following his graduation from high
school; his pre-professional years, including his
induction into the United States Navy in 1945 and
his studies at Philadelphia's Ornstein Music
School; his professional career, including stints
with rhythm & blues and jazz bands such as those
led by Eddie "Cleanhead" Vinson, Bull Moose
Jackson, King Kolax, the Heath Brothers, Dizzy
Gillespie, Earl Bostic, Johnny Hodges, Thelonius
Monk, and Miles Davis; and the formation of the
Coltrane band.

Laced with quotes from a number of individuals
who knew Coltrane in his formative years and in his
mature years--musicians such as Benny Golson, Hank
Mobley, Cal Massey, Eddie Harris, Billy Taylor,
Sonny Rollins, Jimmy Cobb, McCoy Tyner, critics
Martin Williams and Ralph Gleason, impresario
George Wein, saxophone technical expert Tony Rulli,
a mysterious "Trane's Lady," and others--the work
treats aspects of Coltrane's life and career such
as: how he hired and fired his sidemen; his
mid-career matriculation at the Granoff School of
Music in Philadelphia; his relationships with his
two wives; his drug and alcohol habits and how he
quit them; his character, such as his tendency
toward extremes; his spiritual/mystical orientations, beliefs, and behaviors and their relation to
his music, particularly to the creation of the
album A Love Supreme; and his tour of Japan, where
he was "the most popular musician in Japan"
(p. 208). The comments on and insights into
Coltrane's musical purposing, his method of
practicing, and his constant search for knowledge
and perfection are informative and revealing.

Reviews: Booklist 72:279 O 15 '75; Choice 12:856
S '75; Coda n141:33-34 S '75; Coda n146:27 Ap
'76; Creem 7:63 Au '75; Down Beat 42:35+ Ju 5
'75; Instrumentalist 31:22 D '76; Jazz Forum
n39:21 '76; Jazz Forum n42:67 '76; Jazz Journal

John Coltrane

29:26 Jy '76; Jazz Podium 26:38-39 Jy '77; Kirkus Reviews 43:229 F 15 '75; Kirkus Reviews 43:392 Ap 1 '75; Kliatt Young Adult Paperback Book Guide 11:39 Spring '77; Library Journal 100:989 My 15 '75; Melody Maker 51:26 My 8 '76; Music Journal 33:42 S '75; Music Journal 34:30 D '76; New York Times 124:25 Ju 28 '75; New York Times Book Review p16 Au 10 '75; Orkester Journalen 43:11+ O '75; Publishers Weekly 207:76 F 17 '75; Reprint Bulletin--Book Reviews 22:28 O 4 '77

SELECTIVE DISCOGRAPHY

Ascension. Impulse 95, 1965.
The Best of John Coltrane. 3 vols. Impulse 9200-2, 9223-2, 9227-2.
Dizzy Gillespie Sextet. DeeGee 3600/1, 1951.
Giant Steps. Atlantic 1311, 1959.
Interstellar Space. Impulse 9277, 1967.
LeGrand Jazz. Columbia 8079, 1958.
A Love Supreme. Impulse AS-77, 1964.
Meditations. Impulse 9110, 1965.
Monk's Music. Riverside 3004, 1957.
My Favorite Things. Atlantic 1361, 1960.
Round About Midnight. Columbia 949, 1955.
SoulTrane. Prestige 7531, 1958.
Two Tenors. Prestige 7670, 1956.

Andrae Crouch

Crouch, Andrae, with Nina Ball. <u>Through It All</u>. Foreword by Nicky Cruz. Waco, Tex.: Word Books, 1974. 148 pp. photographs.

Born a twin to a father who was a cleaning-shop proprietor and a "bootleggin' street preacher" (p. 19), this gospel singer, pianist, and group leader was early introduced to religion and to the world of the economically and socially unfortunate. Furthermore, Crouch's great-uncle was pastor of a Church of God in Christ and had "been a state overseer" for that denomination "for over forty years" (p. 20). The whole Crouch family "loved music. Dad would buy records and we'd wear them out playing them over and over again" (p. 22). The three Crouch siblings were mischievous, and Andrae gives anecdotes of such activity as he details his childhood experiences. Of his parents' cultural orientations, we learn that "Dad's side was the soulful side, the chitlin and hogmaw side. My mother's people were all God-fearing people--on the conservative side. Her family didn't eat chitlins and hogmaws. They always had fried chicken. They almost never used ain't" (p. 31). At nine Crouch was converted, started testifying "to all my teachers at school," and "loved church so much I never wanted to miss a chance to go" (p. 38). Soon after his conversion he learned to play the piano, started to play for church services, and formed "The Crouch Trio" with his sister and brother. In his high school years he started a church choir and also a singing group called the COGICs which sang at churches, conventions, and colleges.

Soon after he graduated from high school, The Disciples--a group of three singers--were organized. Then he began working at Los Angeles' Teen Challenge Center, where he formed an Addict's Choir, and attending L.I.F.E. Bible College part-time. "After school, I'd have choir rehearsals and then we'd go out to different places for services at night. We also presented programs on the streets and in schools and parks. A staff member led the program or services. We'd sing and give testimonies" (p. 57). Soon Crouch's first song and a song book were published, The Disciples' first album was cut at Light Records, and the group made its first tour of parts of the Orient. In the telling of his life, Crouch discusses his and The Disciples' ministry and music, his illness, incidents of racial prejudice and discrimination against himself, his experiences with demons, his religious philosophy, and his life in music and in Christ.

SELECTIVE DISCOGRAPHY

The Best of Andrae. LC-5678.
Finally. LC-5784.
From Here to Eternity. LC-5546.
I'll Be Thinking of You. LC-5763.
Live at Carnegie Hall. LC-5602.
Live in London. LC-5717.
More of the Best. LC-5795.
No Time to Lose. LC-5863.
Take Me Back. LC-5637.
This Is Another Day. LC-5683.

Wendell Phillips Dabney

Beaver, Joseph T., Jr. <u>I Want You to Know Wendell Phillips</u>
<u>Dabney</u>. Mexico: n.p., 1958. 47 pp.

No more than a brief character sketch and
testimonial, this little pamphlet gives a view of
an early twentieth-century composer, guitarist, and
banjoist who was also widely respected as a
scholarly journalist. Dabney was visited at his
newspaper office in Cincinnati, where he edited <u>The</u>
<u>Union</u>, by a wide variety of individuals: "writers,
and scholars, artists, actors, orators, civic
leaders from various parts of the country, even an
honest-to-goodness cowboy from the Wild West, or an
anthropologist now and then. . . . There were nuns
and teachers, priests, ministers, or just any
layman" who came to seek his counsel, conversation,
and company (pp. 15-16). As an editor, "there were
occasions where his writings betrayed the bitter
theme with respect to the denials of his people, a
minority group, even though his works as a whole I
would say embody some messages for mankind in its
entirety. Those of his own group whom he felt had
shortcomings he rebuked. For those of the
majority, who were deserving, he spared no vent of
hell" (p. 26). Dabney wrote two method books for
the guitar and one reference book and was a "school
teacher, musician and composer, author, member of
the Cincinnati Treasury for 21 years" (p. 23). He
was eighty-five when this pamphlet was written in
1951.

Dorothy Dandridge

Dandridge, Dorothy, and Earl Conrad. <u>Everything and Nothing: The Dorothy Dandridge Tragedy</u>. New York: Abelard-Schuman, 1970. viii, 215 pp. photographs.

This "exotically beautiful singer of the Western World," whose "gross earnings exceeded a million dollars when [she] was in [her] mid-thirties" and who was the first black actress "to achieve both film stardom and a nomination for a best actress Academy Award" tells here of her tragic experiences in seeking acceptance by the white world (pp. 1-2). This story is a frank revelation of her behavior and her attitudes during that search. By the age of three, Dandridge was making stage appearances in Cleveland; and in the late 1920s she and her sister Vivian toured for the National Baptist Convention-- one state a month--as the Wonder Kids, singing, dancing, and doing skits. When she was eight, her fatherless family moved to Chicago, where the Depression was taking its toll and where work was scarce. There, "when Mother was out of the house, Auntie Ma-ma taught us. She brought out books and taught us to read. Yet mostly our learning was of the hard knocks variety, the kind you get out in the world contending with people, doing things, working. Vivian and I hadn't seen the inside of a school building nor had we ever sat in a classroom" (p. 32).

Then came the move to Los Angeles, where the sisters got intermittent film work, traveled to one-nighters all across the country, and entered

public school. Much later, Dandridge was in resi-
dence at the Los Angeles Cotton Club and was
married to Harold Nicholas of the dancing Nicholas
Brothers. Shortly thereafter she joined the Actors
Laboratory, where Anthony Quinn and Marilyn Monroe
were among her classmates. Soon there was a
divorce, and Dandridge became a nightclub singer.
Following her debut at New York's La Vie en Rose,
Look magazine did a feature article on her success
there, likening her style to "a caterpillar on a
hot rock" (p. 84).

While most black performers worked jazz clubs in
the 1950s, Dandridge worked the "carriage trade"
rooms that catered to wealthy whites. Dandridge
did not regard herself as a good singer, "only one
with a sultry or torchy voice. . . . My vocal
range was less than an octave; there was no
mechanism for range or variety" (p. 74). But her
singing of Cole Porter songs allowed her to project
a style of "cosmopolitan sophistication," in which
she acted "the character of each song as determined
by the lyrics" (pp. 80, 83). Between 1951 and 1952
she traveled widely, flying all over the world to
perform in supper clubs and films, and was pursued
by men with financial empires and fortunes. Then
came her extraordinary successes in the lead roles
of the films Carmen Jones, in which she won top
acclaim, and Porgy and Bess, in which she starred
with Sidney Poitier and Sammy Davis, Jr. All the
while, she was "running backward from my bad
marriage and my retarded child, and I wanted to
make it as a woman. I wanted to be in the
backdrops of some man's life" (p. 170). But following her successes, her attitude at that time was
such that "it wasn't possible for people to get too
near me. I dismissed them; I rejected scripts,
writers, deals, advice, men. I made people wait.
Judgment wasn't as important to me as the
opportunity to arbitrarily settle matters as
befitted my whim. Like so many, I too became a
queen" (p. 179).

Dandridge's film career soon declined. She
turned down the role of Tuptin in The King and I,
and by 1962 she was in trouble financially and "had
been through friends, lovers, pictures, two
husbands, two colors, international travels, ups
and downs" (p. 202). By 1964 she was "weary now as
any river that ever flowed: the disasters, the
mistakes, the fortune made and displaced, the loves
held and lost. What do you do when you are still

young, and, so they say, still beautiful, and
nothing much has meaning except to stay, at last,
to hold on, to carry on regardless each day,
wondering sometimes what for. Then what do you
do?" (p. 215).

Reviews: AB Bookman's Weekly 47:1046 Mr 29 '71;
Best Sellers 30:441 Ja 15 '71; Booklist 67:539
Mr 1 '71; Kirkus Reviews 38:721 Jy 1 '70;
Library Journal 95:3768 N 1 '70; Publishers
Weekly 198:71 Jy 27 '70

Miles Davis

Carr, Ian. <u>Miles Davis: A Biography</u>. Foreword by Len
Lyons. New York: William Morrow, 1982. 310 pp. photographs, musical examples. discography. bibliography.
index.

This work documents Miles Davis's career as
stylist, innovator, trumpet player, and bandleader
in jazz genres ranging from bebop to jazz/
rock/fusion. In the process, the author presents
behind-the-scenes accounts of "historic recording
sessions and . . . analyses that came out of them,"
as well as information related to Davis's penchant
for "stylish clothes"; his passion for Ferrari
automobiles; his skill at boxing; his run-ins with
the New York City police; his several injuries and
his precarious health; and his "romance with a
famous actress" (p. 11). This critical and
objective biography is a fine research source,
graced as it is with a good bibliography, effective
musical examples, a complete discography, and a
useful index.

Among the book's eighteen chapters are
provocative ones such as "The First Great Quintet,"
"Is It Jazz," "After Coltrane," "Miles in the Sky,"
and "Jazz Into Rock Will Go." Davis's early home
environment in East St. Louis is discussed in these
and other chapters, as are: his early musical
influences and models; his musical activities in
the St. Louis area; his association with Charlie
Parker, Gil Evans, and others; the significance of
recorded performances such as "Walkin"/"Blue 'n'

Boogie"; his blindfold test successes; his cosmopolitan jazz tastes and his appreciation for music from the entire historical jazz spectrum; the Miles Ahead days; and the emergence of "The First Great Sextet."

More personally, the author treats the motivations and the conditions of Davis's strivings and his accomplishments; the effects of musical and social events on his life and his art; his interactions with his sidemen, colleagues, producers, and impresarios; his "unpredictable and often mystifying behavior" (p. 99); his health regimen, including his boxing and his diet; racial incidents in which he was involved; and the deterioration of his health. Even more important, there are discussions of Davis as composer; of the continuity of his style and his output; of his move from an essentially Western approach to improvisation to the strengthening of the non-Western elements of his style; of his effort to become a "folk hero" in the black community with the production of the album On the Corner; and of the diffuse nature of his later recordings.

Reviews: Best Sellers 42:305 N '82; Booklist 79:178 O 1 '82; British Book News p379 Ju '82; Choice 20:998 Mr '83; Christian Science Monitor 75:B7 Ju 24 '83; Christian Science Monitor 75:11 S 28 '83; Christian Science Monitor 76:B8 Jy 6 '84; Coda n197:21 Au 1 '84; Jazz Journal International 37:20 O '84; Jazz Times p13 F '83; Kirkus Reviews 50:832 Jy 15 '82; Library Journal 107:1662 S 1 '82; Los Angeles Times Book Review p4 D 5 '82; National Review 35:888 Jy 22 '83; New Statesman 103:24 Mr 5 '82; New York Times Book Review 87:11 S 12 '82; New York Times Book Review 89:30 Jy 15 '84; Publishers Weekly 222:50 Jy 2 '82; Village Voice 28:76 Ju 28 '83; West Coast Review of Books 8:45 N '82; Wall Street Journal 201:30 Ja 26 '83

Chambers, Jack. Milestones I: The Music and Times of Miles Davis to 1960. Toronto, Buffalo, and London: University of Toronto Press, 1983. xii, 345 pp. photographs. bibliography. index.

_____. Milestones II. New York: Beach Tree Books, 1985. 416 pp. photographs. bibliography. index.

Miles Davis

This impressive work

is organized into two volumes, which
subdivide Davis's long and extra-
ordinarily productive career into its
main phases. Milestones I traces the
emergence of the teenaged Davis from East
St. Louis, Illinois, into post-war New
York City, where he joined the ranks of
the bebop revolutionaries, worked out his
individual style, and took his place in
the forefront of jazz music by late 1959.
Davis's activities during this period are
covered in two main movements: the first,
under the heading of "Boplicity," details
his apprenticeship, first in his hometown
and later under the aegis of Charlie
Parker and Dizzy Gillespie, culminating
in his first masterwork with the
short-lived experimental nonet of 1948;
the second, titled "Miles Ahead,"
concerns his creative recess during his
years of heroin addiction and his
dramatic return to form in the 1950s,
culminating in the years of the first
great quintet and sextet. Milestones II
takes up his music and his times from
1960, also in two main movements: it
begins, in "Prince of Darkness," with his
formal reorganization of bebop in the
second great quintet and continues in
"Pangaea" with his restless search for
further formal expansions, leading to
fusions with free form, rock, and other
music (p. xi).

These volumes offer many more details of the
trumpeter's musical development than any of the
other studies on him, and they contain valuable
information on the workaday relationships, musical
contributions, and accomplishments of Davis's
sidemen. A realistic view of all aspects of the
jazz life is given, including recording sessions,
the formation and dissolution of bands,
exploitation by and of members of the jazz
community, heroin addiction, tensions and conflicts
between jazzmen and the community at large, life on
"the road," and so forth.

Reviews: Milestones I: Book World 14:10 F 26
'84; Books in Canada 13:11 Ja '84; Booklist
80:780 F 1 '84; Cadence 10:22-23 Mr '84;

Canadian Forum 64:34 My '84; Choice 21:1143 Ap '84; Coda n197:21-23 Au 1 '84; Jazz Times p18 Jy '84; Notes 42:60-61 nl '85; Quill & Quire 50:36 F '84; Variety 314:114 F 15 '84. Milestones II: Notes 42:60-61 nl '85

Cole, Bill. Miles Davis: A Musical Biography. New York: William Morrow, 1974. 256 pp. discography. bibliography. transcriptions. index.

The book begins with a short introduction that provides a very brief and lightly encapsulated background to the events and people in jazz from bebop in the late 1930s to the jazz of the late 1960s. The first two sections of the book, "Biography" and "Style," contain the text about Miles Davis. The first section is primarily a chronology of Miles's recordings, with details on the members of some of Davis's recording sessions and the songs that were played on them, between 1945, when Davis began recording, and the early 1970s, when Bitches Brew was recorded. Among those mentioned as participating in Davis's bands and recording sessions are Sonny Rollins, Thelonius Monk, Horace Silver, Art Blakey, Max Roach, J. J. Johnson, Kenny Clarke, John Coltrane, Paul Chambers, Red Garland, Bill Evans, Cannonball Adderley, Ron Carter, Herbie Hancock, and Wayne Shorter. The "Biography" section begins with Davis's early musical experiences in East St. Louis and with Charlie Parker and Dizzy Gillespie in New York. It then treats his collaboration with Gil Evans beginning in 1948; his problems with drugs in the early 1950s; his first performance at the second Newport Jazz Festival in 1955 and the critical acclaim that accompanied it; his throat operation and permanent vocal chord injury; his increasing interest in brass/rhythm sonorities as a result of his participation in Columbia's Music for Brass album; his trip to Japan in the mid-1960s; and his move toward using electric instruments in the late 1960s.

The second section of the book, titled "Style," includes analyses of some of Davis's solos on recordings. It characterizes Davis as a player who performs best at moderate tempos in mid-register, who plays short phrases that are often most interesting rhythmically, who plays with a great deal of intensity, and who is a lyrical player who "utilizes space brilliantly, with accents falling all over the place" (p. 133). "His use of triplets makes a traceable evolution throughout his career; his use of the chromatic scale for runs is another one of his patented devices" (p. 163). The third section of the book contains a list of the recording sessions in which Davis played from May, 1945, to September, 1972. Accompanying the date and place of each session is a list of the pieces played, with those composed by Davis indicated, and a list of the personnel on the date. The book concludes with a section of thirteen transcriptions from selected Davis solos on record.

Reviews: Book World pF10 F 6 '77; Booklist 71:366 D 1 '74; Choice 11:1644 Ja '74; Coda 12:31-32 n3 '75; Down Beat 42:40+ Mr 13 '75; Jazz Journal 27:16 O '74; Jazz Podium 24:26 F '75; Kirkus Reviews 42:558 My 15 '74; Music Journal 32:24 D '74; New York Times Book Review p6 Au 18 '74; Publishers Weekly 205:62 My 20 '74

James, Michael. Miles Davis. Kings of Jazz. New York: A. S. Barnes, 1961. 89 pp. photographs. discography.

This brief book discusses the development of the trumpeter's technique and style from his days as a novice sideman in Charlie Parker's 1947 combo to the year 1959, when the album Kind of Blue was recorded. Commenting on Davis's strengths and weaknesses, his use of blues inflections and powerful drummers, his phrasing, and his tone, the author treats Davis's evolution in the context of the jazz mainstream, pointing out that by 1954 "he was far more consistent stylistically . . . than he had ever been before" (p. 50). By 1958, we learn, Davis was basing his improvisations on scales rather than on chord progressions, his phrasing had become more sparse, and "the rests in his melodic line more prolonged" (p. 71). Maturing "within the bop idiom to develop a style of improvisation that was clearly his own," he also sought and achieved new modes of expression that would change the shape of the jazz to come (p. 78).

Reviews: Jazz Hot n167:41-42 Jy/Au '61; Jazz Journal 14:36 Jy '61; Jazz Monthly 7:27 F '62

Nisenson, Eric. 'Round About Midnight: A Portrait of Miles Davis. New York: Dial Press, 1982. xi, 244 pp. photographs. discography. index.

The author of this book has written a study of a jazz trumpeter "whose genius [he] perceived as

being as universal as that of Stravinsky, Joyce, or
Picasso" (p. x). The book is an effective chronicle
of Davis's musical life from his childhood through
1981. Pre-professional matters are treated, such
as: Davis's birth into a middle-class family and
his childhood musical development as a member of
his high-school band; Clark Terry's serving as one
of Davis's mentors as the two trumpeters jammed
around St. Louis; and his opportunity to play,
briefly, with the Billy Eckstine band immediately
following his graduation from high school. Davis's
first steady professional job was with the Eddie
Randall band, from which, in 1945, he moved on to
New York to join Charlie Parker. We learn about his
search for Parker after he arrived in New York; his
involvement with the bebop movement; his
apprenticeship under Parker; and the influence of
Thelonius Monk and Freddie Webster on Davis's
style.

In 1947, having played with Parker for more than
a year, Davis played in "the tightest band Bird
ever had, and probably the most coherent bop unit
around" (p. 50). In the next year, 1948, Davis
spearheaded the birth of the "cool" concept, with
the organization of the Miles Davis Band (the
nonet). In 1949 he found his style in the first
recording session of his group. Then he played a
role in the advent of "hard bop." The author
treats Davis's arrival as a recognized and popular
jazz artist in 1955; his band's "becoming one of
the most successful and sought-after jazz groups in
the country" by 1957 (p. 131); his addiction to
heroin and his withdrawal from it; his tours of
Europe; and his "modal" period and its
contributions to the continuing evolution of jazz.

By the late 1950s Davis had become "the brujo of
American music, the great teacher, even the
alchemist of jazz" (p. 131), one whose "business
acumen helped make [him] one of the richest men in
jazz" (p. 158). Having made this point, the author
proceeds to examine the development of the style of
Davis's groups through the 1960s as shown in albums
ranging from Someday My Prince Will Come (1961)
through Sorcerer (1967). Then comes a discussion of
Davis's move toward jazz/rock in the late sixties
with Miles in the Sky and Filles de Kilimanjaro. We
learn that in late 1969 Miles moved in the
direction of "the use of electronics and the
freedom of improvisation; the music of the
moment--that 'thing' that was to him the essence of

jazz--and the multitextured colors that in the past had been possible through scores written for the orchestra" (p. 205). The result of this latter move was the album _In a Silent Way_. Davis explored the possibilities in this direction until 1975, when he retired. In 1981 he returned to the bandstand and the studio with _The Man with the Horn_.

Reviews: Best Sellers 42:385 Ja '83; Booklist 79:178 O 1 '82; Choice 20:998 Mr '83; Jazz Times p13 My '83; Kirkus Reviews 50:1091 S 15 '82; Library Journal 107:1881 O 1 '82; Publishers Weekly 222:70 S 24 '82; Quill & Quire 49:41 F '83; Village Voice 28:76 Ju 28 '83; Wall Street Journal 201:30 Ja 26 '83

SELECTIVE DISCOGRAPHY

Birth of the Cool. Capitol N-16168.
Bitches Brew. Columbia PG-26.
In a Silent Way. Columbia PC-9875.
Kind of Blue. Columbia PC-8163.
The Man with the Horn. Columbia FC-36790.
Miles Ahead. Columbia PC-8633.
Miles Davis. 2 vols. Blue Note 81501E/2E.
Miles Smiles. Columbia PC-9401.
Milestones. Columbia PC-8633E.
My Funny Valentine. Columbia PC-1906.
Porgy and Bess. Columbia PC-8085.
Sketches of Spain. Columbia CK-08271.
The Very Best of Bird. 2 WB-3198.
You're Under Arrest. Columbia FC-40023.

Sammy Davis, Jr.

Davis, Sammy, Jr., Burt Boyar, and Jane Boyar. <u>Yes I Can:</u>
<u>The Story of Sammy Davis, Jr.</u> 1965. 2nd ed. New York:
Pocket Books, 1966. 626 pp. photographs.

From the poverty of black vaudeville Sammy Davis,
Jr., rose to a position as "the greatest
entertainer in the world" (p. 523). In this
powerful autobiography the reader follows the life
and career of an extraordinary individual from his
beginning in Harlem in a poor family and his start
in show business in 1928. At the age of three he
joined his father and his partner in their act,
later joining them permanently when they became the
Will Mastin Trio. As the story unfolds, the reader
gets a clear and true picture of: what it was like
to be the world's greatest entertainer and an
Afro-American in a racist society between the 1930s
and the 1960s; Davis the individual--"dynamic,
cocky, flamboyant, naive, defiant . . . spontaneous, clever, generous, sophisticated . . . aggres-
sive, egotistical, tough-tender" (front-matter);
and the motivations and enticements of a
show-business career.

Haunting Davis throughout his life and work was
the question "What do I have to accomplish before I
can walk on both sides of the world (black and
white) in peace? With dignity?" (p. 288). It was
a question with which he was to become preoccupied
as he strove to be loyal to both sides. Performing
in night clubs all across the country and becoming
a star in that realm of show business, he moved

onto Broadway with Mr. Wonderful in 1956. "Mr. Wonderful was more than just a hit show. It's the first show in which both Negro and white performers worked together on the same stage and after five minutes nobody cared or even noticed the difference" (p. 403). During its run Davis, an indefatigable entertainer and socializer, in one week did "eight performances of Mr. Wonderful, appeared at nine benefits, rehearsed and performed on the Steve Allen Show . . . appeared on radio with several disc jockeys . . . entertained parties of eight to twelve every night for dinner," and "ended [his] evenings with parties at his apartment" (p. 383). Such a practice was typical of his active professional and social life.

In the course of his career, which was primarily night-club oriented, Davis made several films, including Anna Lucasta with Eartha Kitt, Porgy and Bess, and Ocean's Eleven. Davis also discusses his relationships with a variety of friends and acquaintances, such as Bill "Bojangles" Robinson, Frank Sinatra, Humphrey Bogart, George M. Cohan, Jr., Tony Curtis, Jerry Lewis, Mickey Rooney, and Nat Cole. The book ends with accounts of the humiliations he suffered before and during his marriage to Swedish actress May Britt in the 1960s and the pleasantries of his hopes for their future: "Perhaps all the success and the failures, all that I did, were necessary for me and for those I love so that now, after thirty-five years, this is really only the beginning" (p. 626).

Reviews: AB Bookman's Weekly 36:948 S 20 '65; Best Sellers 25:263 O 1 '65; Book Week p1 S 19 '65; Booklist 62:38 S 1 '65; Booklist 62:320 N 15 '65; Choice 2:762 Ja '66; Christian Science Monitor 57:11 S 30 '65; Christian Science Monitor 57:B2 D 2 '65; Horn Book Magazine 42:334 Ju '66; Kirkus Reviews 33:656 Jy 1 '65; Kirkus Reviews 33:694 Jy 15 '65; Library Journal 90:3277 Au '65; Library Journal 90:5114 N 15 '65; Life 59:21 N 5 '65; National Observer 4:24 O 4 '65; Negro Digest 15:94 Ja '66; New Statesman 70:844 N 26 '65; New Yorker 41:246 O 30 '65; New York Review of Books 5:15 Ja 20 '66; New York Times Book Review p1 S 19 '65; Observer (London) p28 N 7 '65; Publishers Weekly 190:70 Au 15 '66; Punch 249:938 D 22 '65; Saturday Review 49:35 O 29 '66; Saturday Review 49:38 D 17 '66; Times Literary Supplement p1044 N 25 '65

Sammy Davis, Jr.

SELECTIVE DISCOGRAPHY

"As Long As She Needs Me." Reprise 20138, 1963.
"The Candy Man." MGM 14320, 1962.
Closest of Friends. DBX EC-7041.
Hey There (It's Sammy Davis, Jr. at His Dynamite Great-
    est). MCA S2-4109.
"I've Gotta Be Me." Reprise 0779, 1958.
"Love Me or Leave Me." Decca 29484, 1955.
"Me and My Shadow." Reprise 20128, 1962.
"The People Tree." MGM 14426, 1972.
"Sam's Song." Reprise 20128, 1962.
That Old Black Magic. MCA 20198.
Treasury of Hits. Reprise 96096.
"What Kind of Fool Am I?" Reprise 20048, 1962.

R. Nathaniel Dett

McBrier, Vivian Flagg. R. Nathaniel Dett: His Life and Works (1882-1943). The Sigma Pi Phi Series. Washington, D.C.: Associated Publishers, 1977. xi, 152 pp. photographs, musical examples. appendixes.

Dett was a composer, lecturer, teacher, choral conductor, piano recitalist, author, and editor/compiler. In this book we learn of Dett's youth in Niagara Falls and his first experiences in improvising at the piano; his first piano recital, which included several of his own compositions, at thirteen; his study at the Oberlin Conservatory; his teaching career at Lane College in Jackson, Tennessee, at Lincoln Institute in Jefferson City, Missouri, at Hampton Institute in Hampton, Virginia, and at Bennett College in Greensboro, North Carolina; and the continuation of his studies with Nadia Boulanger in Fontainebleau, France, and at the Eastman School of Music. He was the recipient of the honorary doctorate from Howard University and from Oberlin College; he served as president and was a long-time member of the National Association of Negro Musicians; he was the recipient of the Harmon Award for excellence in composition; and he saw the formation in Washington, D.C., of the Nathaniel Dett Choral Society.

During his studies at Oberlin, Dett came into contact with the music and aesthetic philosophy of Anton Dvořák. Of this music the author says, "Here indeed was the concept--the use of traditional folk melodies in art music--which was to direct and control his creative efforts throughout his life" (p. 11). The publication of his compositions began in 1912 and continued throughout his life; he served as editor and compiler of two books: Religious Folk Songs of the Negro (1927) and the Dett Collection of Negro Spirituals (1936). The book contains brief analytical discussions of several of Dett's compositions, including "Juba Dance" from In the Bottoms Suite, Listen to the Lambs, and The Ordering of Moses. The appendixes include a list of Dett's works, reprints of several of his recitals and concerts, and "Examples of Techniques and Style." The latter illustrates "(1) the ways in which Dett used the Negro spiritual and Negro idiom; (2) various compositional techniques used; (3) and the general characteristics of his style" (p. 134).

SELECTIVE DISCOGRAPHY

"Balm in Gilead." Period SPL-580, c1950.
The Chariot Jubilee. Audio House AHS-30F75, 1975.
"Go Tell It on the Mountain." RCA Camden CAL-344, c1950.
"I Couldn't Hear Nobody Pray." RCA Camden CAL-344, c1955.
In the Bottoms. Desto DC-7102/3, c1971.
"Listen to the Lambs." Columbia ML-6235/MS-6835, 1965.
The Ordering of Moses. Silver Crest TAL-42868-S, 1968.

Baby Dodds

Dodds, Warren. The Baby Dodds Story, as told to Larry Gara. Los Angeles: Contemporary Press, 1959. xiii, 96 pp. photographs. index.

Born in New Orleans in 1894, drummer Warren "Baby" Dodds "was inspired by music all around," especially by that of his musical family, which included a father, uncle, mother, and sisters (all of whom were accomplished musicians), and his brother Johnny, the famed clarinetist (p. 2). Dodds studied the drums privately and early did street-parade work with Bunk Johnson. Subsequently, while still living in New Orleans, he was, in succession, a regular member of Frankie Dusen's Eagle Band, Celestin's band, and the Fate Marable riverboat orchestra. Dodds was with Marable from 1918 to 1921. He joined King Oliver's Creole Jazz Band in 1921, soon settling in Chicago; and in 1924 he joined his brother's band at Kelly's Stables night club, remaining with that band until his brother's death in 1940. Thereafter, he played with a variety of groups, including that of Bunk Johnson when the latter made his comeback in 1944. In 1948 he went to France with a group led by white clarinetist Mezz Mezzrow. Later he performed in New York with a number of integrated groups led by white musicians Miff Mole, Art Hodes, and Conrad Janis. In the early 1950s, Dodds had three strokes, and although having lost strength and considerable coordination, he felt confident that "someday I will again carry out with my drumsticks and drum sets the ideas that I am now carrying around in my head" (p. 96).

As he tells his story, Dodds gives considerable information about and insight into early jazz and jazz culture in New Orleans; his musical philosophy; his innovations, including playing on the rims of the drums, striking the cymbal with the drum sticks ("I worked that out around 1919" [p. 26]); the inner workings of the King Oliver Band; his friendships and relationships with Louis Armstrong, Lil Hardin, his brother Johnny Dodds, Joe Oliver, Freddie Keppard, guitarist Lonnie Johnson, Kid Ory, and others; and his role as an ensemble drummer: "I studied each player individually. I had to study their method of improvising and to know what they intended to do. And when the band came in as a whole, in ensemble, I had to do something different again" (p. 39). In addition, he discusses the "Paul Mares sessions," in which he and his brother jammed with a number of white musicians whose names would become well known; the circumstances, conditions, and details of many of his record sessions; his work at various Chicago clubs such as Lincoln Gardens, Kelly's Stables, Three Deuces, Lamb's Club, New Plantation, 29 Club, Lower Deck, K-Nine Club, New Stables, Dreamland, Club Bagdad, Midway Gardens, Jeffrey Tavern, and the 9750 Club. Dodds died in February, 1959.

SELECTIVE DISCOGRAPHY

Jelly Roll Morton and His Red Hot Peppers, Volume 3. RCA (France) 731.059, 1926-1927.
King Oliver's Jazz Band. Smithsonian Collection, R-001, 1923.
Louis Armstrong and Earl Hines. Smithsonian Collection R-002, 1928.

Johnny Dodds

Lambert, G. E. <u>Johnny Dodds</u>. Kings of Jazz. London: Cassell, 1961. 90 pp. photographs. discography.

Focusing on clarinetist Johnny Dodds's role in the King Oliver Creole Jazz Band and Louis Armstrong's Hot Five and Hot Seven recording bands, this brief book begins with Dodd's birth in 1892 and his childhood environment, telling of his musical family, his own musical start on a toy flute, and his first stint with the Oliver band in 1920. Of his musical prowess, the author writes:

> On the stomps and rags, Dodd's part is a tremendous stimulus to the other musicians, his counterpoint continually apt, the clarinet moving with ease round the lead in a continual line of singing melody. The rhythmic drive of the group is tremendously enhanced by Dodd's biting, stomping up-tempo manner, while the natural blues inflections of his playing keeps the music away from the shallow, novelty sound of a clarinettist like Larry Shields, Dodd's counterpart in the Original Dixieland Jazz Band (p. 22).

Dodds is presented as "the only player who could even occasionally match Armstrong in ensemble jazz, and one of the very few who could create solos of a caliber not to be completely outshone by Armstrong's supreme genius" (p. 69).

Johnny Dodds

Reviews: Jazz Hot n167:41-42 Jy/Au '61; Jazz
Journal 14:36 Jy '61; Jazz Monthly 7:29 Ja '62

SELECTIVE DISCOGRAPHY

The Greatest Jazz Recordings of All Time: Kings of New
    Orleans Jazz/Jelly Roll Morton, King Oliver, and Sidney
    Bechet. Franklin Mint Record Society Tapes 17-20, 1983.
Jelly Roll Morton and His Red Hot Peppers, Volume 3. RCA
    (France) 731.059, 1926-1927.
Johnny Dodds. 2 vols. MCA (France) 510.089/510.106, 1926-
    1940.
Johnny Dodds: Sixteen Rare Recordings. RCA LPV-558, 1926-
    1929.
Johnny Dodds and Kid Ory. Epic 16004, 1926-1928.
Louis Armstrong and Earl Hines. Smithsonian Collection
    R-002, 1928.

Eric Dolphy

Simosko, Vladimir, and Barry Tepperman. Eric Dolphy: A Musical Biography and Discography. Washington, D.C.: Smithsonian Institution Press, 1974. photographs. discography. bibliography.

Not an actual biography, this work chronicles the development of the musical style and recorded legacy of this saxophonist, bass clarinetist, and flutist, discussing his influences, predilections, and strengths. It is the chronicle of a legacy which "defines an artist of unique versatility and enormously vital spiritual resources" (p. 17). In discussing "His Medium," "His Musical Biography," and "His Recordings," the authors mention Dolphy's birth in 1928 to parents of West Indian ancestry; his start in music as a clarinetist and later as an oboist in his high-school band; his fine musicianship in high school and his winning of a scholarship to attend the University of Southern California Music School; and his service in the Army and later attendance at and graduation from the "U.S. Naval School of Music in Washington, D.C."

The authors discuss Dolphy's joining the Chico Hamilton Quintet in 1958; his move from California to New York in 1960, where he free-lanced and played with the Charlie Mingus Quartet; his membership in a sextet led by John Coltrane; the formation of his own group in 1962; his professional activity in Sweden; and his settling in Paris in 1964. The stylistic treatment stresses

and is based on his recordings with Hamilton,
Mingus, Coltrane, Gunther Schuller, Oliver Nelson,
Ken McIntyre, Abbey Lincoln, Ornette Coleman,
Booker Little, Ron Carter, Orchestra U.S.A., and
others. The authors portray Dolphy as

> a totally dedicated artist, one for
> whom music was more important than
> considerations of economics, race,
> culture, or even ego: witness how often
> groups performing on records released
> under his own name are, by his own
> statement, cooperatives where every man
> is granted an equal role in determining
> the direction and content of the music.
> The exuberant joy and total passion of
> his best solos are the signs of a man
> completely immersed, fully committed to
> the act of creation (pp. 23-24).

Reviews: Down Beat 41:44 D 19 '74; Jazz Forum
n35:66 Ju '75; Jazz Hot n310:10 N '74; Music
Educators Journal 62:69-70 My '76; Music Journal
32:21-22 S '74

SELECTIVE DISCOGRAPHY

Charles Mingus Jazz Workshop. 3 vols. America (France)
30AM003/4/5, 1964.
Charlie Mingus Jazz Workshop. Candid CJM-8005/CJS-905,
45-601, 1960.
Chico Hamilton Quintet. Sesac Repertory N-2901/2, AD-45,
1959.
Eric Dolphy Quintet. Blue Note BLP(BST8)-4163 and BST-
88904, 1964.
George Russell Sextet. Riverside RLP(9)-375, 1961.
Gunther Schuller and His Orchestra. Atlantic LP/SD-1365,
1960.
John Coltrane Combo. Atlantic LP/SD-1373, SD-1553,
1961.
John Coltrane Quintet. Historic Performances HPLP-1/5,
1961.
John Coltrane Quintet/Sextet. Impulse A(S)-42, ASD9223-2;
Impulse A(S)-10, ASD9228-3, 1961.
John Lewis and His Orchestra. Atlantic LP/SD-1425, 1962.
Oliver Nelson Quintet. New Jazz NJLP-8255, 1961.
Ornette Coleman Double Quartet. Atlantic SD-1588,
LP/SD-1364, 1960.
Roy Porter's 17 Beboppers. Savoy 944 and Savoy MG-9026,
1948-49.

Duke Ellington

Ellington, Edward Kennedy. <u>Music Is My Mistress</u>. New York: Da Capo Press, 1973. xv, 522 pp. photographs, musical examples. discography. music bibliography. book bibliography. appendixes.

In this book Ellington presents pictures of the events of his life up to the early 1970s, including his childhood in Washington, D.C.; early learning experiences with ragtime pianists such as Oliver "Doc" Perry, Louis Brown, and Louis Thomas; his business as a booker of bands in Washington; the first extended engagements of The Washingtonians at the Kentucky Club and the Cotton Club in New York; the nationally broadcast live radio show from the latter club; the 1941 musical show titled <u>Jump for Joy</u>, "a show that would take Uncle Tom out of the theatre, eliminate the stereotyped image that had been exploited by Hollywood and Broadway, and say things that would make the audience think" (p. 175); his various Carnegie Hall concerts beginning in 1943; the State Department tour in 1963 that took the band to the Middle East, India, Afghanistan, Southeast Asia, and some of the Mediterranean countries; the Sacred Concerts--the first in 1965 presented at Grace Cathedral in San Francisco; his White House appearances beginning in 1969; the seventieth birthday party given by President Nixon in Ellington's honor; and numerous and continuous tours that began on a regional basis and expanded over the years to all parts of the globe.

Duke Ellington

In addition to providing the reader with valuable
information about the personnel of his big bands
across the years, Ellington gives us numerous small
vignettes devoted to his relationship to and
perceptions of many musicians and other
acquaintances, including Sidney Bechet, Fletcher
Henderson, Willie the Lion Smith, Will Marion Cook,
Johnny Hodges, Ivie Anderson, Billy Strayhorn, Lena
Horne, Art Tatum, Cat Anderson, Clark Terry, Ella
Fitzgerald, Mahalia Jackson, and Coleman Hawkins.
An epilogue presents an interview with Ellington.
The appendixes list honors and awards received by
Ellington, as well as lists of "The Singers,"
"Arrangers and Lyricists," "The Symphony
Orchestras," and "Band Boys and Barbers." Although
the book lacks an index, its detailed table of
contents provides adequate access to its contents.

Reviews: AB Bookman's Weekly 52:2191 D 24 '73;
Best Sellers 33:412 D 15 '73; Black Perspective
in Music 2:211-212 n2 '74; Black Scholar 12:87
Mr '81; Black Scholar 12:92 Mr '81; Choice
11:105 Mr '74; Guardian Weekly 111:21 Au 3 '74;
High Fidelity/Musical America 24:MA30 Mr '74;
Instrumentalist 29:24+ Au '74; Jazz Journal 27:3
Ap '74; Jazz Magazine n219:4-5 F '74; Kirkus
Reviews 41:1066 S 15 '73 Library Journal 98:3368
N 15 '73; Listener 92:252 Au 22 '74; New
Statesman 88:130 Jy 26 '74; New York Times Book
Review p6 Au 18 '74; New York Times Book Review
p74 D 1 '74; Music Journal 32:21 Ja '74; Musart
27:46 n2 '74; Orkester Journalen 42:14 Jy/Au
'74; Pan Pipes 67:39 n2 '75; Popular Music and
Society 3:46-47 n1 '74; Publishers Weekly 204:47
S 17 '73; Punch 267:236 Au 7 '74; Second Line
26:22-23 Winter '74; Spectator 233:307 S 7 '74;
Village Voice 18:41 D 13 '73

Ellington, Mercer, with Stanley Dance. Duke Ellington in
Person: An Intimate Memoir. 1978. reprint. New York: Da
Capo Press, 1979. xii, 236 pp. photographs. appendixes.
index.

This memoir, by the son of the musician, gives an
insider's view of the father's personality and
character. The discussion ranges from perspectives
on Ellington's early life as told to the son by
relatives and by Ellington himself; Ellington's
motivations, attitude, and method of working,
including his disdain for formal training; his
approach to composing and arranging; his devotion
to his mother--the inspiration behind some of his

compositions; his composing around black themes and social issues; and his method of handling the press to avoid negative publicity. In the process the author treats matters such as Ellington's wisdom and cleverness; his religious beliefs and orientation; his strengths and weaknesses; his method of coping with fame; his personality quirks and superstitions; his acumen as a businessman; his relationships with his sidemen; and Ellington as father, family man, ladies' man, hustler, showman, jazzman, and composer. Also discussed are the importance of marketing in fashioning Ellington's career; his creative orientation and aesthetic beliefs; his tours overseas; and his orientation toward race relations in America and the world. Included as one of the appendixes is a list of copyrighted Ellington compositions that were "unaccountably omitted from the listing in Music Is My Mistress" (p. 222).

Reviews: Best Sellers 38:159 Au '78; Booklist 74:1156 Mr 15 '78; Christian Century 95:542 My 17 '78; Coda n176:22 D 1 '80; Down Beat 45:59 N 2 '78; International Musician 77:12 Ja '79; Jazz Forum n58:49-50 '79; Jazz Podium 28:38-39 S '79; Kirkus Reviews 46:215 F 15 '78; Library Journal 103:756 Ap 1 '78; New Boston Review 4:7 D '78; New Leader 61:25 Jy 17 '78 New Statesman 96:599 N 3 '78; Publishers Weekly 213:121 F 13 '78; Second Line 31:29-30 Summer '79

George, Don. Sweet Man: The Real Duke Ellington. New York: G. P. Putnam's Sons, 1981. 272 pp. photographs. index.

A collection of vignettes, interviews, reminiscences, and portraits of events, places, and people comprise this book. Their content reveals a portrait of Ellington the man, as the author relates and discusses events and activities in the daily life of the renowned composer/bandleader/pianist. Claiming that "Duke and I were teammates, two buddies in the old sense; the real way," the author writes of very personal matters in Ellington's life and speaks more briefly and in generalities about his musical accomplishments. For example, he writes:

> He was the first to combine Latin and jazz. . . . He was the first to put jazz in a church. He was the first to write jazz as serious music. He was the first orchestra leader and composer to ever

write music especially for an individual
instrumentalist, like a Puccini might
fashion an aria for an opera. He had the
sensuousness of a black artist and the
polish and savoir faire of what people
wanted of a Ray Noble, a Guy Lombardo or
a Benny Goodman. He insisted on elegance
in the presentation of his music. He was
particular about the lighting and the
scrim. He appealed to the senses in a
way that few other musicians did. He was
as sensuous with his music as he was with
his women (pp. 93, 102-103).

Of the more personal matters, such statements as
"Duke probably out-Gabled Gable and out-bedroomed
Valentino and was certainly one of the great
Lotharios of the twentieth century" are
complemented and embellished with details and
explanations, as are his statements pertaining to
Ellington's intellectual and biological gifts and
interests such as, "Genetically, biologically,
cerebrally and in terms of the emotions, Duke was a
superior being" (p. 109). "There was a sense of not
just the four sides of a square but an extra
dimension that he possessed" (p. 110). Of Ellington's capacity for work and of his artistic
orientation, the author has much to say. He sums
it up by citing Ellington's response to Louis
Armstrong when the the latter suggested a vacation:

> Louie, what would I do? Where would I
> go? In my work I go all over the world.
> There's no place for me to take a
> vacation. . . . I enjoy the whole thing
> just the way it is, because I have a band
> waiting. The day after I compose
> something, I can hear the music. Who can
> do that? A playwright has to wait for a
> producer to produce a play, but I have an
> immediate playback on what I've
> composed. That's what keeps me going.
> That's what interests me the most. It's
> not the gigs themselves, Louis. The gigs
> keep the band going. What keeps me going
> is to be able to compose and do the work
> (p. 133).

In this work we also learn that Ellington was "an
avid reader" of books: "He had the desire and the
need constantly to learn, constantly to recharge
his batteries and become a new source of energy for

something different. . . . He was starving and thirsty for knowledge at all times" (p. 136). His tastes ran from Shakespeare to The Adventures of Alice in Wonderland; for him, "life was one great big stage and living was a big fairy story and he was Prince Charming throughout the whole thing" (p. 147). Also treated are dozens of other aspects of Ellington's life and of his death, including the writing of various of his compositions; his religious orientation; his 1969 birthday celebration at the White House; his views on race and equality; his death and his funeral; and his relationships with figures such as Billy Strayhorn, Nat King Cole, Yehudi Menuhin, Martin Luther King, Jr., Geoffrey Holder, Tony Bennett, Otto Preminger, and members of the Ellington band. Most books about Ellington treat his career; none treat his music; and this is the first to treat the man. Perhaps the next will treat the music and also bring it together with Ellington's career and his personal life.

Reviews: Booklist 78:276 O 15 '81; International Musician 80:8 D '81; Kirkus Reviews 49:1053 Au 15 '81; Library Journal 106:1929 O 1 '81; National Review 34:73 Ja 22 '82; Publishers Weekly 220:48 S 4 '81; Times Literary Supplement p691 Ju 25 '82

Gutman, Bill. Duke: The Musical Life of Duke Ellington. New York: Random House, 1977. 184 pp. photographs. discography. index.

Although designed for young readers, this small work effectively chronicles the musical developments of the Ellington band over the nearly fifty years of its existence. The reader is informed that this bandleader/composer/pianist was born in Washington, D.C., in the year 1899 into a hard-working middle-class family and that he was taken with art and music classes in his school days, seriously studying drawing, piano, and music theory. "He could turn simple exercises into adventures by improvising--playing a melody with new variations each time" (p. 21). He soon became a member of the "gig" bands of Louis Thomas, a ragtime pianist who provided bands for society functions, but he quickly started an identical booking business for himself, sending out four or five bands a night, all the time operating his own sign-painting business. By the age of eighteen he had enough money to buy his own house and car, "an amazing accomplishment for any young man of his age in 1918" (p. 26). Subsequently he moved to New York and broke into the music scene there.

Taken with the notion that jazz "is a music with an African foundation which came out of an American environment," Ellington sought, in developing his own style, to "keep the music expressive of the New Orleans bands, yet . . . as elegant as that of the best musicians of the East," bringing together "African rhythms, black people's worksongs and spirituals, the blues, ragtime piano, brass bands" (p. 35). In this way he gradually emerged from a "society" musician to a bonafide jazzman. He got his New York start at Barron's night club in Harlem, moved downtown to the Hollywood Club, which later took the name Kentucky Club, and stayed at the latter four years (1923-1927). From there he moved, in 1927, to the celebrated Cotton Club, where he remained until 1931. He left to take his band across the country on a string of one-nighters and short engagements that would continue uninterrupted for the next forty years.

During the Cotton Club years Ellington enlarged his band, moving from its original five pieces to ten, then toward what would eventually become a seventeen-piece organization; developed "a totally new concept of sound" (p. 65); wrote several masterpieces; broadcast nightly, coast to coast, on network radio; and recorded more than 150 titles on disk. In 1933 the band toured Europe. In the 1940s the group, with stars at every position, reached its peak. It had a deeper and fuller sound that made it "sound even bigger than it was" (p. 110). In the 1960s Ellington began to feature himself on piano, was turned down for a Pulitzer Prize (1965), and wrote the First Sacred Concert (1965) and the Second Sacred Concert (1968).

This book characterizes Ellington as being "at once secretive but sentimental, loyal but unavailable, popular but alone. He found his own happiness and contentment in a way that would frustrate and possibly destroy a different kind of man" (p. 170). The work also treats Ellington as "World Traveler" in the fifties and sixties (p. 136); mentions his scores of the motion pictures Anatomy of a Murder (1959) and Paris Blues (1960); reveals Ellington "The Private Man" (p. 161); and describes the end of the man and his band.

Duke Ellington

Reviews: Booklist 73:1490 Ju 1 '77; Booklist
73:1496 Ju 1 '77; Cadence 3:33 F '78; Center for
Children's Books Bulletin 31:32 O '77; English
Journal 66:81 N '77; Jazz Podium 28:50 Ap '79;
Kirkus Reviews 45:494 My 1 '77; Music Journal
36:37-38 Mr '78; Orkester Journalen 46:14 F '78;
School Library Journal 24:129 S '77

Jewell, Derek. Duke: A Portrait of Duke Ellington. New
York: W. W. Norton, 1977. 264 pp. photographs. chronology. discography and bibliography. index.

This book presents an overview of the major events
in Duke Ellington's life and career. Arranged
chronologically, the book discusses Ellington's
concert appearances and tours; his major
compositions; the changing personnel of the
Ellington band; his relationships with friends and
family members; and personal elements, such as the
women who were important in Ellington's life, his
eating and drinking habits, his superstitions, his
foibles about clothing, his hypochondria, and his
philosophy of life. Although the quotations in the
text are undocumented and sometimes even
unattributed, the book includes statements about
Ellington's personality and personal habits by his
friends and bandsmen.

The book begins with Ellington's childhood in
Washington, D.C., where he was raised in a middle-
class family and where he was exposed to black
music by poolroom pianists like Oliver "Doc" Perry
and to conventional harmony by Henry Grant, one of
his high-school teachers. In 1917 he became a
booker for bands at social events in the Washington
area while, at the same time, running a sign- and
backdrop-painting business. The following year he
married Edna Thompson; his son, Mercer, was born a
year later. The nucleus for his band was formed by
1922, when Duke (piano), Sonny Greer (drums), and
Otto Hardwick (C melody saxophone) traveled to New
York City to find work. They returned to New York
the following year and were hired, at Ada
"Bricktop" Smith's instigation, by Barron Wilkins
at his club, Barron's. Later in 1923 they began a
four-year stint at the Kentucky Club, interspersed
with tours outside the confines of New York City.

The big break for the Ellington band came in
1927, when they were hired as the house band at the
famous Cotton Club; during their tenure they were

featured in a nightly radio broadcast, which greatly increased their popularity and fame. Throughout the 1930s Ellington and his band made almost constant railroad tours across the United States and intermittent trips to Europe. The book treats Ellington's habit of composing to the strengths of particular bandsmen, and his habit of writing on trains under all types of conditions. In 1940 Billy Strayhorn joined the band as arranger; he was to become Ellington's "alter ego" and to collaborate with Ellington in compositions until his death in 1967. Demand for performances of the Ellington band slumped in the early 1950s. That trend was turned around in 1956 by an appearance at the Newport Jazz Festival; from that time until his death in 1974, Ellington toured with his band in ever-increasing activity. In 1965 Ellington was invited to participate in the celebration of the completion of Grace Cathedral in San Francisco; thus began the Sacred Concerts, an important part of Ellington's creative output during the last decade of his life.

As the chronology progresses, Jewell treats the personnel of Ellington's bands, which included, among others: Johnny Hodges (alto saxophone), Cootie Williams (trumpet), Bubber Miley (trumpet), Barney Bigard (clarinet), Harry Carney (baritone saxophone and clarinet), Lawrence Brown (trombone), "Tricky Sam" Nanton (trombone), Ben Webster (tenor saxophone), Jimmy Blanton (bass), Rex Stewart (cornet), Ray Nance (trumpet and violin), Jimmy Hamilton (tenor saxophone and clarinet), Russell Procope (alto saxophone and clarinet), Cat Anderson (trumpet), Clark Terry (trumpet), Tyree Glenn (trombone), Don Byas (tenor saxophone), Paul Gonsalves (tenor saxophone), Louis Bellson (drums), Mercer Ellington (trumpet), Sam Woodyard (drums), and Rufus Jones (drums). Jewell discusses tours made by the Ellington band to Europe, South America, the Middle East, the Far East, Japan, Australia, and Russia.

Among the larger compositions included in the chronology are "Black and Tan Fantasy" (1927), Jump for Joy, a musical stage show (1941), "Black, Brown, and Beige" (1943), "The Perfume Suite" (1945), "The Deep South Suite" (1946), "The Liberian Suite" (1947), "Harlem Suite" (1950), "Such Sweet Thunder" (1957), "The Queen's Suite" (1959), "Suite Thursday" (1960), My People (1963), "The Far East Suite" (1964), "The Virgin Islands

Suite" (1965), "The Latin American Suite" (1968),
"The New Orleans Suite" (1970), "The Goutelas
Suite" (1971), The River (1970), "Togo Brava!"
(1971), and three Sacred Concerts (1965, 1968, and
1973). Throughout his long life, Ellington was
accorded many honors and awards, the most important
of which were the President's Gold Medal, presented
by Lyndon Johnson; the Medal of Freedom, presented
by Richard Nixon at Ellington's seventieth birthday
party at the White House; many honorary doctorates
from prestigious colleges and universities; the
French Legion of Honor; and Ethiopia's Emperor's
Star.

Reviews: Atlantic Monthly 239:100 My '77; Best
Sellers 37:111 Jy '77; Booklist 73:1698 Jy 15
'77; Cadence 3:32 Au '77; Choice 14:1072 O '77;
Christian Science Monitor 69:19 Ju 10 '77;
Christian Science Monitor 69:23 Ju 10 '77;
Clavier 16:9 n4 '77; Crescendo International
15:8 Ju '77; Guardian Weekly 116:22 Ap 17 '77;
High Fidelity/Musical America 27:167 O '77; Jazz
Forum n48:56 '77; Jazz Journal International
30:32 Ju '77; Jazz Journal International 30:23 S
'77; Jazz Podium 28:50 Ap '79; Jazz Report 9:17
n4 '77; Kirkus Reviews 45:200 F 15 '77; Library
Journal 102:927 Ap 15 '77; Listener 97:547 Ap 28
'77; Music Journal 36:37-38 Mr '78; Observer p27
Ap 3 '77; Orkester Journalen 45:22 D '77;
Publishers Weekly 211:70 F 21 '77; Punch 272:556
Mr 30 '77; Radio Free Jazz 18:10 Jy '77; School
Library Journal 24:70 O '77; Times Educational
Supplement p51 D 16 '77; Times Literary
Supplement p449 Ap 15 '77

Lambert, G. E. Duke Ellington. Kings of Jazz. New York: A.
S. Barnes, 1961. 88 pp. photographs. discography.

The focus in this short work is on the Ellington
band from its genesis in Elmer Snowden's five-piece
"sweet" unit through the fifteen-piece 1940 group
that was "an all-star band indeed!" to its high
level of achievement in the 1950s (p. 20). In
tracing the band's progress the author touches on
Ellington's compositional prowess, the longevity
and survival capacity of the band, its music as
"American Negro music" (p. 47), its unrivaled "solo
strength and ensemble ability" (p. 71), and
Ellington's "preeminence in jazz because of the
very high aesthetic standard of his output"
(p. 72). The author writes of the comings and
goings of Ellington's sidemen over the years, of

the evolution of the band's sound and its uniqueness, and of Ellington's compositional style and ability.

Ulanov, Barry. Duke Ellington. New York: Creative Age Press, 1946. x, 322 pp. photographs. discography. index.

This early study of the person and the band of Edward Kennedy Ellington is "an attempt . . . to present the career of Duke Ellington and the collective greatness of the Ellington orchestra . . . [and] to delineate the atmosphere and conditions of the jazz world" (p. ix). Made possible by the cooperation of Ellington's "band and associate organizations . . . his family and friends . . . and Duke himself" (pp. ix-x), the work covers the composer/bandleader's early life in his hometown of Washington, D.C., where he began his piano studies, was nicknamed "Duke" when he was eight, developed a talent for drawing, studied harmony in high school, and learned ragtime piano outside school. By 1916, at seventeen, Ellington had decided to be a professional pianist, forsaking his talent for art. His first composition, "Soda Fountain Rag," was written in 1916. The years 1917-1919 saw the beginnings of the development of The Washingtonians. During this time Ellington was married (1918) and saw the birth of his son, Mercer (1919).

In Ellington's formative years, Eastern ragtimers--e.g., James P. Johnson and Lucky Roberts--visited Washington, and Ellington heard them all, as well as Washington ragtimers and "stomp" players. By the time he was twenty Ellington had five bands playing society balls for him in Washington, and his earnings averaged $150 to $200 a week. In 1922 Ellington left Washington for New York. There he initially played with Wilbur Sweatman, met and was influenced by Willie the Lion Smith, "cruised" the music and house-rent party scenes with The Lion, James P. Johnson, Fats Waller, and "a professional character" pianist called Lippy (p. 28). He returned to Washington after a short stay, then went again to New York in 1923, when he and his band settled at Barron's in Harlem, mixing "soft volume and organized voicings with traditional gutbucket sounds" (p. 33). In 1926, the author tells us, the Ellington band made its first records and became associated with impresario Irving Mills. With these events, "big

business took over and the rise of the Ellington
orchestra was made inevitable" (p. 56).

In 1927 the band made its radio debut,
broadcasting from the Kentucky Club, then, in the
following year, from its new location, the Cotton
Club, over the Columbia Broadcasting System. With
the latter opportunity came "the ineluctable growth
from music for its own sake to music for big
business, from booking one's own jobs to booking
through Irving Mills, from seven pieces to ten,
eleven, twelve and fifteen, from wildcat recording
of a dozen companies under as many pseudonyms to a
contract with Victor, then with Brunswick, from
appearances in late spots on their own volition for
the kicks of playing to paid jam sessions and tony
benefits" (pp. 69-70). In 1933 the band made its
first trip to Europe, visiting England, where
Ellington made an "imprint upon the national
consciousness [which] was deep and indelible," and
Paris, where they visited with Bricktop and where
the French were delighted to hear the original
music that had been imitated so often by "Les
Six"--Milhaud, Honegger, Poulenc, Germaine
Tailleferre, Auric and Louis Dutry (p. 145). The
band also made its first trip to the southern
United States, appearing in Dallas and New Orleans.

By 1934 it had become fashionable in critical
circles to berate Ellington's work as "arty" and
pretentious, in spite of the fact that "they swung
as no other swing bands swung, with greater
looseness and more drive than their competitors.
They presented greater soloists than other bands
could" (p. 175). In 1937, with significantly
enhanced reputation and stature, Ellington and his
band returned to the Cotton Club. In 1939 the band
made another trip to Europe, traveling to France,
Sweden, Denmark, Norway, Holland, and Belgium. It
was also in this year that Billy Strayhorn joined
Ellington as an arranger. By 1943 Ellington was
unequivocally at the top of the jazz world, giving
a number of Carnegie Hall concerts, winning Down
Beat, Metronome, and Esquire polls, and making his
"Pastel Period" radio broadcasts.

With a discussion of events surrounding the
latter accomplishments, the author brings the book
to a close, having treated, at points throughout,
such other matters as: Ellington's prowess in using
the microphone in radio broadcasting; Will Vodery's
influence on Ellington's arranging and composing;

Duke Ellington

the illnesses and deaths of Ellington's mother,
father, and close friends in the 1930s; Ellington's
three marriages; the career of Billy Strayhorn and
the details of the Ellington-Strayhorn
collaboration; Ellington's musical, Jump for Joy,
and its social and musical significance; Black,
Brown and Beige and the controversy that followed
its Carnegie Hall premiere; and the band's
singers.

Reviews: Booklist 42:199 F 15 '46; Cleveland
Open Shelf p7 Mr '46; Kirkus Reviews 14:63 F 1
'46; Library Journal 70:1088 N 15 '45; New York
Times p18 Mr 10 '46; New Yorker 21:79 F 2 '46;
Saturday Review 29:13 Au 3 '46; Theatre Arts
30:556 S '46; Weekly Book Review p24 Mr 31 '46

SELECTIVE DISCOGRAPHY

Black, Brown and Beige. Columbia Special Products JCS-
8015.
Daybreak Express. RCA LPV-506, 1931-1934.
The Drum Is a Woman. Columbia Special Products JCL-951.
Duke Ellington--1938. Smithsonian Collection R-003, 1938.
Duke Ellington--1939. Smithsonian Collection R-010, 1939.
Duke Ellington--1940. Smithsonian Collection R-013, 1940.
Duke Ellington--The Pianist. Fantasy F-9462, 1966.
Duke Ellington and His Orchestra. For Discriminate
Collectors FDC-1002, 1943.
Duke Ellington at the Cotton Club. Camden CAL-459, 1929-
1931.
The Duke Ellington Carnegie Hall Concerts--January, 1943.
Prestige P-34004, 1943.
The Duke Ellington Carnegie Hall Concerts--1944. Prestige
P-24073, 1944.
The Duke Ellington Carnegie Hall Concerts--1946. Prestige
P-24074, 1946.
The Duke Ellington Carnegie Hall Concerts--1947. Prestige
P-24075, 1947.
Duke Ellington's Greatest Hits. Columbia CS-9629.
Ellington, 1899-1974. DE-5, 1977.
The Ellington Era. 4 vols. Columbia CL-2047/2048/2364/
2365, 1927-1940.
Flaming Youth. RCA LPV-568, 1927-1929.
Giants of Jazz: Ellington. Time-Life Records J-02, 1926-
1956.
Hot from Harlem. 2 vols. World Records SHB-58, 1927-1930.
Masterpieces by Ellington. Columbia Special Products JCL-
825.
Money Jungle. Blue Note BNP-25113, 1962.
Music of Duke Ellington. Columbia Special Products JCL-

558.
New Orleans Suite. Atlantic 1580, 1970.
Such Sweet Thunder. Columbia Special Products JCL-1033,
    1956-1957.
Suite Thursday/Controversial Suite/Harlem Suite. Encore
    P-14359.
Toodle-Oo Duke Ellington. Decca DL-9224, 1926-1928.
The World of Duke Ellington. Columbia CG-32564, 1947.

Tom Fletcher

Fletcher, Tom. 100 Years of the Negro in Show Business. New introduction and index by Thomas L. Riis. New York: Da Capo Press, 1984. xx, 350 pp. photographs. index.

Reminiscence as much as autobiography, this work by singer/drummer/entertainer Tom Fletcher was written "to put on record the names of unsung great pioneers who blazed trails for those who followed" (p. 39). Tracing his own family from his maternal grandfather who "was born on the Gold Coast of West Africa" and his birth in Portsmouth, Ohio, in 1873, Fletcher tells of his early exposure to and entry into show business by way of circuses, medicine shows, and minstrel shows (p. 3). We learn that in 1888, at fifteen, Fletcher joined the Howard's Novelty Colored Minstrels show, where he remained for "a few seasons," playing primarily in Ohio, Virginia, West Virginia, Kentucky, and Indiana (p. 10). Later he joined a show called In Old Kentucky as a bass drummer in the show's "Pickaninny Band." Later he joined Ed Winn's Big Novelty Minstrels as a trap drummer. In 1897 Fletcher joined the Georgia Minstrels, a troupe that "travelled in our private car, sleeping and eating there" (p. 57).

> In those towns where there was a matinee we would parade from the car to the theater, change into our parade clothes and make our regular street parade, change back into our street clothes and parade back to our car.

Tom Fletcher

> After eating our dinner we would parade
> back to the theater, play a concert in
> front of the theater, get dressed for the
> performance, change back into our street
> clothes and parade back to the car. We
> would then eat our supper and parade back
> to the theater, do our concert and change
> clothes for the night show. After the
> show that night all the colored people
> connected with the show would get
> together and parade down to the car. If
> there were no trains leaving that night
> we would hire an engine and get right out
> of town without delay (p. 78).

In 1901 Fletcher became a member of the Alabama
Troubadors, which featured Sam Lucas. In the
winters--the off-season for minstrel shows--
Fletcher "sang at such first class hotels as the
Waldorf Astoria, and the Hoffman House, also at the
Yale, Princeton, Harvard University and Metropolitan clubs, and top restaurants like Rector's,
Delmonicos, Sherry's and Healy's" (p. 117). Just
before the turn of the century he joined the Rabbit
Foot Minstrels for a short run in New Jersey, then
worked in vaudeville sometime after the new century
began. Around 1900 he worked in moving pictures,
making a great deal of money on an innovation that
he regarded lightly, as something that "would never
get any place" (p. 121). In 1919 Fletcher joined
Will Marion Cook's New York Syncopated Orchestra as
a comedian and technical manager; then, in 1921,
moved into "private entertaining" (p. 278).

By World War II Fletcher's type of entertainment
had gone into a decline, and he took a day job as a
bank messenger. Active at a time when "performers
had to be good singers and dancers and also be able
to do characters" (p. 50), Fletcher's narrative is
filled with historical information and
perspective. For example, he reports that "James
Bohee of Bohee Brothers, gave banjo lessons to King
George V of England, and the Duke of Windsor. Jim
Bland wrote special songs and material for
royalty. Billy Kersands gave dancing lessons"
(p. 41). In the course his reminiscences, Fletcher
also tells of his several "firsts" as an
entertainer; racial incidents that he encountered;
details of the formation, organization, life, and
demise of the Clef Club; development of the Clef
Club Orchestra; and his relationships with Gussie
L. Davis, Leigh Whipper, Sam Lucas, James Bland,

Billy McClain, Abbie Mitchell, Ernest Hogan, Chris
Smith, and Wilbur Sweatman. He gives career
portraits and descriptions of the acts and arts of
entertainers and musicians such as Billy Kersands,
Will Vodery, Florence Mills, the vaudeville team of
Miller and Lyles, W. C. Handy, Bert Williams, James
Reese Europe, Will H. Tyers, and Bill "Bojangles"
Robinson.

Review: Jazz Times p17 Au '84

SELECTIVE DISCOGRAPHY

"Late Hours"/"He's a Cousin of Mine." Ebony 105, 1946.
"Nobody Knows the Way I Feel This Morning"/"When It's
Goin' Out and Nothin' Coming In." Decca 48184, 1950.

Pops Foster

Foster, George, and Tom Stoddard. <u>Pops Foster: The Autobiography of a New Orleans Jazzman</u>. Introduction by Bertram Turetzsky. Interchapters by Ross Russell. 1971. paperback. Berkeley, Los Angeles, and London: University of California Press, 1973. xxii, 208 pp. photographs. bibliography. chronology. discography by Brian Rust. index.

This is the autobiography of "the first famous double bass player in jazz" (p. xi), one who "helped the double bass push aside the tuba as the preferred instrument in jazz" (p. xv). Traversing the history of the genre from its beginnings to the 1960s, Foster performed with many other musical greats, ranging from John Robichaux and Louis Armstrong to Charlie Parker and Dizzy Gillespie. In his effort to "straighten a lot of things out" (p. 1), Foster takes issue with some of the myths of jazz history as he describes "the everyday events that were accompanied by live music in New Orleans" in the early days (p. 59); caste distinctions in New Orleans between about 1900 and 1920; musical and social activity in "The District" (Storyville), where he performed and sometimes lived; musical life on the Mississippi riverboats and during prohibition in Los Angeles and St. Louis; and musical activity in New York from 1929 through the 1940s. The work is shot through with the anecdotes, descriptions, portraits, stories, and valuable comments that might be expected from one who performed with such jazz greats as Buddy Petit, Jack Carey's Band, The Silver Leaf Band,

Frankie Drusen's Eagle Band, the Magnolia Band,
Freddie Keppard, Kid Ory, Fate Marable, Jelly Roll
Morton, Leadbelly, Willie the Lion Smith, and a
host of others. The foreword explains how the book
was put together and written. The introduction is
a brief but informative discussion of Foster's
technique, performance style, and influence.

Reviews: AB Bookman's Weekly 48:1239 O 25 '71;
American Music Teacher 23:43-44 n4 '74; Best
Sellers 31:442 Ja 1 '72; Booklist 72:561 D 15
'75; Choice 9:222 Ap '72; Footnote 4:35-36 n6
'73; Jazz & Blues 3:20 N '73; Jazz Digest 3:21
Mr '74; Journal of Negro History 58:221 Ap '73;
Library Journal 96:3138 O 1 '71; Music Educators
Journal 60:83 D '73; New Statesman 83:117 Ja 28
'72; Notes 29:454-455 n3 '73; Orkester Journalen
40:8-9 Ap '72; Popular Music and Society 2:83-84
n1 '72

SELECTIVE DISCOGRAPHY

Henry "Red" Allen, Volume 1. RCA LPV-556, 1929.
Luis Russell. 2 vols. Columbia KG32338, 1926-1934.
The Rhythmakers. VJM VLP53, 1932.
Sidney Bechet Jazz Classics. 2 vols. Blue Note BLP1201/2,
   1939-1951.

Erroll Garner

Doran, James M. Erroll Garner: The Most Happy Piano.
Introduction by Dan Morgenstern. Studies in Jazz.
Metuchen, N.J.: Scarecrow Press and the Institute of Jazz
Studies, Rutgers University, 1985. xv, 481 pp. pho-
tographs. discography. filmography. bibliography.
index.

Only the first 156 pages of this work are devoted
to strictly biographical matters; the remaining
pages are given over to the pianist's recorded
output and to end matter. The biographical portion
is "not a complete biography but a straightforward
account of the man and his works told by those
individuals who in some way were able to
reconstruct their part in Erroll Garner's life"
(p. xii). As such, the work is an oral history--raw
data that would serve well for the construction of
a more conventional life-writing. But it is
effective as it stands, recounting Garner's birth
into a modest but enterprising family, in which his
father and his siblings were all reading musicians
(although Erroll, who did not read music, turned
out to be the most accomplished and most famous of
them all); his early training as a tuba player in
his school band; his precocious piano playing when
he was six, according to some accounts, or two,
according to others; his early semi-professional
and professional work as a member of the
Kandi-Kids, the Barrelhouse Four, and the Leroy
Brown Orchestra; and his takeoff into a high-level
career of night-club and concert work. Forty-seven
individuals tell of their relationships with

Garner--family members, childhood friends and music mates, sidemen and other professional associates, producers, road managers, and a lady friend.

After the interview section comes a chronology, "an account of Erroll Garner's ancestral background, as well as personal and professional events which occurred throughout his life. The first section, The Garner Family Chron- ology, is accompanied by a diagram on the following pages to allow the reader to graphically trace the Garner lineage. The second section, Erroll Garner Chronology, provides a detailed account of Garner's life" (p. 129). Then comes the discography, consuming 189 pages, another gold mine for future biographers of Garner but of little use to the casual reader.

Reviews: Cadence 11:21 Jy '85; Down Beat 52:58-59 Jy '85; Keyboard Magazine 11:27 Jy '85; Jazz Journal International 38:21 My '85; Jazz Times p17 S '85

SELECTIVE DISCOGRAPHY

Concert By the Sea. Columbia CBS 9821, 1956.
Early Erroll, 1943 Stride. 2 vols. Jazz Connoisseur JC-001/2, 1978.
Erroll Garner. Vogue LAE-12209, 1947.
Eroll Garner Gems. Columbia CL-583.
Erroll Garner Trio. Columbia CL-883, 1955.
Giants of the Piano (Erroll Garner/Art Tatum). Columbia 33-SX-1557.
The Most Happy Piano. Columbia CL 939, 1956.
Other Voices. Columbia CL-1014, 1956-1957.
Paris Impressions. 2 vols. Columbia C2L9, 1958.
Solitaire. Mercury MG-20063.

Marvin Gaye

Ritz, David. <u>Divided Soul: The Life of Marvin Gaye</u>. New York: McGraw-Hill, 1985. xv, 367 pp. photographs. discography. index.

Interview-based and set in the context of the rise, development, and decline of the Motown empire, this work begins with the singer's upbringing in a Pentacostal House of God environment under the supervision of a kindly mother and a brutal, sadistic, and jealous father. It portrays Gaye as a masochist who sought to attract the attention of his father through antagonism and singing and to "please, support, and to protect" his mother (p. 20). By his high-school days, Gaye's relationship to his father had grown more antagonistic, and he "stepped out into the fifties, into a world of secular singing. One word describes the bewitching style which, together with gospel, blues, and jazz, would shape the future course of Marvin Gaye's music: doo-wop" (p. 26). Gaye was also influenced heavily by Rudy West, Clyde McPhatter, Little Willie John, Ray Charles, and Billie Holiday. In addition, he liked the styles of white singers Frank Sinatra, Dean Martin, and Perry Como. And he "got hooked on Miles Davis, especially the way he played ballads through his mute. His 'It Never Entered My Mind' killed me. Miles cried like a singer, and Billie sang like an instrumentalist, and everything they both did was wrapped in the blues" (p. 30).

Gaye's political alienation grew: "How's the average black kid supposed to buy the Bill of Rights when he sees on the streets that his own rights aren't worth shit" (p. 34). He quit school after the eleventh grade and enlisted in the Air Force: "I went in to learn to fly and wound up peeling potatoes on some God-forsaken bases in Kansas, Texas, and Wyoming" (p. 35). He was soon discharged because he could not "adjust to regimentation and authority" (p. 36). Gaye returned to Washington and joined his first singing group--the Marquees, patterned after the Moonglows. Soon the group was introduced to Bo Diddley, one of "the great root sources of American music," whose relationship with Gaye "would critically alter" the latter's "musical being" (p. 39). Then, in 1954, he joined Harvey and the Moonglows, with Harvey Fuqua his mentor, and left for Chicago. "The real woodshedding had just started" (p. 47). He and the Moonglows sang backup for Chuck Berry at Chess record sessions and also recorded their own sides.

From Chicago Gaye moved to Detroit, "straight ahead into a future of great wealth but even greater pain," where Berry Gordy, Jr., of Motown Records, replaced Fuqua as Gaye's mentor (p. 55). Gaye--"this very shy guy who worried all the time"--courted and soon would marry Gordy's sister, Anna, who helped the "green" and insecure Gaye achieve stardom (p. 66). Trying both to blend in and stand out at Motown, Gaye strived to be a "black Sinatra," making six albums, over a four-year period, that were aimed at the white pop market (p. 75). They all failed, but he "pressed on, motivated to get money for Mother, to show Father he was a winner, to prove himself, to score any way he could" (p. 76). He did score, when he started to "sing his color" and had his first hit with the song "Stubborn Kind of Fellow" (p. 77). "Hitch Hike" and "Pride and Joy" followed in 1963--the latter crossing to the pop Top Ten--then came "Can I Get a Witness" in the same year.

As part of the "highly driven performers" of Motown, Gaye was motivated and required to work hard for success (p. 90); he developed his own style, and his career soared, with his winning top billing in the Motown Revue. "By winning the hearts of women--his primary market--Marvin Gaye was making money" (p. 95). In 1968 he scored his first

Marvin Gaye

Number-One-across-the-boards hit--"Heard It Through
the Grapevine." By 1970,

> since "Stubborn Kind of Fellow" in
> 1962, he'd sung over thirty hits, which
> spanned an emotional range from sweet
> innocence to sour frustration. He'd
> proven himself as perhaps the most
> dependable money-maker on the Motown
> roster. He'd survived a decade marked by
> volatile musical changes. Yet the one
> thing he wanted most--to become a ballad
> singer--still eluded him (p. 135).

In the sixties his repertoire was devoted to his
relationship with his first wife; in the seventies,
with his second. In between, in 1970, he created
"a socioreligious work of astounding originality,"
concerned with "soul and salvation"--the album
What's Going On, his first "self-produced, self-
written album" (pp. 136, 148). With this album,
Gaye "revolutionized soul music by expanding its
boundaries. He changed the direction of Motown by
showing the sales potential of thought-provoking
inner monologues. In winning the fight for his own
integrity, others--equally talented and capable of
creating their own art--benefitted," including
Stevie Wonder and Michael Jackson (pp. 152-153). In
1973 Gaye recorded the biggest hit of his
career--the album Let's Get It On. Here, My Dear,
the album which reviewed Gaye's marriage to Anna
and which was made to pay his divorce settlement to
her, came in 1978.

By the next year Gaye had a large federal tax
debt, was behind on his alimony and child-support
payments, and had been left by his second wife.
One of his homes and his recording studio were
padlocked by federal agents, and his empire was
collapsing. He spent the winter and spring in
Hawaii, sick and depressed. Finally, "Gaye twisted
his suffering into song. Symbolically, he was
excited by the sight of his own blood. He still
viewed himself as a Jesus figure, someone whose
sacrifice carried heroic significance. He saw
sorrow as necessary to creative expression. In
Hawaii, he used that belief to regain his senses.
Because he had suffered, he now had fresh material"
(p. 268). His Hawaiian exile ended in June, when he
left to begin a European tour. That, too, resulted
in continuing exile from the United States. Living
in London, "his life grew wild and untamed,"

hitting bottom as he was almost incapacitated by free-based cocaine (p. 280).

Rescued by a Belgian businessman, he left England in 1981 to live with his liberator's family in Ostend, near the sea. The two men became business partners, and Gaye moved to a luxurious apartment, began a new European tour, severed his relationship with Motown, and worked out a new deal with CBS Records, the latter settling his debts with the Internal Revenue Service and his two ex-wives. In 1982, his nearly three-year exile ended, he returned to the United States "a radiant success," showered with honors and awards for the single "Sexual Healing" and its album <u>Midnight Love</u> (p. 304). But emotional and mental decline and deterioration would set in, continue for the next year--through his 1983 tour--and worsen until his death in 1984.

Ritz's story presents Gaye as a complex man who did not like himself, was brutally self-critical (a perfectionist), defiant, courageous, talented, of "rare integrity," and full of paradoxes (p. 106).

> But rather than resolving his para-
> doxes, however, Gaye enlarged them. He
> hated show business yet pursued a show
> business career with singular tenacity.
> He believed in the passivism of Jesus
> while identifying with Malcom X's
> explosive anger. He advocated political
> involvement yet, reluctant to alienate
> any part of his audience, wasn't espe-
> cially active himself. As an artist
> arguing against the notion of entertain-
> ment, he nonetheless did everything he
> could to win a mainstream middle-class
> audience, crooning the ballads he thought
> white music lovers wanted to hear
> (p. 107).

Of Gaye's singing techniques the author relates, "Marvin's voice could almost be seen as a thin stream of light between his mouth and the mike. With remarkably little exertion, he could sound loud, gruff, pained or powerful. He could sing on his back. Often he sang reclining on a couch, his favorite piece of furniture" (p. 257). Throughout the book Ritz tells of Gaye's reluctance and refusal to do concerts; his participation in athletics in an effort to enhance his manhood; his

constant use of drugs; the separations and mergings
of the sensual and the spiritual aspects of his
psyche and personality; his "talent for doing
exactly what he wanted and avoiding everything
else" (p. 207); details of his marriages, love
affairs, and domestic life; his practice of missing
engagements and ignoring contracts; his emotional
problems; his fear of going on stage; and his
sexual preoccupations.

Reviews: Melody Maker 60:41 S 7 '85; Village
Voice 30:VLS6 My 7 '85

SELECTIVE DISCOGRAPHY

Anthology. Motown M9-791.
Compact Command Performance (Fifteen Greatest Hits).
  Motown 6069-MD.
The Dream of a Life Time. Columbia FC-39916, 1985.
Every Great Motown Hit of Marvin Gaye. Motown 6058.
Greatest Hits. 2 vols. Tamla S-252/78, 1964.
Here My Dear. Motown 5295, 1978.
Let's Get It On. Motown M5-192, 1973.
Midnight Love. Columbia PC-38197, 1982.
Moods of Marvin Gaye. Motown 5296, 1966.
Trouble Man. Motown 5241.
What's Going On. Motown S-5339, 1971.

Dizzy Gillespie

Gillespie, Dizzy, with Al Fraser. <u>To Be or Not to Bop:</u>
<u>Memoirs</u>. Garden City, N.Y.: Doubleday, 1979. xix, 552 pp.
Chronology. photographs. discography. filmography.
index.

These memoirs of "the brain trust . . . of modern
music" are detailed reminiscences, facts, and
impressions of Gillespie's life and career as told
by the trumpeter himself and by many of his
relatives, friends, and acquaintances from his
early childhood to the late 1970s (p. 240). He
spent his childhood in Cheraw, South Carolina; his
home life included eight brothers and sisters and a
"mean" father who played piano in a jazz band. His
behavior as a youth was "wild", but he was
academically successful. The book also covers the
early influences on Gillespie's development as a
musician; the impact of his father's death on the
family's well-being; and his encounters with racism
as a child. Gillespie got his start in music by
joining his school's beginners' band when he was in
fifth grade, and his first paying job was at the
local white high school. Almost immediately he
began to play "at house parties, dances down at the
Elks Hall, and even gigs in other little towns like
Clio, Hartville, Darlington, Florence, Chester-
field, South Carolina, and Rockingham and Hamlet in
North Carolina" (p. 26). We learn of the influence
of Afro-American church practices on the
development of his art; his matriculation, in 1933,
at the Laurinburg Institute, a high school in North
Carolina, on a trumpet scholarship; and his

participation on the school's football team as a
first-string end. At Laurinburg, Gillespie says,

> Since I didn't have to study too much
> in other areas, I started fooling around
> with the piano and my ideas expanded
> greatly, I practiced constantly, until
> all times of the night, anytime I
> wanted. I'd practice the trumpet and
> then the piano for twenty-four hours
> straight if they didn't come around and
> shut me up when they checked the locks
> every night. I developed a very serious
> attitude about music, and music was the
> only thing I was serious about (pp.
> 38-39).

Approaching his professional life, Gillespie
tells of his move to Philadelphia just months short
of finishing high school and of his becoming part
of a trio there; his subsequent move to big bands;
his use of the piano in the development of his
musicianship; his introduction to Afro-Cuban music;
his introduction to Charlie Parker and their
subsequent collaboration in the development of
bebop; his move to New York and his gigging around
that city; his first stint with a "name" band--that
of Teddy Hill, with which he made his first trip to
Europe--in 1937; the development of his style from
its basis in that of Roy Eldridge to his own unique
bebop manner; his stints with the Earl Hines, Billy
Eckstine, Ella Fitzgerald, and Cab Calloway bands;
the origins and development of the bebop style; and
the organization of his own band in 1947, in which
year he achieved listings as "Best Trumpeter" and
"Best Orchestra" in _Metronome_ magazine.

Among those whose contributions to the book are
represented by transcribed interviews and excerpts,
aside from relatives and hometown acquaintances,
are: Dicky Wells, Buddy Johnson, Woody Herman,
Milton Hinton, Billy Eckstine, Earl Hines, Max
Roach, Kenny Clarke, and Miles Davis. These and
other individuals tell of the bebop movement as a
"school," a kind of undergraduate and graduate
academy for professional musicians; of Gillespie's
superior musicianship and his gracious and
unselfish sharing of ideas; and of Gillespie as
master teacher. These interviewees illuminate
Gillespie's accounts of the birth of the bebop era
in 1944, when a Gillespie/Oscar Pettiford-led band
opened at the Onyx Club on New York's 52nd Street;

his short-lived big band of 1945; and his second
and highly successful big band of 1946-1950. What
comes through all the testimony is a portrait of
Gillespie as teacher and professor, head of a
would-be "Gillespie School of Music"; and Gillespie
as revolutionary genius. Gillespie himself tells
us that bebop reached the height of its perfection
when he, Parker, Max Roach, Bud Powell, and Curly
Russell settled in at the Three Deuces; he comments
on the perception of bebop as a cult and on the
misperceptions and unfounded accusations of the
press during the 1940s and 1950s.

We learn of Gillespie's fusion of Afro-Cuban
music and jazz; the first tour of the Dizzy
Gillespie Big Band in 1948; the story behind the
bent horn; the "Jazz at the Philharmonic" tours;
his struggle to establish jazz as a concert music;
his status as "the first jazz musician to represent
the United States on a cultural mission" in 1956
(p. 414); his half-serious candidacy for the United
States Presidency in 1963; his participation in
films as musician and actor; his religious beliefs;
his perception of black music history and
aesthetics; and his honors and awards.

Reviews: Book World 9:5 S 30 '79; Book World
9:13 D 2 '79; Booklist 75:652 D 15 '78; Choice
16:1317 D '79; Christian Science Monitor 71:19
Au 15 '79; Coda n170:18-19 D 1 '79; Down Beat
46:835 Ap 5 '79; Down Beat 47:74 Ja '80; Jazz
Journal International 33:17 Ap '80; Jazz Journal
International 33:17 Ju '80; Jazz Journal
International 33:10 D '80; Jazz Podium 29:44-45
N '80; Kirkus Reviews 47:835 Jy 15 '79; Library
Journal 104:494 F 15 '79; Music Educators
Journal 66:177 Ja '80; National Review 31:1045
Au 17 '79; New York Times Book Review p177 F 3
'80; New Yorker 55:140+ O 29 '79; Orkester
Journalen 47:2 D '79; Publishers Weekly 216:93
Jy 9 '79; Stereo Review 43:13 D '79; Times
Literary Supplement p676 Ju 13 '80

James, Michael. _Dizzy Gillespie_. Kings of Jazz. New York:
A. S. Barnes, 1961. 86 pp. photographs. discography.

This brief review of the trumpeter's career
chronicles his artistic development through his
recordings and tours. Some provocative points made
by the author are the facts that the Gillespie
style might eventually have degenerated in the
small-band context but had its vitality ensured in

the experimental context of the big bands; that
Gillespie's "playing had evolved between 1946 and
1950 towards a virtuoso presentation" (p. 39); that
with the sudden disappearance of the big-band
setting, Gillespie's "solo work had to be adapted
to meet the needs of the changed environment"
(p. 39); that the recordings with "big-band and
Afro-rhythm" reveal a remarkable rhythmic
complexity and expressive intensity; and that the
trumpeter reached artistic maturity in the late
1950s. In the course of the narrative the author
also discusses, among other things, the fortunes
and misfortunes of Gillespie's big band and his
tours to Europe and their relationship to his
development.

SELECTIVE DISCOGRAPHY

Billy Eckstine and His Orchestra. Smithsonian Collection
 R004-P13456, 1944.
Cab Calloway and His Orchestra. Smithsonian Collection
 R004-P13456, 1940.
Dizzy Gillespie All-Star Quintet. Phoenix
 LP2, Prestige P-24030, Smithsonian Collection P-11895,
 1945.
Dizzy Gillespie and His Orchestra. Arco LP-8, 1947.
Dizzy Gillespie and His Orchestra. Hi-Fly H-01, 1946.
Dizzy Gillespie and His Orchestra. Norgran MGV 1084;
 Verve MGV 8017, 1956.
Dizzy Gillespie Sextet. Savoy SJL 2209, 1951.
Dizzy Gillespie Sextet. Smithsonian Collection R004-
 P13457 and P11895, 1945.
Dizzy Gillespie y Machito. Pablo 2310-771.
Dizzy Gillespie's Band. Roulette RE-105, 1947.
Duke Ellington and His Orchestra. For Discriminate
 Collectors FDC-1002, 1943.
Free Ride. Pablo 2310-794.
Teddy Hill and His NBC Orchestra. Victor LPV-530, 1937.

Babs Gonzales

Gonzales, Babs. <u>I Paid My Dues: Good Time--No Bread</u>. East Orange, N.J.: Expubidence Publishing Corp., 1967. 160 pp. discography.

Born Lee Brown, this bebop singer/pianist/drummer, the son of a madame, was a hustler and numbers runner in his hometown of Newark, New Jersey, by the age of thirteen, and was living away from home in his own rented room by the age of fourteen. "With my paper route, my gambling in school and my other hustles, I was able to acquire a radio and two new drape suits. Every afternoon after school I'd rush home to listen to the 'bands from the Savoy' and head for my mother's to practice the piano a couple of hours" (p. 19). Graduating from high school at fifteen, he went on the road as a band boy with Jimmy Lunceford; Lunceford became his idol, educationally and musically. Soon he was back in Newark, playing with a local group. By 1940 he was actively engaged in desegregating public facilities in New Jersey.

In 1943, in an effort to escape racial discrimination, he moved to Los Angeles, wearing turbans and assuming the name Ram Singh to give the impression that he was a foreigner. There he met many established musicians, got a day job, and frequented the night spots that featured bands. Soon he took the name Babs Gonzales. Among his friends in Los Angeles were Don Byas, Nat King Cole, Billy Strayhorn, Gerald Wilson, Benny Carter, Dexter Gordon, Freddy Webster, and Curley Russell.

- 135 -

Babs Gonzales

In 1944 Gonzales returned to Newark, avoided the military draft, and moved to New York. He began to frequent Minton's, worked as a clothing salesman, and began playing gigs. In 1946 he formed his own group, Babs' Three Bips and a Bop, which included pianist Tad Dameron, guitarist Pee Wee Tinney, bassist Art Phipps, and himself on drums. In 1947 he added saxophonist Rudy Williams and cut his first records. One of the tunes, "Oop-Pop-a-Da," became a hit around New York. But a lawsuit he filed against his record company caused a reaction against him, and he was unable to get additional work. In 1949, however, he signed a contract with Capitol Records and organized a nine-piece group which included, among others, J. J. Johnson, Benny Green, and Sonny Rollins. The group's first sides brought them national attention, and they opened for the Clique, a new night club, played a concert at Town Hall, and did the Perry Como Show.

Success did not last:

> I had written a "Bop Dictionary" that I was selling at fifty cents each to help sustain me. . . . I was shocked again to find out that "Capitol" had reproduced thousands without my consent and were giving them away at record shops, etc., in their promotional program. The irony of it all was that "Benny Goodman," "Woody Herman," and all the big artists got the "LARGE" billing, while at the bottom, I was given credit as the author in very small print (p. 60).

In 1951 Gonzales traveled to Sweden and Paris. On his return to New York later that year, he and James Moody formed a band, recorded for Mercury, opened at the Harlem Club in Philadelphia, and went on the road; and Gonzales wrote the song "Moody's Mood for Love." After two years he left Moody and returned to Europe, arriving in Stockholm in April, 1954. After a brief stay he went back to Newark, where he worked as a disk jockey. Then he moved to Chicago and teamed up with Johnny Griffin at the Bluenote. Again he went abroad, touring Paris, Egypt, Holland, Spain, Switzerland, and London. Next he returned to Chicago, where he worked at the Flame Lounge. In 1963 Gonzales ran his own club in Harlem—the Insane Asylum—for a short time. Then he took a winter job in Tampa, moving on to Atlanta, Los Angeles, and San Francisco.

Gonzales was proud of his romantic inclinations and abilities and his insider's knowledge of show business. He also believed that he paid his dues but that his breaks never came because of the proclivity of other artists toward their own professional self-preservation. "I've helped at least ten people who are now stars, but not one has ever put me on a theatre or concert date with them. They know my work and figure I would distract from their star status performance" (p. 155). Gonzales also claims to be the "Creater of the Bebop Language" (p. 2).

Reviews: Book World 4:17 Ap 12 '70; Down Beat 35:37 Mr 7 '68; Jazz Journal 21:14 Ju '68; Jazz Hot n255:41 N '69; Jazz Magazine n169/170:17 S '69; Jazz Monthly n169:28 Mr '69; Melody Maker 43:8 S 21 '68; Orkester Journalen 36:16 D '68

SELECTIVE DISCOGRAPHY

Babs Gonzales: Live at Small's Paradise. Chiaroscuro Records CR2025.
Sunday at Smalls. Audio Fidelity.
Tales of Manhattan. J. Arthur Rank.

Taylor Gordon

Gordon, Taylor. <u>Born to Be</u>. Introduction by Muriel Draper. Foreword by Carl Van Vechten. Illustrations by Michael Covarrubias. New Introduction by Robert Hemmenway. 1929. Reprint. Seattle and Washington: University of Washington Press, 1975. liv, 236 pp. photographs, drawings.

This rather unusual biography of a man with even more unusual experiences provides "an account of Harlem in the twenties vividly true to the era" (p. x). It is an account of the life of a singer who, born in 1893, "spent his formative years carrying messages from civic leaders to Madame, hauling water to bawdy houses, serving drinks to the 'sports,' setting bowling pins to a gambler's advantage, and selling 'hop' in a rustic opium den" (p. xi). Although Gordon left little record of his musical activities, we know, as this book tells us, that he "traveled for three years with a vaudeville act organized by J. Rosamond Johnson called the 'Inimitable Five,' playing the Keith circuit from New York to Los Angeles, St. Louis to Moose Jaw," and that in 1925 his "singing career took off, rising in almost direct proportion to the increasing interest in the phenomenon of the Harlem Renaissance" (p. xiii). Gordon and Johnson toured England and France in 1927, and they were an intimate part of the Harlem Renaissance movement, Gordon's "rich tenor and his sensitivity to spirituals" being known "far and wide" (p. xviii). Gordon's autobiography is "the story of the only black family in the booming Montana town of White Sulphur Springs; of Emmanuel Gordon Taylor's rise

from messenger for a thriving local brothel to
chauffeur, cook, and private railway car attendant
for the financier and circus impressario John
Ringling; and of Gordon's international career as a
singer of Afro-American spirituals" (cover 4).

W. C. Handy

Handy, W. C. <u>Father of the Blues: An Autobiography</u>. Edited by Arna Bontemps. Foreword by Abbie Niles. 1941. Reprint. New York: Collier, 1970. xvi, 333 pp. photographs, musical examples. music and book bibliography. index.

This story of W. C. Handy's life is also a first-hand account of the development of black popular music during the second and third decades of the twentieth century. Handy was born and raised in Florence, Alabama. He toured the Midwest and South with Mahara's Minstrels, playing the cornet; joined the faculty of Alabama A. & M. University in Huntsville, Alabama, for a short tenure; and settled in Memphis, Tennessee, where he led and booked bands regionally. A tune he composed for the election campaign of a local politician was published with new lyrics and became famous as the "Memphis Blues." Handy tells of its composition:

> The melody of <u>Mr. Crump</u> was mine throughout. On the other hand, the twelve-bar, three-line form of the first and last strains, with its three-chord basic harmonic structure (tonic, subdominant, dominant seventh) was that already used by Negro roustabouts, honky-tonk piano players, wanderers and others of their underprivileged but undaunted class from Missouri to the Gulf, and had become a common medium through which any such individual might express his personal feelings in a sort

> of musical soliloquy. My part in their
> history was to introduce this, the
> "blues" form to the general public, as
> the medium for my own feelings, and my
> own musical ideas. And the transitional
> flat thirds and sevenths in my melody, by
> which I was attempting to suggest the
> typical slurs of the Negro voice, were
> what have since become known as "blue
> notes" (p. 103).

Handy's experiences with the publication of
"Memphis Blues" and his partnership with Harry Pace
led to the establishment in 1918 of the publishing
firm of Pace & Handy in New York.

Throughout the book, the reader is exposed to the
development of black music, from its rural styles
to its more sophisticated manifestations in the
classic blues, Tin Pan Alley thirty-two-bar and
hybrid forms, and in the more extended forms
created by such composers as James P. Johnson and
William Grant Still. Also included are Handy's
views on social and political matters as they were
related to the prevailing cultural climate--in the
form of the Harlem Renaissance--of that period, and
his perception of the blues and its evolution:

> Negroes react rhythmically to every-
> thing. That's how the blues came to be.
> Sometimes I think that rhythm is our
> middle name. When the sweet good man
> packs his trunk and goes, that is
> occasion for some low moaning. When
> darktown puts on its new shoes and takes
> off the brakes, jazz steps in. If it's
> the New Jerusalem and the River Jordan
> we're studying, we make the spirituals.
> The rounders among us, those whose aim in
> life is just to become bigger
> rounders--well, they're the ones we can
> thank for the Frankie and Johnnie songs.
> In every case the songs come from down
> deep (p. 86).

Particularly valuable are Handy's comments about
other important figures of the period.

Reviews: AB Bookman's Weekly 46:465 Au 24 '70;
Choice 7:84 D '70; Music Educators Journal 57:91

W. C. Handy

O '70; Publishers Weekly 197:84 Mr 2 '70; Sing
Out! 20:40-41 n2 '70

SELECTIVE DISCOGRAPHY

"Memphis Blues." On <u>Fletcher Henderson 1934</u>. MCA 1318,
    1934.
"St. Louis Blues." On <u>The Empress</u> (Bessie Smith). Columbia
    CG-30818.

Hazel Harrison

Cazort, Jean E., and Constance Tibbs Hobson. <u>Born to Play:</u>
<u>The Life and Career of Hazel Harrison</u>. Contributions to
the Study of Music and Dance, No. 3. Westport, Conn. and
London: Greenwood Press, 1983. xviii, 171 pp. photographs. appendixes. bibliography. index.

This book chronicles the musical activities of
Hazel Harrison (1883-1969), America's first black
musician to establish an international reputation
in the area of concert and recital music. Her
activities are traced from her first piano lessons
when she was five, through her pre-World War I
studies in Berlin with Busoni and Petri and her
return to the United States with the onset of the
war, to the expansion of her career as a concert
pianist in the 1920s and 1930s. Also treated are
her brief stint as a teacher at the Chicago
University of Music and her more lengthy tenures at
Tuskegee Institute (1931-1936), Howard University
(1936-1955), and Alabama State University (1958-
1963). Among the many persons whose professional
relationships with Harrison are treated in the book
are: Harry T. Burleigh, E. Azalia Hackley, R.
Nathaniel Dett, Alain Locke, Frederick Hall, Abbie
Mitchell, William Dawson, Roy Tibbs, Camille
Nickerson, Todd Duncan, and Louise Burge. One
important feature of the book is the insight it
provides into Harrison's teaching methods--insights
gleaned from several of her many students.

Hazel Harrison

Reviews: Black Perspective in Music 12:133-135
nl '84; History: Reviews of New Books 12:46 N
'83

Hampton Hawes

Hawes, Hampton, and Don Ascher. <u>Raise Up Off Me: A
Portrait of Hampton Hawes</u>. New introduction by Gary
Giddins. 1974. Reprint. New York: Da Capo Press, 1979.
xiii, 179 pp.

This biography of a bebop pianist "was the first
book to give an insider's view of the most
provocative and misunderstood movement in jazz--the
modernism of the '40s" (p. 6); it is the story of a
musician who played a role in translating the style
of saxophonist Charlie Parker to the piano, one
whose art "set the stage for many of the soul
pianists who became prominent in the late '50s, and
also influenced many of the more facile keyboard
technicians on the West Coast including Oscar
Peterson and the mystifying successful Andre
Previn" (p. xi). Hawes tells of his childhood and
teen years in Los Angeles as a precocious
preacher's son who was, by nine, imitating Fats
Waller and Earl Hines at the piano. He then
relates his first encounter with Parker's music and
his drug habit, acquired after he graduated from
high school in 1947. Hawes moved to New York and
Harlem, where he immersed himself in the bebop
subculture, and subsequently returned to Los
Angeles, where he had his first personal encounter
with heroin. Inducted into the U.S. Army in 1952,
he committed and experienced AWOLs and courts
martial in the Uunited States and in Japan, and he
became "strung out" on drugs in Japan. When he
returned to civilian life, however, he had a
successful jazz career, holding jobs at New York's

Embers, Basin Street, and other clubs and winning
Down Beat and Metronome polls in 1956.

Hawes also discusses his friendships and musical
relationships with Wardell Grey, Billie Holiday,
Oscar Peterson, Thelonius Monk, Charles Mingus,
jazz patroness Baroness Nica Rothschild, and
others; his futile voluntary commitments to
hospitals in order to discard his drug habit; his
arrest and sentencing to prison for drug dealing,
his "kicking" his habit there, and his eventual
pardoning by President John F. Kennedy; his return
to his career, including successful tours of
Europe; and his relationship with and eventual
separation from his wife. The pianist also
comments on the cutting-contest phenomenon, racial
discrimination, and his eventual decision to move,
stylistically, beyond bebop.

Reviews: Best Sellers 34:218 Au 1 '74; Choice
11:1149 O '74; Kirkus Reviews 42:458 Ap 15 '74;
Library Journal 99:2147 S 15 '74; Library
Journal 99:2308 S 15 '74; Publishers Weekly
205:71 Ap 22 '74; Radio Free Jazz 21:8 Mr '80;
Village Voice 19:26 Au 29 '74

SELECTIVE DISCOGRAPHY

All Night Session. 3 vols. Contemporary Records
   C-7545/6/7, 1956.
As Long As There's Music. Artists House AH-4, 1977.
The Challenge. RCA JPL1-1508.
For Real. Contemporary Records C-7589, 1958.
The Green Leaves of Summer. Contemporary Records C-7614,
   1963.
Hampton Hawes at the Piano. Contemporary 7637, 1977.
A Little Copenhagen Night Music. Arista AF-1043, 1968.
Live at the Montmartre. Arista AL-1020.
Piano: East/West. Fantasy/Original Jazz Classics OJC-1705.
The Trio. Contemporary Records C-3505/15/23, 1956.

Coleman Hawkins

McCarthy, Albert J. <u>Coleman Hawkins</u>. Kings of Jazz. London: Cassell, 1963. 90 pp. photographs. discography.

Born in St. Louis, Missouri, in 1904, this saxophonist joined Mamie Smith's accompanying band in 1919 or 1920, then joined Fletcher Henderson in 1924. During his ten years in the latter group, "Hawkins was . . . preoccupied in a personal development that was to see the crude, slap-tongue methods of the average saxophonist of the period evolve into a less staccato style that was rhythmically flexible, concerned with shading and capable of a variety of emotional nuances" (pp. 5-6). By 1926 his own individual style was emerging, and by 1929 he was the undisputed master of his instrument; his playing was the "yardstick by which others were to be judged" (p. 9). Between 1934 and 1939 he lived and played in Europe. By 1944 his recorded output had reached its peak and, despite his "swing" orientation, he began to play with bebop musicians. In the fifties Hawkins played a large number of "Jazz at the Philharmonic" tours. As late as 1963 he was "as firmly established as he was during his great position of eminence during the 'thirties" (p. 19), and "he remains, after forty years as a jazz musician, one of the most enthusiastic and impassioned improvisers in jazz" (p. 20). The author also discusses Hawkins's continuing stylistic development throughout his career and mentions his impact on John Coltrane, Sonny Rollins, and other tenor saxophone players of the late fifties and early sixties.

Reviews: Jazz Journal 16:13 O '63; Jazz Monthly
10:27 Mr '64; Orkester Journalen 31:10 D '63

SELECTIVE DISCOGRAPHY

At Ease with Coleman Hawkins. Fantasy/Original Jazz
  Classics OJC-181.
Bean and the Boys. Prestige P-7824.
Blues Groove. Prestige P-7753.
Classic Tenors. Contact CM-3, 1943.
Coleman Hawkins. Archives FS-252.
Coleman Hawkins. Commodore XFL-14936, 1940-1943.
Coleman Hawkins: Swing. Fontana FJL-102, 1944.
Coleman Hawkins Meets Duke Ellington. Impulse A-26.
Coleman Hawkins Meets the Big Sax Section. Savoy SJL-1123,
  1958.
The Complete Coleman Hawkins, Volume 1. RCA (France)
  FMS-17325, 1929-1940.
Fletcher Henderson: Developing an American Orchestra,
  1923-1937. Smithsonian Collection, R-006.
Further Definitions. Impulse S-12, 1961.
The Great Tenor Encounters: Dedication Series, Volume 10.
  Impulse IA-9350/2.
The Greatest Jazz Recordings of All Time: Jazz Masters of
  the Sax. Franklin Mint Record Society, 1984.
Hawk Eyes. Prestige P-7857.
The Hawk Flies. Milestone M-47015, 1944-1946.
The Hawk in Holland. Jasmine JASM-2011, 1935-1937.
Hollywood Stampede. Capitol M-11030, 1945.
Jam Session in Swingville with Pee Wee Russell. Prestige
  P-24051.
Night Hawk. Prestige P-7671.
Paris 1935 and 1937. Swing 8403.
The Real Thing. Prestige P-24083.
Shelly Manne 2, 3, 4. Impulse S-20, 1962.

Roland Hayes

Helm, MacKinley. <u>Angel Mo' and Her Son, Roland Hayes</u>.
Boston: Little, Brown, 1943. [xi], 289 pp. photograph.

Although this book is undocumented and contains no
index, it gives the reader a picture of the
upbringing and life events of concert artist Roland
Hayes from his childhood to the eve of World War
II. The book is written in the first person, as
though it were an autobiography. In the narrative,
we learn of Hayes's reverence for his mother and of
the life-long influence of her attitude of
single-minded dedication to a goal. During his
childhood on a Georgia farm, Hayes was exposed to
the quills, bones, fiddle, straws, and banjo--
musical instruments used to accompany country
dances--and the methods of playing them. He
learned to read music notation from a shaped-note
hymnal. Through the author's pen, he speaks of the
African roots of black folk music and the
similarities between its sacred and secular forms
and speculates about the possible roots of
spirituals in the early 1800s. He gives details of
the church services of his youth, particularly the
music involved in them. We learn of his move to
Chattanooga, Tennessee, in 1900, where he worked in
the steel mills; his participation in a
street-corner quartet called the Silver-Toned
Quartet; his voice lessons at sixteen with a
graduate of Oberlin Conservatory; his studies at
Fisk University, where he was supported by one of
the teachers, gave concerts in the city of
Nashville, and performed with the Jubilee Singers;

- 149 -

his move to Boston in 1911, where he began to study
with Arthur J. Hubbard and received help in
securing singing jobs from the secretary of the
American Missionary Association office in Boston;
and his being asked to sing duets with Harry T.
Burleigh for lectures by Booker T. Washington.

In 1917 Hayes began his concert career with a
successful performance at Symphony Hall in Boston;
he sang classical repertoire and a group of
spirituals. The following year he began his
association with accompanist Lawrence Brown, who
was later to play for Paul Robeson. Beginning in
1920 his concert tours included venues in Europe as
well as the United States. He gave command
performances for the British royalty, met the great
and near-great in many countries, and sang in their
homes as well as on the concert stages of England,
Germany, Spain, France, Italy, Austria, Czechoslovakia, Russia, and other European countries. His
concert programs consisted of Negro spirituals and
of art songs by such composers as Handel, Schubert,
Bach, Caccini, Montiverdi, Ravel, Debussy, and
Griffes. In the closing comments of the book, the
author provides insight into the conditions of the
lives of black people on the eve of World War II
and decries the lack of production of Negro art.

SELECTIVE DISCOGRAPHY

The Art of Roland Hayes: Six Centuries of Song. Vanguard
  VRS-448/9, 1954.
Art Songs and Spirituals. Veritas VM-112, 1967.
An Evening with Roland Hayes. Heritage LP-SS-1204, 1956.
The Life of Christ as Told Through Afro-American Folksong.
  Vanguard Everyman SRV-352-SD, 1976.
My Songs: Aframerican Religious Folk Songs. Vanguard
  VRS-494, 1957.

Fletcher Henderson

Allen, Walter C. <u>Hendersonia: The Music of Fletcher Henderson and His Musicians. A bio-discography</u>. Highland Park, N.J.: Walter C. Allen, 1973. xiv, 651 pp. photographs, map, reproductions of advertisements and record labels. bibliography. indexes. appendixes.

As indicated by the descriptive title, this book is more than a biography. Each chapter is devoted to a particular period in Henderson's career and consists of three parts. Each chapter begins with narrative information about the events of the period to which it is devoted; discussion of the venues played by the Henderson bands; the personnel of the bands, based on documented recollections of bandsmen and their contemporaries, newspaper accounts and advertisments, and the aural evidence of recordings; and recordings made by the band. The second section consists of an outline of the "Known Playing Engagements" of the group to whom the chapter is devoted, including information about others on the various bills and an indication of the sources of the information about the dates. Each chapter is concluded with a discographical section in which each known recording by Henderson, his band, or his sidemen is listed, together with the date of the recording, variant titles of the record, a list of the personnel or probable personnel and their instruments, a list of the titles of the songs recorded, the matrix and take numbers, catalog numbers, an outline of the solos performed, and notes about the circumstances of the recording and surrounding matrix numbers. Along

the way, much information is imparted about groups
other than Henderson's (as well as non-performance
information such as the membership of the Crescendo
Club in 1940), and myths and misinformation
perpetuated by earlier discographies and works are
corrected. By using the corroborative evidence of
oral-history interviews, newspaper accounts, and so
forth, Allen demonstrates to researchers the
potential pitfalls of relying on a single account
of an event and the necessity of seeking corrobo-
ration.

In the biographical sections, the reader learns
that Henderson grew up in an educated and musical
family, graduated from Atlanta University in 1920,
and began his musical career as demonstration
pianist for the publishing firm of Pace & Handy. He
became musical director of Pace Phonograph Corp.'s
Black Swan label when Harry Pace split with W. C.
Handy the following year. His early recordings
were made as accompanist for such artists as
Alberta Hunter and Ethel Waters. Late 1921 saw him
touring the eastern half of the country with Waters
and the Black Swan Troubadors.

Except for the periods June 1939-end
1940, and again late 1947, when he was
with Benny Goodman, and from May 1948 to
November 1949, when he was Ethel Waters'
personal accompanist, he was the leader
of his own bands from January 1924 until
his stroke in December 1950. His band
always functioned as a DANCE orchestra;
for many seasons, he was a regular at
Roseland Ballroom in New York, and later
at Connie's Inn in Harlem and at the
Grand Terrace in Chicago. His RECORDINGS
showed primarily his band's talents as a
jazz orchestra, although his in-person
performances were probably not that much
oriented toward "le hot." Out of his
total longevity as a leader, he was
considered preeminent by his contemporaries during the period 1924-1932, and
again briefly starting in 1936. He had
the pick of the best musicians. . . . By
1932, only the intense loyalty of his men
kept the band together in spite of
layoffs and lax discipline; and
Fletcher's lackadaisical personality and
disinclination to stand up to the
extortions of his agents and promoters

- 152 -

more than once caused the deterioration of a band which looked great on paper but played poorly in public. But during the '20s, when Duke Ellington was an upstart newcomer, Smack's band was THE band to hear and to be able to play in, and not the standard which others tried to emulate (p. 546).

As an ARRANGER, it is here that I think that Fletcher left his most lasting mark, the one which touched the greatest number of listeners and exerted the greatest influence on his peers. From the start of his arranging career about 1931, until the emergence of Sy Oliver and Eddie Sauter about the periods 1938-40, Fletcher's was the dominant arranging style during the years of the classic swing style, which I would bracket as about 1934-40 (p. 547).

The book concludes with a discussion of Henderson's arrangements and style, a list of the known arrangements, and a short discussion and a detailed listing of his compositions. The end matter includes: a bibliography; "Index of Recording Groups;" "Roster of Henderson Musicians, 1921-1950," including a short biographical statement about each; "Roster of Henderson Vocalists," again with biographical statements; "Itinerary Index;" "Index of Names and Subjects;" "Index of Tune Titles;" and "Index of Catalogue Numbers."

Reviews: AB Bookman's Weekly 53:328 Ja 28 '74; Coda 12:31-32 nl '74; High Fidelity/Musical America 25:MA36-37 Ja '75; Jazz Digest 2:41-42 N/D '73; Jazz Journal 27:31+ Ju '74; Jazz Podium 23:31 F '74; Jazz Research 5:178 '73; Library Journal 97:2551 '72; Matrix nl02/103:21-22 My '74; Music Journal 32:21 Ja '74; Orkester Journalen 42:26-27 D '74; Second Line 25:22 Fall '73; Village Voice 19:19 F 21 '74

SELECTIVE DISCOGRAPHY

The Complete Fletcher Henderson. Bluebird (RCA) AXM2-5507, 1927-1936.
Fletcher Henderson: Developing an American Orchestra. Smithsonian Collection R-006, 1923-1937.
Fletcher Henderson 1934. MCA 1318, 1934.

Fletcher Henderson Orchestra. Biograph BLP-12039, 1923-
   1927.
Fletcher Henderson's Orchestra. Biograph BLP-C-12, 1924-
   1941.
Smack. Ace of Hearts AH-41, 1926-1931.
A Study in Frustration. 4 vols. Columbia CL-1682/3/4/5,
   1927-1938.

Jimi Hendrix

Henderson, David. 'Scuse Me While I Kiss the Sky: The Life
of Jimi Hendrix. 1978. Reprint. New York, London, Toronto,
and Sydney: Bantam Books, 1983. xi, 411 pp. photographs.
discography.

An ingenious blend of research and conversation,
this effective biographical narrative treats the
social, cultural, and familial circumstances into
which Hendrix was born and by which his world view
was formed. It chronicles his career from his
teenage membership in a group called "The Rocking
Kings" to his fronting of the world-renowned "Jimi
Hendrix Experience" and the later "Band of
Gypsies," and his arrival as the "most spectacular
Electric Guitarist in the World" (p. 187). The work
traces Hendrix's musical growth from his birth in
1942 to his death in 1970, treating his early
musical experiences; his learning to play the
guitar; his service in the U.S. Army and his
musical development there; stints with rhythm &
blues stars such as Little Richard, Ike and Tina
Turner, Jackie Wilson, B. B. King, The Isley Brothers, King Curtis, and others. Also treated are his
sojourn in Harlem and his reaching maturity in New
York's Greenwich Village cafe scene in the middle
1960s; the birth of the "Jimi Hendrix Experience"
in England in 1966 and his rise to fame there,
together with his activities in the British rock
culture; his role in creating the musico-
technological revolution of the 1960s, in which
feedback, distortion, overdubbing, mixing, and the
like became common in rock and other forms of pop

Jimi Hendrix

music; how Hendrix took advantage of these advances
to extend and improve his sound, invention, and
delivery; the JHE's smash debut in the United
States; details of Hendrix's triumph at the first
Monterey International Pop Festival in 1967 and the
subsequent tours in Europe and the United States;
details of and surrounding the Woodstock Festival
of 1969 and Hendrix's triumph there; and his
relationships with his friends, fellow musicians,
management and production people, and hangers-on.

Written in the style of a novel, this work is
filled with bits of pop-music history; colorful and
effective descriptions of Hendrix's recorded
performances; and vivid descriptions of Hendrix's
behavior and attitudes, with special insight into
his character and personality. Discussions of the
construction, capabilities, and potential of
Hendrix's Stratocaster guitar are informative, as
are the details on how he used and exploited the
instrument. Extensive material from interviews
with Hendrix's father and quotations from such
celebrities as Eric Clapton, Larry Coryell, and
Mike Bloomfield and from Hendrix's intimates and
acquaintances add breadth, depth, and insight to
this engaging and information-packed book. The
author's "Coda" analyzes the circumstances
surrounding Hendrix's death and the surprising
financial revelations and legal developments that
followed, the posthumous release of recorded
performances, and the adoption by others of
Hendrix's musical style following his death. The
engaging narrative compensates for the lack of
scholarly documentation and indexing.

Reviews: Audio 68:41 O '84; Best Sellers 41:302
N '81; Book World 11:12 O 18 '81; Kliatt Young
Adult Paperback Book Guide 16:67 Winter '82;
Stereo Review 46:81 D '81

Hopkins, Jerry. Hit and Run: The Jimi Hendrix Story. New
York: Perigee Books, 1983. 336 pp. photographs. discography.

Quite simply, Jimi Hendrix was one of
the most significant musical contrib-
utors, not just of our time but of all
time. In only a few years he defined the
spectrum of the electric guitar--or
rather, redefined it--and influenced
thousands of guitarists, many of whom
went on to become worldwide stars. There

Jimi Hendrix

> are things he did on the guitar no one
> yet can explain or duplicate, not even
> given the electronic assistance that's
> been developed since his death (p. 11).

Born in Seattle, Washington, Hendrix taught himself
to play the ukulele when he was about twelve. He
developed a left-handed playing technique that he
retained when he shifted to the electric guitar a
short time later. Hendrix played with several
dance bands during his high-school years. His
experiences with drugs began at that time, and he
was arrested in 1961 for stealing a car. He was
given a chance to avoid imprisonment by enlisting
in the Army. He took it, and was assigned to a
paratrooper unit until he broke an ankle and
received a medical discharge.

For a year Hendrix played with groups in
Nashville and Seattle. Then he was invited to "go
on the road with one of the most influential and
outrageous performers in the history of
rock-and-roll," Little Richard, with whom he played
for the next two years (p. 54). He gradually
developed a style that included imitations of urban
sounds such as "the rushing chatter of New York's
subway trains, the high-pitched release of the air
brakes on a bus, the energetic honk of a
saxophone"; playing his guitar behind his back or
head, or with the neck of the guitar between his
legs like an "erect phallus"; and playing the
guitar with his teeth or tongue (p. 59). Following
his tours with Little Richard, Hendrix moved to New
York, where he tried to find work in clubs in
Greenwich Village and sold drugs to his fellow
musicians when there was no work. Thus began a
life of "sex, drugs, and rock 'n' roll: the tripod
that held up the sixties, the fuels that made the
pop scene go" (p. 75).

In 1966, Brian "Chas" Chandler became his
producer and took Hendrix to London. Chandler and
his partner, Mike Jeffrey, booked Hendrix to play
at the Olympia Theatre in Paris, and the rush began
to find appropriate backup musicians. Thus was
formed the "Jimi Hendrix Experience," with Hendrix
(lead guitar), Noel Redding (bass guitar), and John
"Mitch" Mitchell (drums). The group toured England
and western Europe and made an album titled Are You
Experienced? They made their American debut at the
1967 Monterey International Pop Festival, where
their performance concluded with Hendrix's setting

fire to his guitar, a gimmick he had begun to use
as a curtain-closer almost two years earlier. The
Experience continued to perform in Europe and the
United States, commanding top fees; their
recordings were top sellers and remained at the top
of the record charts for extended periods of time.
This phase of his career culminated in the rock
festival at Woodstock in August, 1969. The late
1960s saw increasing tension among the members of
the Experience and resulted in its periodic breakup
beginning in 1969. Hendrix became increasingly
embroiled in legal battles over representation,
contested recording contracts, and an arrest in
Toronto for drug possession. Alcohol and drugs
were increasingly a part of his daily life: on
September 17, 1970, he died of an overdose of
sleeping pills.

Reviews: Best Sellers 43:329 D '83; Creem
15:48-49 My '84; Guitar Player 18:10 F '84;
Kirkus Reviews 51:751 Jy 1 '83; Library Journal
108:1141 Ju 1 '83; Publishers Weekly 224:68 Jy
29 '83; Trouser 10:48 N '83; Village Voice 28:72
D 20 '83

Welch, Chris. Hendrix: A Biography. New York: Delilah/
Putnam, 1978. 100 pp. photographs. discography.

This book chronicles the development of the musical
style and character of Jimi Hendrix and his bands
as their recordings were released. It also treats
the social and personal experiences that affected
Hendrix. The reader learns that, early in his
career, guitarist James Marshall Hendrix worked as
a backup artist with B. B. King, Sam Cooke, Solomon
Burke, Chuck Jackson, Jackie Wilson, Ike and Tina
Turner, Little Richard, the Isley Brothers, and
Joey Dee and the Starlighters. Based in the South
and traveling almost from coast to coast with these
musicians, he was "thinking all the while about
what I wanted to do" (p. 16).

In about 1965 Hendrix moved to New York, formed
his own group--the Blue Flames--and changed his
name to Jimmy James. Very soon he moved to London,
formed a new band--the Experience--had a
sensational reception in the clubs there, and
recorded his first hit single--"Hey Joe"--in
December, 1966. His first album, Are You
Experienced?, was released in May of the next year;
it was "a tremendously exciting and stimulating
compilation of ideas and musicianship. Nothing

quite like it had ever been heard before. . . .
The combination of jazz and Dylan influences in the
construction of Jimi's vocal line was unheard of at
that time in rock music" (p. 18). In 1967 Hendrix
visited the United States as an accomplished and
successful performer and bandleader, conquering the
Monterey International Pop Festival; he was
enormously successful in 1967 and 1968. In the
latter year the group made an extensive tour of the
United States, traveling from coast to coast and
from Texas to Canada. During 1968/1969, he played
the Woodstock Festival and the Experience broke up;
in 1970, he formed the Band of Gypsies, using old
American friends as sidemen.

Hendrix had a wonderful sense of humor, was
largely apolitical, and was an avid student of the
blues. His style was bound up with electronics,
for he "started out with 75 watts and ended up with
six four by twelve Marshall cabinets, a four by
twelve monitor, and four 100 watt Marshall tops,
all souped-up and coupled up through fuzz, wah-wah
pedals and a Univibe! He had a special box of
gadgets and the fuzz and wah-wah pedals acted as
pre-amps" (p. 72). He used drugs but was not an
addict. Toward the end of his career his technical
proficiency and his musical maturity increased
tremendously, and he was moving in new directions
as evidenced the by posthumously released War
Heroes album.

Review: Library Journal 98:3638 D 15 '73

SELECTIVE DISCOGRAPHY

Axis. Reprise 6281.
Electric Ladyland. 2 vols. Reprise S-6307.
The Essential Jimi Hendrix Experience. 2 vols.
    2RS-2245/HS-2293, 1978, 1979.
Jimi Hendrix Experience. Reprise S-6261-S.
Nine to the Universe. HS-2299, 1980.
Woodstock Two. Cotillion SD-3-500.

Billie Holiday

Chilton, John. Billie's Blues: Billie Holiday's Story, 1933-1959. Foreword by Buck Clayton. New York: Stein and Day, 1975. [vii], 264 pp. photographs. bibliography. index.

Chilton's treatment of Billie Holiday's life begins with the onset of her recording career in 1933 and includes information about her first engagement at the Apollo Theater; her appearance in 1935 in the film Rhapsody in Black; her relationship with her agent Joe Glaser; her long-lasting friendship with Lester Young; her father's death in 1937; her tours with Count Basie's band in 1937 and with Artie Shaw's band in 1938; the story of the composition of "Strange Fruit"; her tour with her own big band in the early 1940s; her New York Metropolitan Opera House Concert (1944); her Town Hall concert in 1946; her appearance in New Orleans with Louis Armstrong; her arrest on drug charges in 1947 and her subsequent jail term; her Carnegie Hall comeback concert following her release from jail; her exclusion from performing in New York clubs because the authorities refused to grant her a cabaret card; her television appearances in the early 1950s; her appearance in Duke Ellington's "25th Anniversary in the Music Business" concert (1952); her European tour under the aegis of Leonard Feather in 1954; her appearance in the first Newport Jazz Festival; the publication of her autobiography, Lady Sings the Blues; the "Lady Sings the Blues" Carnegie Hall concert in 1956; her Central Park summer concert series (1957); her

appearances in the Timex "Seven Lively Arts" series
(1957) and the Monterey Jazz Festival (1958); the
death of Lester Young and its effect on Holiday;
and Holiday's own death in 1959.

Also included are reminiscences about Holiday's
singing by several critics and fellow musicians;
discussion of her personal habits and attitudes
regarding sex, clothes, alcohol, drugs, and
cooking; details of her recording dates throughout
her career; her several marriages; and discussion
of her singing style. Among the people whose lives
touched hers are John Hammond, Cozy Cole, Teddy and
Irene Wilson, Roy Eldridge, Ben Webster, Jimmie
Lunceford, Ella Fitzgerald, Fletcher Henderson,
Jimmy Rushing, Zutty Singleton, Dizzy Gillespie,
Lena Horne, Sid Catlett, Buck Clayton, Trummy
Young, Red Allen, Rex Stewart, Coleman Hawkins,
Sarah Vaughan, Miles Davis, Oscar Peterson, Jo
Jones, and Benny Carter. Throughout the book,
Chilton points out differences between Holiday's
autobiography, Lady Sings the Blues, and other
sources that are, in his opinion, more reliable.

Reviews: Best Sellers 35:215 O '75; Booklist
72:278 O 15 '75; Books & Bookmen 20:53 Jy '75;
Coda nl43:27 N '75; Jazz Journal 28:48 My '75;
Kirkus Reviews 43:632 Ju 1 '75; Library Journal
100:1327 Jy '75; Melody Maker 50:40 My 3 '75;
New Statesman 90:175 Au 8 '75; Orkester
Journalen 43:19 Jy/Au '75; Publishers Weekly
207:79 Ju 16 '75; Punch 269:74 Jy 9 '75

Holiday, Billie, with William Dufty. Lady Sings the Blues.
paperback. New York: Lancer Books, 1956. 191 pp. photographs.

This autobiography begins with Holiday's recollections of her childhood in Baltimore: "Mom and
Pop were just a couple of kids when they got
married. He was eighteen, she was sixteen, and I
was three" (p. 5). Her reminiscences include her
mistreatment by her cousin Ida, with whom she lived
in her first years; her errand running for a local
madame, in return for which she was allowed to
listen to recordings of Louis Armstrong and Bessie
Smith; her near-rape at ten and subsequent
placement in a Catholic school for girls; and her
move to New York at thirteen to join her mother.
Holiday recalls her first singing job at Pod's &
Jerry's in Harlem; her first meeting with promoter
John Hammond, agent Joe Glaser, and such

established performers as Red Norvo and Mildred Bailey; her first record date with Benny Goodman; and her first appearance at the Apollo Theater. In her narrative style, Holiday tells us of meeting and performing with saxophonist Lester Young; her work as an actress on radio and in the movies, her tours with the Count Basie band, the Artie Shaw band, and her own short-lived groups; her problems with drugs and the resultant trouble with the authorities and prison confinement; her several marriages; and her performances in clubs and theaters across the United States and in Europe. The book contains many recollections that are disputed by Holiday's friends and colleagues and are presented in Chilton's biography of her life.

Reviews: Jazz Today 1:52 O '56; Jazz Journal 11:31 S '58; Library Journal 81:1805 '56; Record Changer 14:21-22 Ja '57

SELECTIVE DISCOGRAPHY

Billie Holiday: The Golden Years. 6 vols. CBS
  BPG-62037/9, BPG-62814/6, 1933-1942.
The Billie Holiday Story. 2 vols. Columbia PG-32121/7.
The Billie Holiday Story. MCA MCA2-4006, 1944-1950.
The Complete Billie Holiday on Verve. Verve J-34809,
  1946-1959.
God Bless the Child. Columbia CG-30782.
Strange Fruit. Atlantic SD-1614, 1939-1948.
Swing Brother Swing. Encore P-14388, 1935-1938.

Lena Horne

Haskins, James, with Kathleen Benson. <u>Lena: A Personal and Professional Biography of Lena Horne</u>. New York: Stein and Day, 1984. 226 pp. photographs. index.

This book takes the reader from Horne's childhood in a middle-class Brooklyn neighborhood to her one-woman show that closed in 1982. We learn of her unstable and insecure youth; her employment as a show girl at the Cotton Club at sixteen; her brief tenure as a singer with the Noble Sissle Society Orchestra; her first marriage and the birth of her two children; her appearances in a film, <u>The Duke Is Tops</u>, featuring Duke Ellington, and in a "Broadway revue, Lew Leslie's <u>Blackbirds of 1939</u>" (p. 46); her early recordings; and her engagements in New York at the Café Society Downtown and in Hollywood at the Trocadero.

In the 1940s Horne signed a film contract with MGM and was often included in separately shot musical segments that could be edited out of the films when they were released in the South.

Her trademark through the 1940s [was] singing while leaning against a pillar. The image of Lena, always elegantly gowned, singing while draped around a marble column in a lavishly produced musical sequence, would become virtually standardized. Only her ability to appear enigmatic prevented her from being completely exploited in these stock

sequences; she managed to carry them off
with a dignity that, coupled with her
aloof and detached delivery, enhanced
both her mystery and her audience appeal
(p. 73).

Among the films in which she appeared are <u>Cabin in
the Sky</u> and <u>Stormy Weather</u>. In 1947 Horne married
Lennie Hayton. In the early 1950s she was "denied
work in radio, TV, films, and recording" as a
result of being blacklisted for possible Communist
affiliation (p. 136). Toward the end of the decade
she starred in a Broadway show, <u>Jamaica</u>, which "ran
for over a year, closing in the spring of 1959"
(p. 146). The 1960s saw her support for and
participation in the civil-rights movement. The
film in which she starred, <u>Death of a Gunfighter</u>,
gave her an opportunity to act in a serious role
that did not present her in a stereotypical
fashion; it was released early in 1969.

A few years later Horne suffered the loss of her
father, son, and husband within a few short
months. In the course of recovering from the
losses, she began to return to her singing career.
She and Tony Bennett embarked on an extended tour
of Europe and the United States. Later she played
the part of Glinda the Good Witch in the film
version of <u>The Wiz</u>. In 1980 she made her farewell
tour--which turned out not to be a farewell at
all. The next year began <u>Lena Horne: The Lady and
Her Music</u>. "To make the first half of the show a
reminiscence of Lena's past and the second half a
statement of Lena in the present," the songs in the
one-woman show were chosen with care (p. 196). "The
show was 'a triumph!' and since the show was Lena
and Lena was the show, she was a triumph. For at
least a decade, even critics who could find nothing
particularly notable about her voice had mentioned
her 'presence' onstage; but now she <u>commanded</u> the
stage. And she commanded her material" (pp.
197-198). She celebrated her sixty-fifth birthday
performing the show.

A comparative avalanche of awards
. . . poured in on her as her city and
her profession honored her. <u>Lena Horne:
The Lady and Her Music</u> received, in
addition to the special Tony award, a
Drama Desk Award and a special citation
from the New York Drama Critics' Circle.
The sound track of the show, produced by

Quincy Jones, received two Grammy
awards. Lena herself received New York
City's highest cultural award, the Handel
Medallion, and she was honored by any
number of other local organizations. In
the space of nine months, she got more
awards and more national press coverage
than she had received in any nine-year
period previously, and she also achieved
a notoriety that was unexpected as well
as unique (pp. 203-204).

The book ends with commentary on "Lena, Senior
Citizen."

Reviews: Best Sellers 44:17 Ap '84; Booklist
80:660 Ja 1 '84; Choice 21:1474 Ju '84; Kirkus
Reviews 51:1160 N 1 '83; Library Journal 109:95
Ja '84; Los Angeles Times Book Review p9 Mr 11
'84; Publishers Weekly 224:78 D 2 '83; Variety
314:38 F 29 '84

Haskins, James. Lena Horne. New York: Coward-McCann, 1983.
160 pp. photographs. index.

"Well-born in Brooklyn" in 1917, young readers will
learn, singer/entertainer Lena Horne was left, at
three, with her grandparents when her father and
mother departed, separately, to seek their
individual successes (p. 11). Immediately, her
grandparents began to raise her to be "an aware,
articulate, educated young lady" (p. 16). Soon
after she started school however, her mother, who
had become "an obscure traveling actress," took her
away and traveled to Philadelphia, Miami (where she
experienced prejudice, from whites and blacks, for
the first time), Alabama, southern Ohio, and Macon
and Ft. Valley, Georgia (p. 18). All the while, her
mother was traveling to even different cities to
perform and would leave Lena in the care of
strangers. By the time Lena returned to Brooklyn,
"she was nearly fourteen years old, but she had
lived more places and met more strangers than most
people twice her age. She had also suffered more
mistreatment. She had been abused, both physically
and psychologically. She had been exposed to
terrifying and hateful things" (p. 27).

Following the death of her grandparents when she
was fifteen, young Lena was put to work by her
mother and stepfather to help support them all.
Thus she started to work as a dancer in the

exclusive chorus line of the Cotton Club in Harlem. Her mother accompanied her there almost every night, since Lena was underage. Soon, though, she fled New York and the gangsters who owned the club and joined the Noble Sissle band as a singer; shortly thereafter, she was married. In 1938 Horne got the opportunity to appear in a film--The Duke Is Tops--which starred Duke Ellington and his orchestra. In the following year she appeared in the Broadway revue Blackbirds of 1939. Her work and relationship with Lew Leslie in the latter show, and with his family, made her aware "that there were white people who were not prejudiced against Negroes" (p. 53).

Late in 1939 she left her husband and their two children and moved to New York to find work. But work was hard to find: "Lena didn't fit the commonly accepted image of a Negro. Her skin was too light, her hair was too straight, her features too aquiline. Besides, she didn't sing the blues" (p. 60). But opportunities did begin to come along, leading to her role in the movie Cabin in the Sky and, in 1943, Stormy Weather. Encountering discrimination in California and becoming active in civil-rights organizations, she also became more civic minded. But her main activities continued to consist of her singing and entertaining on the cabaret circuit. In 1947 she made her first trip to Europe and was married there to conductor Lennie Hayton. In 1957 Horne left the cabaret circuit for Broadway, where she first starred in the calypso musical Jamaica. In 1967 her television special, Monsanto Night Presents Lena Horne, was aired on NBC. Then came her good role in the movie Death of a Gunfighter, opposite Richard Widmark. In 1974 Horne made triumphant tours of Great Britain and North America with Tony Bennett. In 1978 she played Glinda the Good Witch in the movie version of The Wiz. In 1981 her one-woman show, Lena Horne: The Lady and Her Music, opened on Broadway.

Details of a number of these and other events and concerns are given: Horne's first marriage, when she was eighteen, and the difficulties she experienced while it lasted; her problems on the road as a singer with the all-white Charlie Barnett band; how her attitude about her racial heritage, her race pride, and her self-image was shaped by white club-owner Barney Josephson and by Paul Robeson, Josh White, Hazel Scott, and Billie Holiday; her stand "against the Hollywood practice

of stereotyping all Negroes" (p. 119); the snubs
she received from black actors and actresses in
Hollywood in the early 1940s; the difficulties she
and her husband Lennie Hayton faced before and
during their marriage; her insecurities and her
strengths; her involvement in the struggle for
black social equality in the 1960s; and her
relationships with her children, her mother, and
her father.

Reviews: Book Report 3:39 My '84; Booklist
80:675 Ja 1 '84; Center for Children's Books
Bulletin 37:109 F '84; Children's Book Review
Service 12:52 Ja '84; Choice 21:1474 Ju '84;
Kirkus Reviews 51:J212 N 1 '83; Reading Teacher
37:889 My '84; School Library Journal 30:172 Mr
'84; Voice of Youth Advocates 7:46 Ap '84

Horne, Lena, as told to Helen Arnstein and Carlton Moss.
In Person: Lena Horne. New York: Greenberg, 1950. 249 pp.
photographs.

The singer/actress writes of her life and career,
beginning with her early introduction to the
entertainment business by her mother, an actress
and member of Harlem's Lafayette Players. Growing
up in Brooklyn and other locations, she had her
first lesson in "race" in Miami, Florida, and was
later exposed to the problem in other Southern
cities, including Jacksonville, Florida, and Ft.
Valley, Georgia. In 1933, at fifteen, Horne and her
mother returned to New York, where the singer lived
first with her paternal grandmother and, later,
with a childhood friend of her mother, all the time
nurturing a burning desire to be an actress.
Seeking knowledge about the theater, she "haunted
our school library; and when that failed me, I went
to the public library . . . hunting for everything
about the theatre I could get my hands on. I read
the classics, committing to memory many of the
roles great actresses like Sarah Bernhardt, Maude
Adams, and Ethel Barrymore had made famous"
(p. 30). Horne was encouraged and guided by high-
school teachers and a drama coach.

At sixteen, in 1934, she quit school to become a
Cotton Club dancer, her mother acting as her
chaperone, manager, and mentor; serving as
inspiration were Cotton Club artists Ada Ward, Avon
Long, Cab Calloway, Flournoy Miller, and others.
Horne began to take singing lessons, and in just a
few months she became one of the club's featured

singers. Not long after, she quit the Cotton Club
to join the Noble Sissle Orchestra as a vocalist.
All the while

> my career was Mama's entire existence.
> She ate, slept, dreamed, planned,
> breathed it. Nothing else--not warmth,
> nor cold, nor comfort, nor illness, nor
> convenience--had any meaning for her.
> I'm sure she couldn't have realized that
> this was her one big topic of
> discussion. She talked about it from
> every angle with everyone she considered
> qualified to comment. She turned to the
> musicians for criticism and for advice.
> She was there when newspaper reporters
> came backstage. She listened to the
> comments of theatre managers, press-
> agents, other performers. And when she
> wasn't backstage with me, she'd be out in
> the audience while I was on the stage,
> straining to catch every word that was
> said about the show and about me (pp.
> 71-72).

In 1936 Horne left the Sissle band and her career
for marriage and Pittsburgh, Pennsylvania. In 1939
she accepted an offer to star in Lew Leslie's
short-lived revue Blackbirds of 1939, returning to
Pittsburgh and her family when the show failed.

By 1940 her two children had been born, and she
had left her husband and to seek work in New York.
There she finally landed a job as vocalist with the
Charlie Barnett band, then moving to Café Society
Downtown, where she performed for a few months
alongside pianists Teddy Wilson, Meade Lux Lewis,
Albert Ammons, and Pete Johnson. Next came
Hollywood and her first motion pictures--Panama
Hattie, Cabin in the Sky, and Stormy Weather. After
the latter film, however, "My setting was almost
identical with that of Panama Hattie, and my
situation was certainly the same. I was a night
club entertainer in a cafe visited by the main
characters in the story. I came on, sang a song,
disappeared, and that was that!" (p. 218). During
the war Horne continued to make films and do club
work. She also did radio transcriptions for
broadcast to American servicemen and made tours of
army camps. The book ends with Horne having: 1)
secured release from her MGM contract to "take the
risk of making pictures independently," commenting

that "though I feel that my 'glamour days' are rapidly disappearing, it seems to me that the most important part of my life is ahead of me" (p. 243); and 2) married, in 1947, for the second time.

Horne gives the reader glimpses of life backstage at the Cotton Club and on the road with Noble Sissle and of racism as it affected herself and other black entertainers; the growth of her understanding of racism in the United States; the shameful treatment she received from the public and the industry while traveling with the all-white Charlie Barnett band; and her friendships with Paul Robeson, Josh White, and Billy Strayhorn.

Horne, Lena, and Richard Schickel. <u>Lena</u>. New York: Doubleday, 1965. 300 pp. photographs.

This book effectively elaborates and expands upon the information presented in <u>In Person</u> and extends the story by fifteen years. In the process the singer/entertainer gives a more detailed view of many of the events and circumstances of her life: her childhood loneliness; the late formation of her own immediate family unit--an interracial one, "which meant we had no place among either Negroes or whites" (p. 46); her relationships with folk singer Josh White, pianist Teddy Wilson, Duke Ellington, Billy Strayhorn, Cole Porter, boxer Joe Louis, singer Hazel Scott, actor Canada Lee, actor/director Orson Welles, Count Basie, actress Hattie McDaniel, singer/actress Ethel Waters, Cab Calloway, her husband Lennie Hayton, pianist Luther Henderson, actor James Mason, Perry Como, and Paul Robeson, who "was used against me later, when the political witch hunts were on, when I was actually banned from radio and television for a time" (pp. 118-119).

Some of the details in this book differ slightly from the same events as they are described in <u>In Person</u>, and both the content and the photographs have more variety; the racial factor is stronger here, the text being shot through with incidents and her perceptions of the problem. Additionally, she tells of her becoming at last "a solidly professional singer in the late war years and the early post-war years" (p. 198); her insistence on non-discriminatory clauses in her night-club and theater contracts; her return trips to Europe in 1950 and 1956; details of her 1946 trip to Europe and her being married there; her attitude toward performing in Las Vegas; her being listed in <u>Red Channels</u>, which effectively blacklisted her from performing on television; her dramatic triumph in the musical <u>Jamaica</u> in 1957; and her participation in and observations on the civil-rights movement of the early 1960s.

Reviews: American Record Guide 32:560-561 F '66; Best Sellers 25:333 N 15 '65; Book Week p14 Ja 23 '66; Booklist 62:391 D 15 '65; Books & Bookmen 11:28 Ap '66; Harper's Magazine 231:132 N '65; Jazz Journal 19:22 Ju '66; Kirkus Reviews 33:869 Au 15 '65; Kirkus Reviews 33:921 S 1 '65; Library Journal 90:4062 O 1 '65; Negro Digest 15:94 Ja '66; New Statesman 71:738 My 20 '66; Observer p27 My 8 '66; Publishers Weekly 190:91 O 3 '66; Saturday Review 48:47 O 2 '65

SELECTIVE DISCOGRAPHY

<u>Ageless/Timeless</u>. Brylen S-4413.
<u>Jazz Master</u>. DRG MRS-501.
<u>Lena in Hollywood</u>. Liberty LN-10194.
<u>Lena Goes Latin</u>. DRG MRS-510, 1985.
<u>Live on Broadway</u>. Qwest 2QW-3597.
<u>Lovely & Alive</u>. RCA Victor LSP 2587.
<u>This Is the Decade of the 30's</u>. Victor VPM-6058.
<u>20 Golden Pieces of Lena Horne</u>. Bulldog 2000.
<u>We'll Take Romance</u>. Intermedia 5051.

Mahalia Jackson

Goreau, Laurraine. <u>Just Mahalia, Baby</u>. Waco, Tex.: Word Books, 1975. x, 611 pp. photographs.

Through Goreau's story-telling ability, the facts and events of Mahalia Jackson's life are interestingly and effectively presented. In this detailed work the reader learns that the great gospel singer was born in New Orleans in 1912, grew up in an environment that was "mainly Afro--some speaking French--laced with Italians, Irish, and Germans, their children flowing in and out of each other's homes, sure of a little something from the kitchen, black or white: spaghetti, or gingercake, or flour biscuits sopped with syrup" (p. 16); and that she reached the pinnacle of fame at about fifty, having earned many honors and awards, including the Silver Dove Prize for her album <u>Mahalia Jackson Sings</u> "for work of quality doing the most good for international understanding" and the Grand Prix du Disque in 1966 (p. 324).

The book vividly describes Jackson's early physical, mental, and musical growth and development, painting a picture of an impoverished childhood among a variety of influences (e.g., blues, jazz, sport, and voodoo), a rather oppressive home life and her refuge from it in church activities, her father's rejection of her from birth, and her "conversion" and singing when she "<u>knew</u> she had religion; there was not a doubt. Then she came through with that long meter and she set that church on <u>fire</u>" (p. 45). Written largely

- 171 -

in the style of black vernacular, the work
discusses the details of Jackson move, at fifteen,
to Chicago, where she did domestic work and sought
opportunities to listen to Earl Hines and Louis
Armstrong to "hear a little bit of that Loosiana
jazz music 'cause it reminded her of home" (p. 53)
and the attempts of these two famous musicians to
engage her to sing with their bands. She
eventually joined the Johnson Singers Quartet--a
religious group--the author tells us, and because
of her style, ran into resistance, attacks, and
denunciation from ministers who considered her
singing "blasphemous" and jazzy (p. 54). She met
Thomas A. Dorsey in 1929, sang and peddled his
gospel songs on street corners, and helped him form
the first black gospel chorus in 1930. Later she
became involved in Chicago and national politics,
supporting William L. Dawson, Franklin D. Roosevelt, John F. Kennedy, and others over the years.

In discussing other aspects of the life of this
singer who rose from "the swamps of the Mississippi
to the streets of Paris" (p. 207), the author gives
details about: Jackson's travels with Dorsey
between 1929 and 1942; her conquests of skeptical
audiences that were uninformed about and unexposed
to gospel music; her contacts, associations, and
friendships with the young Della Reese, the even
younger Aretha Franklin, Rev. James Cleveland, Alex
Bradford, Duke Ellington, Dinah Shore, Roberta
Martin, Sister Rosetta Tharpe, Albertina Walker,
Studs Terkel, Chicago Mayor Richard Daley, S. I.
Hayakawa, Nat King Cole, Dr. Martin Luther King,
Jr., and many others, including foreign heads of
state. Also treated are her trips to Europe in
1952, 1961, and 1963-1964 and to Africa, Japan, and
India in 1970; her many appearances on local and
national radio and television; the tremendous
impact of her gospel songs on jazz critics; her
marriages, long-term illness, and unfulfilled dream
to build a "temple" where young people might study
gospel music, religion, and academics; and the
turbulence of a life of struggles for respect and
security, and of one-nighters, a heavy television
schedule, festivals, rallies, fund-raisers, and
tours.

Throughout the book, the reader senses that the
subject's aesthetic and fervent religious beliefs
were inseparably intertwined (one has to "sing 'til
the Lord come, and when he comes, you sing 'til he
let go" [p. 445]), and that they and her life were

one and the same. The book contains vivid descriptions of Jackson's participation in the civil-rights struggles of the 1950s and 1960s and effective treatments of Jackson at home with friends, visitors, and members of her entourage, with comments on and revealing insights into her love for and cooking of soul food, and her music-making and decision-making procedures. The book ends with her death in 1972.

Reviews: Best Sellers 35:103 Jy '75; Christian Century 92:638 Ju 25 '75; Choice 12:1318 D '75; Melody Maker 52:18 Ja 1 '77; Music Journal 33:42 S '75; Publishers Weekly 207:66 Mr 3 '75; Second Line 27:17-18 Summer '75

Jackson, Mahalia, with Evan McLeod Wylie. Movin' On Up. New York: Hawthorn Books, 1966. 212 pp. photographs. discography.

This famous gospel singer tells of her early life in New Orleans at a time when "they had all the brass bands. There was still music on the showboats on the Mississippi River and there were all the cabarets and cafes where musicians like Jelly Roll Morton and King Oliver were playing. Ragtime music and jazz and the blues were being played all over" (p. 29). In this context she discusses the influence of the blues and the church on the formation of her own musical values and styles. She proceeds to tell of her move from New Orleans to Chicago in 1928 at sixteen and the hardships, inspirations, and accomplishments of her early days in the latter city, including the formation of and her participation in Chicago's first black gospel group--The Johnson Gospel Singers. She offers her opinions on the value and purpose of gospel music, as well as information about and insights into the gospel life.

Accompanying this information are facts and reminiscences of her work as proprietor of a beauty salon and a floral shop; her singing on the black gospel circuit, and her eventual arrival, in 1950, as the world's most famous gospel singer, with appearances on the Ed Sullivan Show, at the National Baptist Convention, and at Carnegie Hall. She goes on to give details about her European tours in 1952 and 1960; her own radio and television shows; her encounters with racism on her tours in the southern United States; her treatment as a celebrity in the North and in Europe; her participation in and observation of the civil-rights movement of the 1950s and 1960s; her views of the racial climate and conditions in the United States; and the impact of discrimination on young performers. There are vivid descriptions of President Kennedy's inaugural celebration, at which she sang the "Star Spangled Banner," and of the 1963 "March on Washington."

Reviews: AB Bookman's Weekly 39:948 Mr 6 '67; Best Sellers 26:379 Ja 15 '67; Book World 3:17 Mr 9 '69; Booklist 63:826 Ap 1 '67; Christian Science Monitor p9 Ja 10 '67; International Musician 66:18 Ja '68; Kirkus Reviews 34:1031 S 15 '66; Library Journal 91:5600 N 15 '66; Negro Digest 16:76 Jy '67; New York Times Book Review 72:46 Mr 5 '67; Publishers Weekly 190:47 O 24 '66; Publishers Weekly 195:67 F 3 '67; Saturday Review 52:35 S 6 '69

SELECTIVE DISCOGRAPHY

Mahalia Jackson--World's Greatest Gospel Singer and Falls-Jones Ensemble. Columbia CL-644, CS-8759.
Mahalia Jackson's Latest Hits. Columbia CL-2004, CS-8804.
My Faith. Columbia CL-2605, CS-9405.
The Power and the Glory. Columbia CL-1473, CS-8264.
Silent Night--Songs for Christmas. Columbia CL-1903, CS-8703.

Michael Jackson

Bego, Mark. _Michael!_ New York: Pinnacle Books, 1984. 180 pp. discography.

This brief biographical sketch of singer/entertainer Michael Jackson introduces Jackson the person and Jackson the entertainer and traces his growth from early childhood in Gary, Indiana. The author treats Jackson's early development in a family of eleven children, details the formation of the Jackson Five, and discusses their television debut on "Hollywood Palace" in 1969. Jackson's career is followed through the chronological release of his record albums and through his television appearances, beginning with the album _Diana Ross Presents the Jackson 5_ in 1969 and ending with Jackson's arrival as a video star in 1983. "A teen idol before he was a teen" (p. 37), Jackson made his first solo album, _Got to Be There_, in 1972. The author traces Jackson's subsequent solo career, during which he worked both as a single and as a member of The Jacksons, the group assuming this latter name when it switched from Motown Records to Columbia's Epic label in 1976. The author here treats the making of and Jackson's participation in the movie version of _The Wiz_ in 1978; the arrival of The Jacksons as "the largest selling rock group, after the Beatles" (p. 88); the _Thriller_ album of 1982, Jackson's views on race, health, and other matters; and his arrival at the top of the entertainment world in 1984. Jackson himself is allowed to tell of his career, his perception of himself, his friendships, his fans, and his professional relationships.

> Reviews: Booklist 80:1230 My 1 '84; Kliatt Young Adult Paperback Book Guide 18:62 Spring '84; Los Angeles Times Book Review p10 Ap 29 '84; Voice of Youth Advocates 7:210 O '84

George, Nelson. <u>The Michael Jackson Story</u>. New York: Dell, 1984. 191 pp. photographs. discography.

> Less a fan biography than other books on Jackson, this little volume discusses or mentions the singer/entertainer's start in the entertainment business and his nurturing in a religious and disciplined household, the emergence of the Jackson Five under the tutelage and management of their father, the influence of the early Motown acts on the Jackson Five's formative years, and the group's recording on Motown Records when Michael was just ten. The author goes on to treat Michael's home and backstage life, elements of his personality and character, and his personal and musical growth and development. The reader learns that in 1973, the Jacksons moved into disco, then toward independence from Motown. Relative to this, the author discusses: the group's break with the corporation in 1976 and their deal with Columbia Records' Epic label; Michael's emergence as a solo voice and entertainer distinct and separate from the Jackson Five; the making of the albums <u>Off the Wall</u> and <u>Thriller</u>; and possible new directions for Michael, including "acting as an integral part of his future" (p. 174).

> Reviews: Variety 314:94 Ap 4 '84; Village Voice 28:72 D 20 '83; Voice of Youth Advocates 7:211 O '84

SELECTIVE DISCOGRAPHY

<u>The Best of Michael of Jackson</u>. Motown M5-194, 1975.
<u>Forever Michael</u>. Motown 5331.
<u>The Jackson Five Anthology</u>. Motown M9-868, 1976.
<u>The Jackson Five's Greatest Hits</u>. Motown M5-201, 1971.
<u>The Jacksons</u>. Epic PE-34229, 1976.
<u>Off the Wall</u>. Epic FE-35745, 1979.
<u>Thriller</u>. Epic QE-38112, 1983.
<u>Triumph</u>. Epic PE-36424.
<u>Victory</u>. Epic 8E8-39576.

Edmund Thornton Jenkins

Green, Jeffrey P. Edmund Thornton Jenkins: The Life and
Times of an American Black Composer, 1894-1926.
Contributions to the Study of Music and Dance, No. 2.
Westport, Conn.: Greenwood Press, 1982. xii, 213 pp.
photographs, map. bibliography. index. list of compo-
sitions and recordings.

This is the biography of the most accomplished son
of the founder of the Jenkins Orphanage in
Charleston, South Carolina. It treats the history
of the orphanage from its establishment in 1892 and
chronicles the musical development of Edmund
Thornton Jenkins from his early training in the
orphanage band through his education at the Royal
Academy of Music in London, England, his teaching
and band leadership in England, and his performance
in night clubs, to his death in Paris in 1926. The
book touches on Jenkins's relationship to the black
progress movement of the period--the leaders and
artists of which included W.E.B. DuBois, Alain
Locke, Paul Robeson, Lawrence Brown, Sidney Bechet,
Will Marion Cooke, John Barbarolli, Florence Mills,
Will Vodery, Shelton Brooks, James P. Johnson, and
others. While the majority of the book is a
recapitulation of the events and persons in
Jenkins's life, some attention is given to the
series of jazz recordings in which Jenkins
participated in the early 1920s.

Reviews: Choice 20:1300 My '83; Jazz Times p16
Au '84; Library Journal 107:2341 D 15 '82

Bunk Johnson

Sonnier, Austin M., Jr. <u>William Geary "Bunk" Johnson: The New Iberia Years</u>. New York: Crescendo Publishing, 1977. 81 pp. photographs, musical examples. discography.

This informative but undocumented handbook includes a brief biographical sketch of Johnson, a chronology of his career, a discography of his works, and biographical vignettes of fourteen other jazzmen from the Louisiana lowlands. It tells of the trumpeter's birth in 1880; his introduction to the trumpet at seven; and the launching of his professional career at seventeen with Adam Oliver's orchestra, a "reading" band in New Orleans. The reader learns that Johnson played in Buddy Bolden's band from 1895 to 1898 and in at least thirteen other bands in his early career, including the Bob Russell band and Frank Dusen's Eagle Band; that he played with minstrel show and circus bands; and that his musical associations included the ragtime pianist Arthur Marshall, bandleader John Robichaux, trombonist Jack Carey, clarinetist George Lewis, trumpeter Louis Armstrong, and clarinetist/saxophonist Sidney Bechet. Known for his "sweet tone, refined taste, and near perfect execution" (p. 5), Johnson toured extensively between 1914 and 1920, moving, in the latter year, to New Iberia, Louisiana, where he married and settled down to manual labor. He gradually lost his inspiration to play, although he did perform there with the Black Eagle and Banner bands and ventured to other locations for short performance stints. In 1932 Johnson stopped playing altogether for ten years,

during which time he worked in the WPA program as a
music teacher and laborer. He was "rediscovered"
in 1942 and began to make sound recordings. His
career revived, and he traveled to California and
New York to record and to restructure his career.
Johnson "was an important guiding light in the
early years of jazz, . . . but his later work was
to be his most important and most significant
achievement" (p. 13).

Reviews: Booklist 73:1698 Jy 15 '77; Cadence
4:39 Au '78; Choice 14:1072 O '77; Coda n162:12
Au 1 '78; Footnote 9:2 n1 '77; Jazz Hot n347:30
Mr '78; Jazz Journal International 32:24 Mr '79;
Jazz Research 10:200-201 '78; Melody Maker 52:32
D 17 '77; Music Journal 36:43 F '78; Orkester
Journalen 46:15 Mr '78

SELECTIVE DISCOGRAPHY

Bunk Johnson. Collectors' Series JCL-829, 1947.
Bunk Johnson: Last Testament. Columbia JCL-829, 1947.
Bunk Johnson 1945. Dan VC-4018, 1945.
Bunk Johnson 1947. Collectors' Series JCL-829, 1947.
Bunk Johnson's Band 1944 with George Lewis. Storyville
    SLP-128, 1944.
Early Bunk, 1942-43. Dan VC-4020, 1942-1943.
Live and Lively, 1945 and 1950. Transark 1000, 197-.
The Sound of New Orleans, Volume 3. Columbia CL-2104, 1945.

James Weldon Johnson

Johnson, James Weldon. <u>Along This Way: The Autobiography of James Weldon Johnson</u>. New York: Viking Press, 1933. 418 pp. photographs. index.

> James Weldon Johnson's name is best known and most cited in connection with the song "Lift Every Voice and Sing," the text of which he composed for musical setting by his brother, John Rosamond. This songwriter, author, poet, educator, and lawyer also served as American Consul to Venezuela and to Nicaragua in the first decade of this century and as Field Secretary and General Secretary to the National Association for the Advancement of Colored People. In focusing on these high points in his life, Johnson tells of his birth; his childhood in Jacksonville, Florida, during which he was intro-duced to and surrounded by books and enjoyed the stimulation of his mother's intelligence; his musical household, in which he studied the piano with his mother and the guitar with his father; and his childhood religious indoctrination and activi-ties, subsequent skepticism, eventual agnosticism, and final arrival at "that conception of religion and that philosophy of life" that became his ethical "guideposts" (p. 31). Following a childhood filled with unique experiences and adventures and a friendly musical rivalry with his brother, Johnson graduated from high school in 1887 and enrolled at Atlanta University. There he received a rather classical education and sang bass in the school's quartet.

James Weldon Johnson

In his youth Johnson witnessed and experienced the birth and growth of Jim Crow following Reconstruction in such places as New York and rural Georgia, where he served as a "student teacher" and began to learn about Afro-Americans "as a race" (p. 119). The entire autobiography is a pene-trating, clear, and effective exposition on race relations in the United States from about 1887 to 1931. It tells of the author's first positions in the world of work--as a high-school principal and, simultaneously, as founder/owner/editor of a news-paper in his hometown; his admission to the Florida bar; his artistic partnership with his brother and their summer excursions to New York "to try for a place in the world of light opera" and the success they had there (p. 150); their meeting, in New York, personalities such as Will Marion Cook, Harry T. Burleigh, Paul Lawrence Dunbar, Theodore Drury, Jack Nail, Bert Williams, George Walker, Ada Overton, Ernest Hogan, and others; and their teaming with Bob Cole to write the trio's first song--a hit--"Louisiana Lize." In New York their efforts to break into show business led the brothers to business dealings with impresarios and publishers such as Florenz Ziegfeld and Joseph Stern. Johnson met W.E.B. DuBois in 1904 and had a close association with him thereafter. He tells of his accompanying his brother and Cole, who had formed a team, as they toured vaudeville; his trips to Europe; his introduction to national politics; his marriage; and black aspirations within the social context of the late nineteenth and early twentieth centuries.

Around 1916 Johnson resigned his position as American consul, settled in New York, where he wrote editorials for the New York Age, helped organize the American Society of Composers, Authors, and Publishers (ASCAP), and became Field Secretary for the NAACP. His activities in these capacities are ably detailed in this work, as are his firsthand observations of the pre-World War I black migration to the North and the many fights of the NAACP for freedom and equality for Afro-Americans. He retired from the NAACP in 1931 to join the faculty of Fisk University. Johnson reports on the literary output of Afro-Americans of the 1920s, including his own, and tells of his and Rosamond's collection and preparation of The Book of Negro Spirituals in 1925 and its sequel in 1926. Johnson's autobiography is a document of the Harlem

Renaissance, reflecting its thought and its values and reporting briefly on some of its activities.

Reviews: Booklist 30:119 D '33; Christian Science Monitor p12 N 11 '33; Commonweal 19:82 N 17 '33; Nation 137:452 O 18 '33; New York Herald Tribune Books p1 O 1 '33; New York Times p4 O 15 '33; North American Review 236:573 D '33; Saturday Review 10:369 D 23 '33; Springfield Republican p7e O 22 '33; Survey Graphic 22:568 N '33; Wisconsin Library Bulletin 29:238 N '33; World Tomorrow 17:20 Ja 4 '34; Yale Review 23:395 Winter '34

SELECTIVE DISCOGRAPHY

"Lift Every Voice and Sing." RCA ARC-1-4421, 1982.

Tommy Johnson

Evans, David. <u>Tommy Johnson</u>. London: Studio Vista, 1971.
112 pp. photographs. bibliography. discography.

    This "portrait of a famous black folk blues singer"
(p. 7), "one of the greatest blues singers ever
recorded" (p. 13), was composed from a large number
of interviews conducted by the author in the 1960s.
The work chronicles the exploits of Johnson and
those of his colleagues, from his childhood to the
1950s. It tells of Johnson the wanderer, a real
itinerant, playing the blues in Crystal Spring,
Drew, Bolton, Jackson, Tylertown, and other
Mississippi towns and on plantations such as the
famous Dockery, where Charley Patton, Willie Brown,
and other renowned blues singers were based. Also
discussed are Johnson's making of his sound
recordings; his lifestyle, personality, and character; and his "Repertoire, Style, and Legacy"
(p. 91). Mention is made of black Alabama and
Mississippi string bands that used the violin,
guitar, banjo, and mandolin. The primary contri-
butors to Johnson's story, quoted extensively, are
his brothers Clarence and Mager, themselves former
bluesmen, and other famous singers, including Rube
Lacy and Ishman Bracey.

    Reviews: Blues Unlimited n84:20 S '71;
Ethnomusicology 17:326-327 n2 '73; Jazz Journal
24:11 Au '71; JEMF Quarterly 8:168-170 pt3 '72;

Tommy Johnson

Journal of American Folklore 85:287-288 n337
'72; Music Teacher 112:864 S '71

SELECTIVE DISCOGRAPHY

The Legacy of Tommy Johnson. Matchbox SDM-224, 1972.
Tommy Johnson, 1928-1930: Complete Recordings in Chronological Order. Wolf WSE-104.

Bessie Jones

Jones, Bessie. <u>For the Ancestors: Autobiographical Memories</u>. Collected and edited by John Stewart.   Urbana: University of Illinois Press, 1983. xxv, 203 pp. photographs. chronology. bibliography. discography. filmography.

Bessie Jones is "the last active member of the original Georgia Sea Island Singers" (jacket notes).   She represents an attempt to carry this tradition of spirituals and game songs into the late twentieth century through workshops, concerts, and recordings.   Born in 1902 in Smithville, Georgia, Bessie Jones grew up in a family of farmers and sharecroppers.   Musical instruments were homemade; music was an important part of her life and the lives of her family members.   "My grandfather made his own bam-bams and he played an accordion. He used to have the kind with the knob on top. And all the men in the family played the guitar and banjos.   They made their own banjos, too.   My uncle, he could make good things. He made for white people and all. He was real tall and could he pick a guitar! Made the best banjos, too" (p. 15).

As a child people always used to say I was very musical, and most of my life has been taken up with music. My mother used to play the auto harp--they were different then from what they are now, the way you used to tune them up--and up in Dawson she bought me an accordion. Later on I bought me a guitar.   I can fram a

guitar now but I can't pick it. In those
days we didn't have parties--so-called
parties--we had frolics. And then we'd
have different musicians with accordions
and banjos and we'd have a big time (p.
30).

Frolics included games (such as apple dunking or
egg cracking), set dances ("There would be a man in
front who called the sets and usually there were
sixteen, or half that number, in the ring" [p.
36]), buck dancing, and, of course, eating. Games
and dances that included songs as an integral part
of their makeup were also a common part of life and
were part of the heritage of slavery. Among those
game-songs and dances were ring games, "Jibber"
("people say Juba, but it's really jibber" [p.
45]), the "Buzzard Lope," and "No No Thread
Needle." The tradition also included stories and
riddles, which often had a moral or a teaching purpose. Jones was active in the musical life of her
church. The book demonstrates the integration of
the musical traditions of the game-song and
play-party into church- related activities. "We
clap our hands and whether it's in church or any-
where else, they're on time. 'Cause if you clap
off-beat it's just--like the Bible say--like taming
a salmon. It's no good. You knock others off
their beat and singing" (p. 47).

Jones's husband, Cassius Davis, was a native of
the Georgia Sea Islands. In 1919 the family traveled to the islands to attend a funeral and stayed
there with Davis's family for three months. Between 1926 and 1933, Bessie lived in Florida. During this time, before she joined the Church of God
in Christ, she "did the blues and rags and things
like that" (p. 135).

When I came to St. Simons, John Davis
and them were already singing here and I
joined them. I started out singing with
Julia Armstrong and them, but we never
sang onstage. We were just in the hotel
on Sea Island, or usually in people's
homes. . . . Alan Lomax was the person
who sent me out to the stage. I first
met Lomax in 1955 when he came to St.
Simons to see John Davis and made a
record (p. 137).

Bessie Jones

Under Lomax's aegis Bessie was to take part in two
movies, <u>The Music of Williamsburg</u> and <u>The Georgia
Sea Island Singers</u>. She began a series of concert
tours and workshops, at first alone and later with
the Georgia Sea Island Singers. Gradually she became the leader of the singers. Through her singing in concerts and workshops, Bessie is continuing
the tradition of folk songs and spirituals with
which she grew up.

Reviews: Choice 21:321 O '83; Come-All-Ye 4:10
Winter '84; Journal of Southern History 50:335
My '84; Library Journal 108:1151 Ju 1 '83

SELECTIVE DISCOGRAPHY

<u>American Folk Songs for Children</u>. Southern Folk Heritage
  Series. Atlantic 1350, 1954.
<u>Deep South--Sacred and Sinful</u>. Southern Journey Series.
  Prestige/International 25005.
<u>Georgia Sea Islands</u>. 2 vols. Southern Journey Series.
  Prestige/International 25001/2.
<u>Georgia Sea Island Songs</u>. New World Records NW-278, 1977.
<u>So Glad I'm Here: Songs and Games from the Georgia Sea
  Islands</u>. Rounder Records 2015, 1975.
<u>Step It Down</u>. Rounder Records 8004.
<u>Traditional Music at Newport, Part I</u>. Vanguard VRS-9182,
  1965.
<u>What a Time</u>. Southern Grass Roots Revival Project, 1980.

Scott Joplin

Haskins, James, with Kathleen Benson. Scott Joplin: The Man Who Made Ragtime. 1978. First Scarborough Books edition. New York: Stein and Day, 1980. xiii, 249 pp. photographs. bibliography. indexes.

The life and musical activities of "The King of Ragtime" from his early days in the 1870s to his death in 1917 are discussed here: the preliminary development and establishment of Joplin's hometown of Texarkana, Texas, within the context of the social, political, and cultural climate of the period; Joplin's early musical influences and training; the life of the itinerant musicians of the period and Joplin's participation in that life; Joplin's years as a professional musician in Sedalia, Missouri, St. Louis, and New York; details about the composition and first production of Joplin's first opera, A Guest of Honor; and the events of "The Last Years," during which Joplin completed Treemonisha, his second and final opera, and endeavored to get it produced. Although the book contains conjecture of which beginning researchers should be wary and a certain musical naïveté, it reveals valuable knowledge of and insight into the development of the entire Joplin musical corpus, and it reconciles previous conflicting claims with new evidence and new perspectives. The "Prologue" discusses details of "The Rediscovery of Scott Joplin," which took place in the 1960s.

Reviews: America 139:91 Au 12 '78; Best Sellers
38:315 Ja '79; Booklist 74:1466 My 15 '78;
Choice 15:1229 N '78; Christian Science Monitor
70:25 Ju 1 '78; Jazz Report 9:13 n5 '80; Kirkus
Reviews 46:413 Ap 1 '78; Library Journal
103:1064 My 15 '78; Listener 101:327 Mr 1 '79;
New York Times Book Review 86:31 Ja 25 '81;
Notes 35:616 Mr '79; Publishers Weekly 213:67 Ap
17 '78

SELECTIVE DISCOGRAPHY

Elite Syncopations. Biograph BLP-1014Q.
Classic Rags Composed by the King of Ragtime Writers.
  Biograph BLP-1008Q.
Piano Rags by Scott Joplin. Joshua Rifkin. Nonesuch H-
  71248/264/305, 1970.
Rare Piano Roll Recordings. Biograph BLP-1010Q.
The Red Back Book. New England Conservatory Ragtime
  Ensemble. Angel S-36060, 1973.
Scott Joplin: Ragtime Pioneer, 1899-1914. Riverside RLP-
  8815.
Scott Joplin, 1916. Biograph BLP-1006, 1916.
Scott Joplin: The Entertainer. Biograph BLP-1013Q.
Treemonisha. Deutsche Grammophon 2707-083, 1967.
The World of Scott Joplin. Vanguard SRV-310-SD, 1973.

B. B. King

Sawyer, Charles. <u>The Arrival of B. B. King</u>. New York: Da Capo Press, 1980. xiv, 274 pp. photographs, musical examples. discography. appendixes. index.

Presented as a black Horatio Alger story, this "social rather than a musical biography" traces King's struggle from an impoverished childhood to his arrival as a consummate artist (p. vii). According to the author, he treats three stories in one: "the first is the development of a personality, the second is the growth of an artist, and the third is the making of a career" (p. 121). The three aspects of the life of this blues singer and guitarist are woven together in a story directed to a general audience, but equally useful to students of music. The book covers: King's first lessons on the guitar with a Sanctified preacher and his singing in a gospel group at the age of nine; the early development of the character traits of racial pride, self-esteem, and self-sufficiency within an impoverished environment; his working as a sharecropper and tractor driver in his youth; his performing in gospel groups and as a blues singer on weekends; and his later turning completely to blues, playing and singing in various towns and cities in the Mississippi Delta; his first trip to Memphis from the lower Delta at twenty; his tutelage there under bluesman Bukka White; and his settling in Memphis as a disk jockey and bluesman in 1948, performing with Robert "Junior" Lockwood, Johnny Ace, and others. Then his professional life is discussed, including: his

first recording in 1949; his first hit record in
1951--"Three O'Clock Blues"; his first national
tour, with the Tiny Bradshaw band, in 1952; his
achievement of "chitlin' circuit" fame in the 1950s
and his move in the 1960s from a main act on the
chitlin' circuit to the opening act on rock & roll
tours to "the prestige entertainment rooms of
Middle America" (p. 105); the hardships of "the
road"; and the "frustration, and later despair,
over the limitations imposed on his career by the
impenetrable racial boundaries that circumscribed
his musical genre" (p. 80).

Additionally, the work examines King's character
and his moral code; his stalwart participation in
the congregation of a Holiness Church and how this
background influenced his music; and his having
been inspired or influenced by such artists as
Blind Lemon Jefferson, Charlie Patton, Lonnie
Johnson, Django Reinhardt, T-Bone Walker, Louis
Jordan, Lester Young, and Ella Fitzgerald. The book
treats his tours of Europe, Australia, the Soviet
Union, Asia, and the world in the 1970s; and it
details and describes his performance and musical
techniques and styles, the motivic basis of his
improvisations, his eclectic musical tastes, the
Southern plantation system and culture as they were
manifest in Mississippi in the mid-twentieth
century, and the Southern race-caste system. The
appendixes: give the reader information on and
insight into "Plantation Organization and
Lynchings"; analyze a B. B. King solo; look "Toward
a Historiography of Oral History"; and identify the
photographers of the many pictures in the book.
The discography is annotated.

Reviews: Booklist 77:662 Ja 15 '81; Cadence 6:23
N '80; Choice 18:964 Mr '81; Library Journal
105:2210 O 15 '80; New York Times Book Review
86:8 F 15 '81; Publishers Weekly 218:361 Au 29
'80; Quill & Quire 47:62 Mr '81; Rolling Stone
n331:40 N 27 '80

SELECTIVE DISCOGRAPHY

Anthology of the Blues/B. B. King, 1949-1950. KST-9011,
1956.

B. B. King

The Best of B. B. King. ABCX-767, 1972.
Blues Is King. BLS-509.
From the Beginning. KST-533, 1956.
Live! B. B. King on Stage. KST-515, 1979.
Live at the Regal. ABCS-509.
Six Silver Strings. MCA 5616.
There Must Be a Better World Somewhere. MCA 27034.

Eartha Kitt

Kitt, Eartha. <u>Alone with Me: A New Autobiography</u>. Chicago:
Henry Regnery, 1976. xii, 276 pp. photographs. index.

This is a slight rewrite of <u>Thursday's Child</u>, with
the last four of its thirty-four chapters being new
material which brings the book up-to-date. These
new pages tell of Kitt's relationships with James
Dean and Marilyn Monroe; her professional life
"from the mid-fifties to the mid-to-late sixties,"
when she "hopped back and forth, logging millions
of air miles and entertaining in 92 countries
besides my own" and, at home, continuing her "work
in legitimate theater" (p. 231). She performed in
the plays <u>Shinbone Alley</u>, <u>Archy and Mehitabel</u>, <u>Mrs.</u>
<u>Patterson</u>, <u>The Skin of Our Teeth</u>, and <u>The Owl and</u>
<u>the Pussycat</u> and in such films as <u>The Mark of the</u>
<u>Hawk</u>, <u>St. Louis Blues</u>, and <u>Anna Lucasta</u>. She ap-
peared as a guest starr on numerous television
shows, including "The Ed Sullivan Show," "Wingless
Victory," "I Spy," and "Batman". And she made
records: three hit singles and a number of record
albums, including five RCA issues that "fought each
other for the top four places on the national
charts for about four years"--<u>Eartha Kitt</u>, <u>That Bad</u>
<u>Eartha</u>, <u>Down to Eartha</u>, <u>St. Louis Blues</u>, and
<u>Thursday's Child</u> (p. 233). Kitt also tells of her
"concert tours through Australia, the Middle East,
Scandinavia, and the rest of Europe" (p. 233); her
numerous benefit and night-club appearances; her
marriage in 1960 and the birth of her only child;
and the "Washington Tea Party" with Lady Bird
Johnson, which led to Kitt's becoming "A CIA

Target" and being blackballed in the United States (pp. 237, 252).

Reviews: Best Sellers 36:81-82 Ju '76; Booklist 72:1082 Ap 1 '76; Kirkus Reviews 43:1267 N 1 '75; Library Journal 101:333 Ja 15 '76; Publishers Weekly 208:50 N 24 '75

Kitt, Eartha. <u>Thursday's Child</u>. New York: Duell, Sloan and Pearce, 1956. photographs.

This singer/entertainer tells of her life and career, beginning with her early childhood in the town of North, South Carolina, around which she, her infant sister, and her mother led a brief vagabond existence; her mother's desertion of her; and her subsequent life on a small cotton farm, where she was treated cruelly by the teenaged members of the family and "heard the songs of the chain-gang criers, and voices of the callers that led the work" (p. 24). "When I was old enough to go to school," she relates, "I was given books, a writing pad, and sent off to a little old school in the yard of St. Peters Church" (p. 22).

Growing up in an environment where she was disliked because of her light complexion and where superstition was widespread, she was generally treated poorly. When she was seven, however, she moved to New York to live with an aunt; in New York she progressed through junior high school, and auditioned for and was accepted into the New York School of Performing Arts. In high school she was relatively happy, but "I began to pity myself and build a hate inside me that was to bring me more pain as I grew older. I began to think of myself as a tortured child. I began to think that I really was a good for nothing. I leaned more and more to myself" (p. 56). Thrown out of her aunt's house while still in school, Kitt, after sleeping "wherever I could, in doorways, on roofs, and at friends' homes for a while, I decided the best thing for me to do was to get a job. . . . I quit school completely. I was myself again after a few days work and a few good meals. I began to laugh all the time, tell jokes, and sing at my machine. . . . Everyone in the factory waited for me to start singing" (pp. 60-61).

Later, in a chance audition with the Katherine Dunham dance troupe, Kitt won a scholarship and attended the Katherine Dunham dance school,

studying ballet and Dunham technique. With the
Dunham company she danced in shows that Dunham
produced or performed in (Carib Song, Bal Negre,
and others), traveled and performed with the
company, lived in Mexico for several months, then
spent time in Hollywood making a film. In 1940
Kitt and the Dunham troupe left the United States
for a European tour, visiting England, France,
Belgium, Italy, Switzerland, Sweden, and Holland.
Back in Paris, Kitt left the tour and the Dunham
troupe to take a job in a Paris night club. In
1951 she was selected by Orson Welles for a major
role, opposite himself, in a stage production that
played Paris and toured cities in Germany and
Belgium. After the play's tour, Kitt worked as a
single in England, Turkey, and Greece. Shortly
thereafter she returned to the United States and
made her American debut at New York's Vie en Rose
night club, on December 11, 1951. From there she
moved to the Village Vanguard, and she starred the
next year in New Faces of 1952 (until 1954). In
April, 1954, she opened in Las Vegas, then moved to
Dallas, Philadelphia, Boston, New York, Lake Tahoe,
and Los Angeles, finally settling again in New York
to rehearse for a new Broadway play titled Mrs.
Patterson, with which appearance "Eartha Kitt had
become a star" (p. 250). In the course of the
discussions in this book, Kitt gives insight into
the Dunham philosophy and her own love life. She
also tells of being "reprimanded by the Negro press
for my relationship in a 'downtown' (white) world"
and "slightly scorned by the downtown press for not
conforming to society" (p. 223).

Reviews: Library Journal 81:2615 N 1 '56; Melody
Maker 32:8 F 2 '57; New York Herald Tribune Book
Reviews p15 D 9 '56; New York Times p26 O 14
'56; New Yorker 32:198 O 20 '56; San Francisco
Chronicle p25 D 2 '56; Saturday Review 39:34 N 3
'56; Springfield Republican p32A N 4 '56

SELECTIVE DISCOGRAPHY

The Best of Eartha Kitt. MCA 1554.
Folk Tales of the Tribes of Africa. Caedmon 1267.
I Love Men. Sunnyview 4902.
Eartha Kitt in Person at the Plaza. CRS 2008.
Where Is My Man. Streetwise 2217.

George Lewis

Bethell, Tom. <u>George Lewis: A Jazzman from New Orleans</u>. Berkeley, Los Angeles, and London: University of California Press, 1977. 378 pp. photographs. bibliography. discography. index.

This is the biography of a musician who, the author claims, embodied the characteristics of the New Orleans jazzman more than anyone else, one who played with "practically every band in New Orleans, on and off," between the 1920s and his death in 1968 (p. 105). The book chronicles Lewis's activities from his participation in the youth "field bands," which imitated the New Orleans "brass bands," to his arrival as a historically important leader of his own group and to his renown as an important figure in the perpetuation and preservation of New Orleans jazz (p. 38). In the process, the author details: Lewis's musical activities in New Orleans during the 1920s, a decade that was "a rich period in the development of New Orleans jazz" (p. 58); his working as a sideman with such stalwart musicians as Bunk Johnson, Tommy Ladnier, Buddy Petit, Lee Collins, Red Allen, Chris Kelly, Kid Rena, Wooden Joe Nicholas, and others; the rediscovery of Bunk Johnson; Johnson's first recording session in 1942; the Bunk Johnson Band in New York in 1945-1946, with Lewis as clarinetist; many of the recording sessions in which Lewis participated, especially the first and famous Climax session of 1943; the historically important <u>American Music</u> sessions; the George Lewis Band's tours in the United States and

England in the 1950s, the three tours of Japan
between 1963 and 1965, and subsequent tours in
Europe to 1967; and details of the opening of
Preservation Hall and Lewis's participation there.

In short, the work is a salient observation and
chronicle of the development of New Orleans jazz
from 1900 to the 1960s. The author's approach is
revisionist, contending that despite earlier claims
to the contrary, "the New Orleans jazz tradition
continued to develop and unfold--to remain alive,
in short--through the 1940s" (pp. 68-69). He
debunks myths about the closing of Storyville,
about "non-reading" early New Orleans jazz
musicians, about jazz moving "up the river" to
Chicago, about "Uptown" and "Downtown" styles and
influences, and about the "New Orleans Revival."
The appendixes are valuable, the first being
Lewis's own discussion of his musical philosophy;
the second, a discography purported to be "one of
the most complete and detailed discographies of a
major jazz figure yet compiled" (p. 291).

Reviews: Booklist 74:1156 Mr 15 '78; Cadence
4:14 My '78; Choice 15:700 Jy '78; Coda
n164/165:37-38 F 1 '79; Footnote 9:19-20 n5 '78;
Jazz Journal International 31:27 Ju '78; Journal
of American Folklore 93:78 Ja '80; Library
Journal 103:170 Ja 15 '78; Music Journal 36:36
My '78; Orkester Journalen 46:15 N '78;
Publishers Weekly 212:134 S 26 '77; Second Line
31:45-48 Winter '79; Swinging Newsletter 8:10
n37 '78; Times Literary Supplement p503 My 5 '78

Fairbairn, Ann. Call Him George. 2nd edition. New York:
Crown Publishers, 1969. 304 pp. photographs.

This is a biography of New Orleans clarinetist
George Lewis, a musician who was an active
performer in the 1920s and whose "ceaseless
inventiveness" led to his belated "discovery" in
the 1940s (p. 121). This touching account of
Lewis's life, written by one who traveled with the
Lewis band for eight years, traces his ancestry
from his grandmother's capture in Africa as an
infant in 1808 and her subsequent childhood and
adulthood as a slave in America, to Lewis's arrival
as a New Orleans jazzman of international fame in
the 1950s and 1960s and his death in 1968. In the
process the author details Lewis's boyhood struggle
to acquire a clarinet; how he taught himself to
play the instrument; his first job as a sideman at

fourteen; the formation of his own band in 1923;
his adult family and musical life in an
impoverished environment; the difficult conditions
under which his first recordings were made; and his
highly successful tours of Great Britain and Europe
in 1957, 1960, and 1961 and of Japan in 1963, 1964,
and 1966.

Laced with poignant examples of the degrading
experiences endured by black people in the American
South up to the 1960s, the author presents myriad
details of Lewis's life, ranging from his childhood
ordeals to experiences he encountered as an
international star. This vivid literary portrayal
of Lewis's life, while it does not treat the music
as thoroughly as does Bethell's account, surpasses
the latter in its social, cultural, and character
analyses, giving attention, as well, to his
personality and behavior. Also of interest in this
regard are such questions as how Lewis managed to
play so beautifully on an instrument that was
always "literally held together by elastic bands
and bits of wire" and how "his clarinet sound
seemed to grow more and more compelling" as he got
older and sicker in a late-blooming career fraught
with poor health (pp. 201, 258).

Reviews: AB Bookman's Weekly 45:128 Ja 19 '70;
Coda 9:10 nll '71; Library Journal 95:1018 Mr 15
'70; Music Journal 28:64 F '70

SELECTIVE DISCOGRAPHY

At Congo Square. Jazzology JCE-27.
Bunk Johnson 1945. Dan VC-4018, 1945.
Bunk Johnson's Band 1944 with George Lewis. Storyville
    SLP-128, 1944.
George Lewis. 2 vols. Blue Note BST-81205/6.
George Lewis: In Concert. Blue Note BST-81208.
George Lewis and His Mustache Stompers. Biograph CEN-1.
George Lewis 1944-45. Storyville SLP=201, 1944-1945.
George Lewis Ragtime Jazz Band. Jazzology GHB-108.
Memorial Album. Delmark DL-203.
New Orleans Jazz Band: Doctor Jazz. Delmark DL-201.
On Parade. Delmark DL-202.

Little Richard

White, Charles. <u>The Life and Times of Little Richard: The Quasar of Rock</u>. New York: Harmony Books, 1984. xvi, 269 pp. photographs. chronology. discography/filmography. index.

This is the story of rock & roll singer Little Richard (Richard Penniman), "a unique and dualistic psyche, an uncontrollable genius whose influence on Western culture has been tormented by outrageous and freakish sexuality and a hunger for public adulation" (p. xii), one whose voice, "with its sheer naked and joyous energy . . . broke through established musical structures and changed the way of life for a whole generation" (p. 76). The author allows Penniman, his mother, his brothers, one of his sisters, producer/manager Bumps Blackwell, impresario Quincy Jones, gospel singer Mahalia Jackson, and a number of other individuals to tell, variously and in their own words, of Penniman's extremely mischievious childhood; his early environment, in which he was exposed to the black folk church, spiritual and gospel songs, touring blues, jazz, and gospel artists; and his first musical training as a saxophonist in his high-school band. Penniman left home at fourteen to join a medicine show as a singer; joined B. Brown and his orchestra, touring Georgia and parts of Florida, "following the seasons" (p. 23); toured with a minstrel show called Sugarfoot Sam from Alabam, the King Brother's Circus, a show called the Tidy Jolly Steppers, and the L. J. Heath Show; and settled for a time with Atlanta's Broadway Follies. In 1951 he joined Percy Welch and his orchestra as a

vocalist, later joined the Tempo Toppers, and finally formed Little Richard and His Upsetters, his
own permanent band, in 1952. We learn of
Penniman's first record, made in 1951; details surrounding his making of such hits as "Tutti Frutti"
and "Long Tall Sally"; his reign as "King of Rock &
Roll"; his two retirements from entertainment to
the ministry; his success in the rock & roll revival of the early seventies; his smashingly successful tours of the United Kingdom; the refusal of
the television networks to televise him until 1968;
and his subsequent appearances on network television in the late sixties and early seventies. The
author also gives details, results, and implications of Penniman's homosexuality, his addiction to
drugs, and his eventual rejection of them both; his
new life as a minister of God; and his current belief that rock & roll music, and its derivations,
is "demonic" (p. 197). The book ends with a sermon
compiled from a variety of Penniman's preachings
and with "Testimonials" to his musicianship and
showmanship by a number of pop-music personalities,
including Elvis Presley, John Lennon, Elton John,
Smokey Robinson, Sam Cooke, Janis Joplin, Chuck
Berry, Professor Longhair, Paul Simon, James Brown,
and Otis Redding.

Reviews: Billboard 96:48 O 27 '84; Kirkus Reviews 52:860 S 1 '84; Library Journal 109:1761 S
15 '84; New York Times Book Review 89:20 O 14
'84; Nation 239:507 N 17 '84; Publishers Weekly
226:68 Au 10 '84; Time 124:70 S 10 '84; Village
Voice 30:VLS6 My 7 '85; Voice of Youth Advocates
8:70 Ap '85

SELECTIVE DISCOGRAPHY

God's Beautiful City. World LP-1001, 1979.
Here's Little Richard. Specialty LP-100 (2100), 1957.
Little Richard Gold. Vee Jay VJS2-1002.
Little Richard's Back. Vee Jay VJS-1107.
Little Richard's Greatest Hits. Vee Jay LP-1124, 1964.
Little Richard's Greatest 17 Original Hits. Specialty
   5082-2113M.
"Long Tall Sally"/"Slippin' and Slidin'." Specialty 572,
   1956.
The Rill Thing. Reprise LP-64006, 1970.
Talkin' 'Bout Soul. Dynasty DYS-7304.
"Taxi Blues"/"Every Hour." RCA 4372, 1951.
"Tutti Frutti"/"I'm Just a Lonely Guy." Specialty 561,
   1955.

Bob Marley

White, Timothy. <u>Catch a Fire: The Life of Bob Marley</u>. New York: Holt, Rinehart and Winston, 1983. xv, 380 pp. photographs. bibliography. discography. index.

This work discusses the life of "international reggae sovereign Bob Marley, hero of black freedom fighters everywhere and the most charismatic emissary of modern Pan-Africanism" (p. 2). It focuses on Marley's relations to and the influences of "the millenarian-messianic cult of Rastafarianism that Marley championed through his music" (p. 5). Essentially, the book is a chronicle of Marley's "rise from wretched poverty to become one of the most renowned figures ever to emerge from the Caribbean" (p. 23). Focusing on Marley's ostensible royal Ethiopian ancestry and shot through with Jamaican folk sayings, folk tales, and legends, the work presents Marley's life against the background of the historical, political, economic, social, and cultural contexts of Jamaican life, giving details of Marley's impoverished but stimulating childhood; his first recording at sixteen in 1961; the origin of Marley's group, The Wailers; his rise to local fame in 1964 in an extremely crowded and competitive Jamaican musical environment; his development from ska to rock steady to reggae; the production of his first reggae album in 1970; Marley as a Rastaman; his arrival on the international scene in the 1970s as the "King of Reggae"; and events leading up to his death in 1981, including treatment for his illness, and the deterioration of his entourage environment. Additionally, filled with accounts of "supernatural events and surreal coincidences" of native mysticism (p. xv), the work treats: the Rastafarian ideological and social influence on ska, rock steady, and reggae; vivid descriptions of Jamaican country and city life; and the violent social and political environment that prevailed in Jamaica at the height of Marley's fame. Based on numerous interviews with Marley's relatives, sidemen, friends, and acquaintances, as well as on data from a variety of archival sources, this work is a start--but only a start--in understanding the basis of mento, ska, rock steady, and reggae music.

Reviews: Audio 69:169-170 Ja '85; Booklist 79:1318 Ju 15 '83; Choice 21:440 N '83; Kirkus Reviews 51:576 My 1 '83; Library Journal 108:1260 Ju 15 '83; Nation 238:56 Ja 21 '84; New York Times Book Review 88:11 Au 14 '83; Publishers Weekly 223:90 My 6 '83; Sing Out! 30:83 nl '84; Spectator 250:21 Au 6 '83; Trouser 10:50-51 O '83; Village Voice 28:52-53 S 20 '83; Voice of Youth Advocates 6:290 D '83; West Coast Review of Books 9:42 N '83

SELECTIVE DISCOGRAPHY

The Best of Bob Marley and The Wailers. GW-0002, 1974.
Bob Marley and The Wailers - The Box Set. BMSP-100, 1982.

Charles Mingus

Priestly, Brian. Mingus: A Critical Biography. London, Melbourne, and New York: Quartet Books, 1982. xii, 308 pp. photographs, musical examples. discography. index.

This biography treats the musical development of Charles Mingus from his early childhood to his death in 1979, tracing his professional career from his pre-New York activity on the West Coast to its peak in the 1960s and 1970s. Relying heavily on record-jacket notes and a variety of published and unpublished interviews, all illuminated by the firsthand observations of Jimmy Knepper and Dannie Richmond (both of whom were longtime members of Mingus's bands) and by comments from Mingus's former wives, Celia and Sue, the work details Mingus's relationships with such jazz artists as Charlie Parker, Jackie McLean, Eric Dolphy, and others; his idiosyncratic behavior; his dealings with record companies and club owners; his compositional tendencies and proclivities; and his influences on contemporary and subsequent bass players. In so doing, the work sheds much light on Mingus's contributions to the continuing development of jazz and on his accomplishments as a bass player and a composer.

Reviews: Coda n193:26-28 D 1 '83; Crescendo International 21:5 Au '83; Down Beat 50:58 S '83; Jazz Times p12 Au '83; Kirkus Reviews 51:443 Ap 1 '83; New Republic 189:36 D 31 '83; Orkester Journalen 51:32 Mr '83; Times Literary

Charles Mingus

Supplement   p319 Ap 1 '83; Village Voice   28:76+
Ju 28 '83

SELECTIVE DISCOGRAPHY

Better Git It in Your Soul. Columbia CG-30628.
Black Saint and Sinner Lady. Impulse A-35.
Blues and Roots. Atlantic 1305.
Charles Mingus--The Impluse Years. Impulse AS-9234-4.
The Charlie Mingus Jazz Workshop/Stormy Weather. Barnaby
   (GRT Canada) 2-6015, 1960.
The Clown. Atlantic 1260, 1961.
The Great Concert of Charles Mingus. Fantasy PR-34001,
   1964.
Jazz Composers' Workshop. Savoy MG-15055.
Mingus-Ah-Um. Columbia CS-8171, 1959.
Mingus at Antibes. Atlantic SD2-3001, 1960.
Mingus in Stuttgart, 1964. 2 vols. Unique Jazz UJ-00718/
   009, 1978.
Nica's Dream: Small Jazz Groups of the 50's and Early
   60's.New World Records NW-242, 1977.
Nostalgia in Times Square: The Immortal 1959 Sessions.
   Columbia JG-35717, 1979.
Oh Yeah. Atlantic 1377.
Passions of a Man (An Anthology). Atlantic SD-3-600, 1956-
   1961, 1973-1977.
Pithecanthropus Erectus. Atlantic 1237, 1956.
Reincarnation of a Lovebird. Fantasy PR-24028.
Tijuana Moods. RCA Victor LPM-2533.

Jelly Roll Morton

Lomax, Alan. <u>Mister Jelly Roll: The Fortunes of Jelly Roll Morton, New Orleans Creole and "Inventor of Jazz."</u> New York: Duell, Sloan and Pearce, 1950. xvii, 318 pp. drawings by David Stone Martin, musical examples. score bibliography. discography.

Jelly Roll Morton's account of jazz history is discussed here, including details of musical life in New Orleans's Storyville district, relationships between the "Uptown" and "Downtown" musicians there, "Battles of Bands" in the early days of New Orleans jazz, relationships between cultures and subcultures in New Orleans, and the development of jazz in other cities he visited. Morton speaks of his travels, his exploits as a gambler and hustler, his beginnings as a musician and composer, and his life in the jazz community. In the process he mentions or discusses Jack the Bear, Bunk Johnson, Buddy Petit, John Robichaux, W. C. Handy, and many other of "The Boys in the Bands" (p. 67). In addition to presenting information about the evolution of jazz and the development of Morton's career, this book gives the reader an idea of the development of Morton's concern for jazz history and the struggles and fulfillments of his life. Lomax, the writer of Morton's account, through the several "interludes" spaced throughout the work, documents, explains, expands upon and, in some cases, corrects Morton's narrative. Throughout the book the writer allows selected contemporaries to give further insight into Morton's life, character, and prowess as a musician.

Jelly Roll Morton

Reviews: Booklist 46:352 Jy 15 '50; Chicago Sun
Times p5 Jy 2 '50; Chicago Sunday Tribune p4 Jy
2 '50; Down Beat 17:7 Au 11 '50; Gramophone
30:71 Au '52; Kirkus Reviews 18:227 Ap 1 '50;
Library Journal 75:868 My 15 '50; New York
Folklore Quarterly 7:165-166 Summer '51; New
York Herald Tribune Book Reviews p6 Ju 18 '50;
New York Times p3 Ju 18 '50; New Yorker 26:120 S
16 '50; Notes 7:567-569 S '50; Melody Maker 27:3
F 10 '51; Melody Maker 28:6 Jy 26 '52; Metronome
66:24 O '50; Musical America 70:37 S '50; Record
Changer 9:5+ S '50; San Francisco Chronicle p16
Ju 19 '50; Saturday Review 33:14 My 13 '50;
Tempo n25:37-38 Autumn '52; Time 55:52 Ju 19
'50; Western Folklore 10:91-92 Ja '51

Williams, Martin. Jelly Roll Morton. London: Cassell,
1962. 89 pp. discography.

Not a biography, this is an analytical essay with a
biographical sketch, but it sheds much light on
Morton's life and work. A concise and condensed
study, this little essay is an effective sketch of
the life and career of the pianist/composer and a
perceptive analysis of his theoretical and musical
sensibilities and contributions. It is an analysis
that remains fresh and important today.

Reviews: Jazz Hot n187:12 My '63; Jazz Monthly
8:24 S '62

SELECTIVE DISCOGRAPHY

Blues and Stomp: Rare Piano Rolls, 1924-1926. Biograph
BLP-1004Q.
The Complete Jelly Roll Morton. 4 vols. RCA (France)
PM-42405/PM-43170, 1926-1929.
The Greatest Jazz Recordings of All Time: Kings of New
Orleans Jazz/Jelly Roll Morton, King Oliver, and Sidney
Bechet. Franklin Mint Record Society Tapes 17-20, 1983.
Jelly Roll Morton, 1923-1924. Milestone M-47018, 1923-
1924.
Jelly Roll Morton (piano rolls). Everest FS-267, 1924.
Jelly Roll Morton: Thesaurus of First Recordings. 2 vols.
Kings of Jazz NLJ-18007/8, 1923-1926.
Jelly Roll Morton, Composer. Columbia M-32587.
Jelly Roll Morton, 1923/24. Milestone M-47018, 1974.
Jelly Roll Morton and His Red Hot Peppers. RCA
(France) 731.059, 1926-1927.

Jelly Roll Morton

The Legendary Jelly Roll Morton, 1885-1941. Murray Hill
  M-52960.
The Library of Congress Recordings. Riverside 9001-12,
  1938.
Music of Jelly Roll Morton. Smithsonian Collection N-006.
New Orleans Memories Plus Two. Commodore XSF-14942, 1939.

King Oliver

Allen, Walter C., and Brian A. L. Rust. <u>King Joe Oliver</u>.
London: Sidgwick and Jackson, Ltd., n.d. xii, 224 pp.
photographs. bibliography. appendixes. indexes.

More of a career sketch and handbook than a
biography, this work is organized into three main
sections: biography, descriptive material, and
discography. The first and second parts treat,
respectively, the various "periods" of the
cornetist's career and matters pertaining to his
character, influence, style, and compositional
output. These two sections account for only 72
pages of the book, with the discography occupying
123 pages and the bibliography and appendixes
taking up the remaining 29 pages. Oliver's
biography is divided into the following periods:
New Orleans Period, 1908-1918; First Chicago
Period, 1918-1921; California Period, 1921-1922;
Second Chicago Period, 1922-1924; On Tour, 1924;
Third Chicago Period, 1924-1927; New York Period,
1927-1931; and Final Period, 1931-1938. While not
much actual biographical information is included in
the book, there is much detail on Oliver's tours,
personnel, and recording activity. Oliver's
relations with to Bunk Johnson, Louis Armstrong,
Jelly Roll Morton, Luis Russell, Sidney Bechet,
Clarence Williams, and other musicians are touched
on, as are the good days of the peak of his career
and the sad days of his declining health and
professional fortunes. The appendixes include an
Oliver itinerary and indexes of recorded titles,

musicians, and catalog numbers of records and cylinders.

Reviews: Down Beat 23:32 F 8 '56; Gramophone 35:116 Au '57; Jazz Journal 10:23 Au '57; Melody Maker 31:6 D 31 '55; Orkcster Journalen 24:15 Au '56; Record Changer 14:14 N 7 '55; Record Research 1:8 D '55

Williams, Martin. King Oliver. Kings of Jazz. New York: A. S. Barnes, 1960. 90 pp. discography.

A brief but effective blend of biography and criticism, this is the story of the career of trumpeter/bandleader Joe Oliver, covering "New Orleans," "The Music of New Orleans," Oliver's work in "Chicago, California, and New York," "Seven Years on the Road," and Oliver's recordings with his Creole Jazz Band, Dixie Syncopators, "His Orchestra," and as a sideman. There is also "An Interim Note on Oliver's Playing." The Creole Jazz Band recordings reveal musical sophistication combined with the strong emotional content of Negro folk music; those of the Dixie Syncopators reveal improvisational abilities, where "Oliver could swing in a rhythmic mode based either on a modified 2/4 rather like Morton's, or a mode based on an even 4/4 like Armstrong's--indeed he may have adopted the latter from certain kinds of 'low' blues playing and passed it on to Armstrong" (p. 71). Williams's conclusion, after examining Oliver's output and his character, is that "it is quite reasonable to contend that without Joseph Oliver, the feeling and form of his music and the techniques he found to express them, jazz could not have happened as we know it. But perhaps without the pride, the dignity, the fortitude, the hope, and finally the joy he gave it, it might not have continued as jazz at all" (p. 88).

Reviews: Jazz Hot 26:8 Jy/Au '60; Jazz Journal 13:15 Jy '60; Jazz Monthly 6:27-28 Au '60; Second Line 11:14-15 n11/12 '60

SELECTIVE DISCOGRAPHY

The Greatest Jazz Recordings of All Time: Kings of New Orleans Jazz/Jelly Roll Morton, King Oliver, and Sidney Bechet. Franklin Mint Record Society Tapes 17-20, 1983.
King Oliver in New York. RCA LPV-529, 1929-1930.
King Oliver's Creole Jazz Band. Riverside RLP-8805, 1923.

King Oliver

King Oliver's Jazz Band. Smithsonian Collection R-001,
   1923.
Louis Armstrong and King Oliver. Milestone M-47017,
   1923-1924.
The Saga of the King Oliver Creole Jazz Band. 2 vols.
   Kings of Jazz NLJ-18003/4, 1923.

Charlie Parker

Harrison, Max. <u>Charlie Parker</u>. Kings of Jazz. New York: A. S. Barnes and Company, 1961. 84 pp. discography.

> This brief volume traces the saxophonist's career from his stints as a "sideman in Mid-Western bands" to his arrival as a significant influence in the history of jazz (p. 5). Parker was nurtured in blues bands, jazz bands, and the bebop cauldron of Uptown New York. By 1945 bebop had matured, and the first definitive examples of the style were recorded. The significant titles were "Groovin' High," "Dizzy Atmosphere," "Salt Peanuts," "Shaw 'Nuff," "Hot House," and "Lover Man." Also in 1945, Parker's November date at the Savoy became "the first session to preserve modern jazz of indisputable greatness, Parker achieved full expression of his musical personality" (p. 31). We learn that the year 1947 was "his most richly creative period," and that the "last session worthy of him" took place in 1953, preserving "Chi Chi," "Now's the Time," "I Remember You," and "Confirmation" (pp. 43, 67-68). Parker's unfortunate road to self-destruction is also discussed.

Russell, Ross. <u>Bird Lives: The High Life and Hard Times of Charlie (Yardbird) Parker</u>. New York: Charterhouse, 1973. 404 pp. photographs, musical examples. bibliography. discography. index.

> This work correctly portrays Charlie Parker as "the last of a breed of jazzmen apprenticed at an early age, styled in emulation of great master players,

- 211 -

tempered in the rough-and-tumble school of the jam
session, a master of his craft by the end of his
teens, and, eventually, the maverick who turned his
back on the big bands to create, almost
single-handedly, the musical revolution of the
Forties" (p. 34). The book details Parker's career
from his childhood in Kansas City to his death in
1955, chronicling his musical development, his
first jam session, his musical education and
apprenticeships, and his arrival as the greatest
jazz musician of his age. Treated are Parker's
stints, relatively early in his career, with the
Harlan Leonard Rockets, the Jay McShann Band, the
Earl Hines Orchestra, the Noble Sissle Orchestra,
and the Billy Eckstine Band; his breaking through
the boundaries of the then-conventional saxophone
and jazz styles to create new techniques and
procedures that would lead to the rise of bebop;
his activity on New York's famed 52nd Street and
the makeup of the character of the Street; the new
sounds, language, mores, and behavior of the bebop
revolution; details of the ups and downs of
Parker's heroin addiction; his sexual exploits and
his family life; the impact of American racism on
Parker's psyche; his relationships to other jazz
greats, such as Kenny Clarke, Ray Brown, Lester
Young, Dizzy Gillespie, Howard McGhee, John Lewis,
Thelonius Monk, Charles Mingus, Max Roach, Jackie
McLean, and Miles Davis; the incredible legal
machinations following Parker's death; and the
author's own relationship to Parker. Informative
discussions related to the development of the
Parker discography appear throughout the book.

Reviews: Best Sellers 33:84 My 15 '73; Black
Perspective in Music 1:181-182 n2 '73; Black
Scholar 12:81 Mr '81; Black World 23:96 N '73;
Book World 7:4 Mr 18 '73; Books & Bookmen 18:100
S '73; Choice 10:1398 N '73; Economist 248:87 Au
4 '73; Educator 5:24 n4 '73; Ethnomusicology
19:315-316 n2 '75; Guardian Weekly 109:21 Jy 7
'73; Jazz & Blues 3:45 Jy '73; Jazz Digest 2:2
Ap '73; Jazz Forum n25:66 O '73; Jazz Forum
n26:64-65 D '73; Jazz Hot n293:15 Ap '73; Jazz
Journal 26:10-11 Ap '73; Jazz Journal 26:12 Jy
'73; Kirkus Reviews 40:1461 D 15 '72; Library
Journal 97:3916 D 1 '72; Listener 90:222 Au 16
'73; Melody Maker 48:40 Ju 30 '73; Music Journal
31:14 Annual '73; National Observer 12:23 Mr 31
'73; New Statesman 86:28 Jy 6 '73; New York
Review of Books 21:14 O 17 '74; New York Times
122:41 My 1 '73; New York Times Book Review p4

Mr 25 '73; New York Times Book Review p36 Ju 10 '73; New York Times Book Review p68 D 2 '73; Newsweek 81:110 Ap 9 '73; Notes 30:268-269 n2 '73; Observer p32 Jy 15 '73; Orkester Journalen 41:15-16+ Ju '73; Publishers Weekly 202:57 S 11 '72; Punch 264:956 Ju 27 '73; Rolling Stone n133:7 Ap 26 '73; Saturday Review 1:81 Ap 7 '73; Saturday Review 1:83 Ap 7 '73; Saturday Review 1:75 Ap 21 '73; Stereo Review 31:12 O '73; Times Literary Supplement p1593 D 28 '73; Variety 270:59 My 2 '73; Village Voice 18:21 Jy 12 '73

SELECTIVE DISCOGRAPHY

Bird: The Savoy Recordings (Master Takes). Savoy SJL-2201, 1944-1948.
Bird at the Roost: The Savoy Years. Savoy Jazz SJL-2259, 1948-1949.
Charlie Parker. 5 vols. Everest FS-214, 1968; FS-232, 1969; FS-254, 1971; FS-254, 1971; FS-315, 1976.
Charlie Parker: The Complete Savoy Sessions. Savoy Records SJ5-5500, 1944-1948.
Charlie Parker: Early Bird. Onyx OR-1221, 1940-1943.
Charlie Parker: The Verve Years 1948-1950. Verve V2-2501.
Charlie Parker: The Verve Years 1950-1951. Verve V2-2512.
Charlie Parker: The Verve Years 1952-1954. Verve V2-2523.
Charlie Parker Encores: The Savoy Sessions. Savoy SJL-1107, 1944-1949.
One Night in Birdland. Columbia J6-34808, 1950.
Summit Meeting. Columbia JC-34831, 1951-1953.
The Very Best of Bird (The "Dial Sessions"). Warner Brothers 2WB-3198, 1946-1947.

Charlie Patton

Fahey, John. <u>Charley Patton</u>. London: Studio Vista, 1970. 111 pp. photographs, musical examples, charts. bibliography. discography. index.

Blues singer/songster

> Charley Patton has been dead for more than [forty] years, yet his name is readily recalled by many Mississippi blacks and some whites. His musical influence, in one way or another, lives on to this day in the recordings and performances of such recently popular blues-singers as Howlin' Wolf (whom Patton taught to play the guitar), Lightnin' Hopkins, (who is known to sing stanzas from "Banty Rooster Blues," which he probably learned by listening to one of Patton's recordings of that song), John Lee Hooker (who knew Patton and also sings some of his stanzas, and others) (p. 8).

Born in the late 1880s, Patton grew up on the Dockery Plantation in the Mississippi Delta and, as a teenager, played roadhouses along Highway 80. By 1908 he had been twice married and by 1912 was having an impact on musicians around the small Mississippi town of Drew, influencing younger bluesmen such as Tommy Johnson, Willie Brown, Howlin' Wolf, and Roebuck Staples. Patton spent the remainder of his life performing in various towns

of the Yazoo Delta--in Mississippi and Arkansas--
leaving only to make records in Indiana, Wisconsin,
and New York.

The author of this brief volume also tells us
that Patton made his first record in 1929 and that
he served as a "subsidiary talent scout" for
Paramount records (p. 25). Patton recorded more
than seventy sides before his death in 1934. "His
recorded repertoire represents a very good sample
of what southern black songsters and blues-singers
were performing between 1915 and 1934, the period
during which Patton was an active entertainer.
There are blues, spirituals and other religious
songs, blues-ballads, folksongs, and even a few
songs probably of Tin Pan Alley origin" (p. 8). The
author presents technical information regarding
modes, scales, and tunings important to the
analysis of black song, a "Tune Analysis" of
Patton's works, information on Patton's "Tune
Families," and an "Examination and Classification
of the Texts" of Patton's songs.

Reviews: Jazz Hot n268:29 Ja '71; Jazz Journal
24:5-6 F '71; JEMF Quarterly 7:192-195 pt4 '71;
Music Teacher 112:141 F '71; Storyville n33:90 F
'71

SELECTIVE DISCOGRAPHY

Charley Patton: Founder of the Delta Blues. Yazoo 1020.
Charley Patton--1929-1934: The Remaining Titles. Wolf
  WSE-103.

Leontyne Price

Lyon, Hugh Lee. Leontyne Price: Highlights of a Prima
Donna. New York: Vantage Press, 1973. 218 pp. photographs. chronology. discography. honors and member-
ships.

> Approximately ten minutes before depar-
> ture time the Price entourage arrived at
> the bus depot. It was in early September
> of 1944 and a torrid sun shone brightly
> from a lucid sky indicating that an
> Indian summer was almost inevitable.
> Mrs. Price, after giving a last-minute
> mother's advice to Leontyne, embraced her
> daughter affectionately. Leontyne turned
> to her Dad, planted a kiss on both his
> cheeks and made her final farewell
> (p. 15).

So begins this chronicle of the great singer's
career. Price was born in 1927 in Laurel,
Mississippi, the daughter of a lumber worker and a
midwife. In 1930, at the age of three, she began
piano lessons. By twelve she was playing for her
Sunday school and church and was making appearances
as a singer as well. Even then, she was a
sensitive and moving singer. In high school she
was an "A" student and, as the most talented singer
in the school, sang soprano in the choir. At the
end of 1943 she was presented in recital, playing
"the 'Prelude in C Sharp Minor' by Rachmaninoff,
'Minuet in G' by I. J. Paderewski and 'Concerto in
B Flat Minor' by Tschaikowsky. Her listeners also

heard her interpretation of popular songs which included the 'Bugle Boy Boogie,' 'The Man I Love' and 'White Christmas.' A special delight of the evening was her own arrangement of 'Deep River'" (p. 33). She was also a drum majorette, she won the Miss Oak Park High School crown, and she graduated from high school cum laude.

Price attended Wilberforce College on a scholarship, "full of enthusiasm, very intelligent and quick to learn" (p. 36); she sang in the Glee Club and the Wilberforce Singers, presented programs, and gave recitals. Throughout her college years she sang more and played the piano less; and by graduation, she had won a scholarship to the Juilliard School of Music, where she made friends easily, studied with Florence Page Kimball (who worked with her on operatic roles and coached her in voice, diction, and lieder), and was viewed as "the Cinderella of the school" (p. 56). Price's first operatic role as a graduate student was that of Aunt Nella in Gianni Schicchi. In 1952, while still at Juilliard, she got her first professional role as Saint Cecelia in the Paris revival of Virgil Thomson's Four Saints in Three Acts.

Later, in 1961, she was engaged for the second and third acts of the Tanglewood production of Aida and was selected to attend the Opera School at the Berkshire Music Center in Boston. In the meantime, in 1952, she played Bess opposite William Warfield's Porgy in that year's revival of Porgy and Bess, where "her acting [was] as fiery as her singing" (p. 66). On the day following the show's closing, Price and Warfield were married. In 1953 Price premiered Samuel Barber's "Hermit Songs," half of which he wrote expressly for her, and his "Prayers of Kierkegaard," the latter with the Boston Symphony Orchestra. Also in 1953 she made her Town Hall solo debut, with Barber at the piano for his songs. Price then performed his opera Knoxville: Summer of 1915. In the same year she premiered works by "Stravinsky, Lou Harrison, Henri Sauget, William Killmayer, and John LaMontaine" (p. 72). In 1955 Price performed the title role in the NBC television production of Tosca, in which she was "stunning and sumptuous sounding" (p. 75), and was quickly cast in other NBC productions: Poulenc's Dialogues of the Carmelites and Mozart's Magic Flute and Don Giovanni.

Leontyne Price

Price's first performance in a major opera house took place in 1957 with the San Francisco Opera Company, where she appeared in the title role of _Aida_. In 1958 she sang the title role in Carl Orff's _The Wise Maiden_, also with the San Francisco Opera. Other performances in other roles followed over the years, with Price celebrating, in 1967, the tenth anniversary of her debut with the company, as Amelia in Verdi's _Un Ballo in Maschera_. Also in 1958 she began singing abroad, debuting in Vienna in _Aida_, following with _The Magic Flute_, and doing opera and concerts in London, Yugoslavia, and Brussels. She performed in Moscow in 1964 and Paris in 1968. In 1961 she had made her Metropolitan Opera debut in the role of Leonora in _Il Trovatore_. After the performance, "for forty-two minutes after the great gold curtain descended, cheers and cries of 'Price! Price!' resounded through the Manhattan hall" (p. 98). Subsequently, in the first nine weeks of the season, she did roles in five different operas and "just laid them in the aisles just one night after the other" (p. 100). From those performances she became a Met mainstay, appearing in successful performances there ever since. In 1966 she opened the new Metropolitan Opera House at Lincoln Center in Samuel Barber's _Antony and Cleopatra_. Since that time, she has been the leading soprano of the Met.

Personally, the author tells us, Price, when working, is "very professional, but when she's in a private situation such as a house party, she gets really friendly and very warm. . . . She likes to dance" (p. 130), and she is always "down to earth" (p. 85). As this story develops, the author tells of Price's friendships and relationships with Andrew Frierson, Betty Allen, Rawn Spearman, Shirley Verrett, George Shirley, Reri Grist, Leonard De Paur, Margaret Bonds, and others; how she prepares for roles; how her art triumphed over racial prejudice; her private life; her relationship with her husband; her concert career; and her honors and awards. The author also discourses on Price's concert career and other black singers at the Met, including Marian Anderson, Reri Grist, Lillian Evanti, Shirley Verrett, Caterina Jaboro, Robert McFerrin, Gloria Davy, Mattiwilda Dobbs, Martina Arroyo, Grace Bumbry, and Felicia Weathers. Liberal quotations from reviews of the singer's performances enhance the narrative.

Leontyne Price

Review: Opera News 38:57 O '73

SELECTIVE DISCOGRAPHY

Five Great Operatic Scenes. RCA LSC-3218, 1972.
Gala Farewell. April 16, 1966. MRF-7, 1967.
Prima Donna, Vol. I. Arias from Purcell to Barber. RCA
   LM/LSC-2898, 1966.
Prima Donna, Vol. II. Arias from Handel to Puccini. RCA
   LM/LSC-2968, 1967.
Prima Donna, Vol. III. Arias from Gluck to Poulenc.
   RCA-3163, 1970.
Sing Low, Sweet Chariot (with the De Paur Choir). RCA
   LM/LSC 2600, 1962.

Prince

Feldman, Jim. _Prince_. New York: Ballantine Books, 1984.
146 pp. appendix. discography. videography.

"Effortlessly blending hard-edged rock, insistent
funk, sweet soul and R&B rhythms, and other styles,
and gluing them all together with ingenious,
feeling synthesizer lines, Prince is that true
rarity--an artist who appeals to people of every
musical and racial stripe," the author writes as
part of his introductory chapter, "Purple Reign."
He then goes on to tell of a childhood in which the
singer/guitarist/multi-instrumentalist was early
introduced to music and pornography, to marital and
other family strife, and to instability; of his
interest and success in sports in his junior
high-school years; and of his growing up on the
"borderline" of black and white cultures (p. 17).
As a child, "Prince got into fights when other kids
teased him about his height, and as he told writer
Jim Farber a few years ago, he had to defend
himself against some people who didn't like the
fact that he dated white girls" (p. 18). Also in
high school Prince played in a band successively
called Grand Central and Champagne. In school "he
made sure to keep his grades up, but only so he
would be able to concentrate on his two burning
interests, music and girls" (p. 20). In 1976,
following high school, Prince concentrated on
songwriting, hired a manager, left Champagne, cut a
demo record, and won the opportunity to produce,
write, arrange, and perform his debut album--the
Warner Brothers release _For You_ (1978). In 1979 he

released his second album, <u>Prince</u>. <u>Dirty Mind</u> (1980) followed, and in 1981 he made a promotional tour and received his first major television exposure on "Saturday Night Live." The year 1982 brought the triple-platinum album <u>1999</u>, and 1984 brought the movie <u>Purple Rain</u> and its soundtrack album by the same name.

In developing his narrative the author treats details of other matters in Prince's life, including his social, political, and ethical beliefs; his sexual orientation; his professional relationship to the rock group Time; his "girl" groups, Vanity 6 and Apollonia 6; the development, writing, and making of the movie <u>Purple Rain</u>; Prince's dress and other personal adornments; and his refusal to give interviews. In addition to the discography and videography, the appendix contains a genealogy and fan club information.

Ivory, Steven. <u>Prince</u>. New York: Perigee Books, 1984. 175 pp. photographs. discography.

This is a brief life and career sketch of Prince Rogers Nelson, a singer/guitarist who, in the author's estimation, "is the most invigorating thing to happen to rock music since Michael Jackson's <u>Thriller</u> became the largest-selling album in the history of recorded music" (p. 14). With his 1982 album <u>1999</u> having sold more than four million copies and with his having been compared favorably to Jimi Hendrix and already "an international phenomenon," Prince promises to be a superstar comparable to Michael Jackson (p. 167). Born in 1958 in Minneapolis to jazz musicians, "Prince came up largely on a musical diet of Beatles, Rolling Stones, Jimi Hendrix, and Sly and the Family Stone" (p. 19). The author tells of Prince's musical and personal development in a childhood group called Grand Central; the details of his search for a company to record his work and his eventual signing with Warner Brothers Records; his arrival as a recording artist; and his producing of his own first album, from which came his first hit single, "Soft and Wet," in 1978. Then the reader learns of Prince's introduction to and activities on the concert circuit as the opening act for Rick James; his development and progression through his post-beginner groups Champagne, The Time, The Revolution, and The Family; the making of the successful rock movie <u>Purple Rain</u> (1984), "the smartest rock 'n' roll movie ever made," in which

Prince and his band were the principals; and the peculiarities of his personality and character (p. 165).

Review: Billboard 96:48 O 27 '84

SELECTIVE DISCOGRAPHY

Around the World in a Day. Warner Brothers. 25286-1, 1985.
Controversy. Warner Brothers. BSK-3601, 1981.
Dirty Mind. Warner Brothers. BSK-3478, 1980.
For You. Warner Brothers. BSK-3150, 1978.
1999. Warner Brothers. 2-23720, 1982.
Parade. Warner Brothers. 1-25895, 1986.
Prince. Warner Brothers. BSK-3366, 1979.
Purple Rain. Warner Brothers. 1-25110, 1984.

Ma Rainey

Lieb, Sandra R. <u>Mother of the Blues: A Study of Ma Rainey</u>.
Amherst: University of Massachusetts Press, 1981. xvii,
226 pp. photographs, musical examples, facsimiles.
discography. bibliography. appendixes. index.

This is an effective and scholarly study of
"America's first major woman blues singer" (p. vi),
a great "vocalist, minstrel show performer, and
commedienne, as well as a fine songwriter, dancer,
and one of the most popular blues recording stars
of the 1920s" (p. 6). It is also a good study of
Rainey's professional life and her classic blues
output. The scholarly apparatus is thorough and
effective, and the index of song titles is a
bonus. The purpose of the book is to explore the
singer's "life and performance style and to analyze
the themes of her recorded song lyrics" (p. xiv).
In realizing these goals, the author tells a story
that "encompasses such diverse topics as the
relationship between black and white minstrelsy,
the great northward migration of rural black people
in the early twentieth century, the development of
jazz, the history of the blues, and the birth and
growth of the recording industry" (p. 2).

Rainey began to perform professionally in tent
shows and revues at about fourteen and graduated to
black minstrel shows, such as the Rabbit Foot
Minstrels and Silas Green from New Orleans. Her
first recordings were made in 1923--"Bad Luck
Blues" and "Moonshine Blues"--on the Paramount
label. We learn about her bisexual inclinations

and her penchant for jewelry; her performances on the Theater Owners' Booking Association (T.O.B.A.) circuit; her good artistic and financial fortunes and high standard of living in the 1920s; events and circumstances surrounding the "diminishing sphere of black recording" around 1927, when classic blues singers were phased out "in favor of male country blues singers" (p. 40); Rainey's diminished economic condition following 1928; the termination of her Paramount contract in 1928 because "her downhome material had gone out of fashion" (p. 41); her fading "into obscurity in the early thirties" (p. 47); and her death in 1939 at the age of fifty-two.

The book has four chapters: the first gives biographical information; the rest attempt to delineate Rainey's style and "analyze her recorded songs as a poetic unity, discussing themes and imagery," treating "the structure of Ma Rainey's songs . . . [and] her debt to folk blues, popular blues, and black entertainment," focusing on and examining "the development of her recordings from 1923 to 1928" (p. 49). In the process the author clearly defines the elements and characteristcs of traditional and classic blues styles, presenting a good and effective discussion of Rainey's recorded output in the context of the musical, social, cultural, and technological environments of the time. The book has a general index and an "Index of Song Titles."

Reviews: Black Perspective in Music 11:83-84 nl '83; Choice 19:1256 My '82; Down Beat 49:70 Ju '82; Jazz Journal International 35:11 My '82; Journal of American Studies 16:481 D '82; Library Journal 107:96 Ja 1 '82; Recorded Sound n83:107-108 Ja '83; Orkester Journalen 51:32-33 Ap '83

SELECTIVE DISCOGRAPHY

Blame It on the Blues. Milestone MLP-2008.
Blues the World Forgot. Biograph BLP-12001.
Down in the Basement. Milestone MLP-2017.
The Immortal Ma Rainey. Milestone MLP-2001.
Ma Rainey. Milestone M-47021.
Oh My Babe Blues. Biograph BLP-12011.
Queen of the Blues. Biograph BLP-12032.

Otis Redding

Schiesel, Jane. The Otis Redding Story. Garden City, N.Y.:
Doubleday. 143 pp. photograph. discography.

A juvenile book, this study teaches that the singer
was born in 1941, grew up in Macon, Georgia, and
was nurtured in the church, where he was cultivated
by the gospel sound, and in his home, where he
listened, to the chagrin of his father, to his
favorite rhythm & blues singers--Little Richard,
Dee Clark, James Brown, Sam Cooke, and others. As
a teenager, the reader learns, Redding performed
with local groups, dropped out of high school,
began to write his own songs, and played dates with
a group called Johnny Jenkins and the Pinetoppers
at high schools, colleges, and other venues in the
area. In 1958 Redding was married and by 1962 had
two children. In the latter year, Redding
accidentally got his break to make a record, and in
1965 he recorded his great album, Dictionary of
Soul, for Stax Volt. In 1967, after a string of
"chitlin' circuit" and record successes, Redding
toured Europe, taking it "by storm" and, in the
meantime, established two music business
promotional firms (p. 107). The year 1967 was a
fateful one: Redding's appearance at the 1967
Monterey International Folk Festival was highly
successful; he won the 1967 Melody Maker poll as
number-one male vocalist; and he died, at age
twenty-six, in the crash of his private plane.

Reviews: Best Sellers 33:430 D 15 '73; Kirkus
Reviews 41:1209 N 1 '73; Library Journal 98:3715

Otis Redding

D 15 '73; New York Times Book Review p10 D 30
'73; Publishers Weekly 204:70 Jy 23 '73

SELECTIVE DISCOGRAPHY

The Best of Otis Redding. Atlantic 81282-4.
Dictionary of Soul. Atco 33-249.
Dock of the Bay. Atco 33-288.
History. Atco S33-290.
Otis Redding. Atco 33-261.
Otis Redding at the Monterey Pop Festival. Reprise 2029.
Pain in My Heart. Atco 33-161.
Sings Soul. Atco S33-284.

Lionel Richie

Plutzik, Roberta. <u>Lionel Richie</u>. New York: Dell, 1985. 185 pp. photographs. discography.

The author says it best:

> This is the story of one nice guy who, through tremendous hard work and faith in his own developing abilities, decided he would finish first, no matter how long it took. It's about a man who paid his dues, and approached the idea of success with a mixture of common sense and the willingness to take risks, even if somebody laughed at him now and then. It's about a man who chose his friends well and, by cherishing those professional and personal relationships, finds himself at the top with so many people to share it with. It's about a man who kept himself healthy and never took his eye off his goals, no matter how unattainable they sometimes seemed. Finally it's about a man who cares about people (p. 18).

This singer/entertainer, born in 1949, was nurtured and matured in Tuskegee Institute, Alabama, in an environment based on the cultural legacy of Booker T. Washington. At Tuskegee Institute High School Richie played clarinet in the orchestra and was an avid tennis player. When he was in the eleventh grade, his family moved to Joliet, Illinois, where he encountered elements of "the hoodlums, thugs, the local gangs like the War Lords and Blackstone Rangers" (p. 34).

Upon graduation from high school Richie returned to Tuskegee, enrolled, with his childhood friends, at Tuskegee Institute to major in "finance and accounting," and became part of a new band that came to be known as The Mystics (p. 36). Later in the year Richie's group combined with several members of another, and became The Commodores, rapidly improving to a point where they played in Montgomery "alongside many revered names on the southern black music circuit: Billy Stewart, Ike and Tina Turner, and comedian Dewey 'Pigmeat' Markham" (p. 42). In the summer of 1965 Richie began working in a Joliet bomb plant, "pouring TNT in shells," but in July he and The Commodores traveled to New York to seek their musical fortune (p. 45). After a short while they were booked into the legendary Smalls Paradise--and they were impressive. Word spread:

> The club was packed every night with jazz afficionados, lovers of R and B, and such community luminaries as Redd Foxx and James Brown. Wilson Pickett impressed the Commodores by swooping into the club in a massive cape. Anyone who wanted to be seen was there, and on the street, people said, "The place is smokin'." Even the local gangsters came, parking their Cadillac limos outside, curious to see these wet-behind-the-ears musicians, and when they did, they nicknamed them "the Schoolboys" (p. 49).

The Commodores then moved to midtown Manhattan, where they again triumphed. In the fall term the group returned to Tuskegee, took classes, toured the Southern circuit, and began to travel and play in distant places (as on the French Riviera, in Canada, New York, and Atlantic City) and accompanied the Jackson Five on a forty-two-date tour. All the while, Richie continued his studies at Tuskegee, where "those around him considered him a natural actor, outgoing and self-possessed, funny and light-hearted" (p. 67). At Tuskegee he met his wife-to-be, Brenda Harvey, who would in 1972 be "named Miss Tuskegee, and [go] on to reach the semifinals of the Miss Alabama pageant--the first black woman to do so" (p. 69). In 1975 they were

married; the Commodores signed with Motown, though
they did not immediately make records, and
continued to tour. Even after making their first
hit singles--"Machine Gun," "Rapid Fire," and
"Sanctified"--they continued to serve as a warm-up
group, opening for established acts such as Stevie
Wonder, Earth, Wind and Fire, and the O'Jays.
Through the 1970s and into 1980 the Commodores
produced hit singles and albums, which included the
songs "Easy" (1977) and "Three Times a Lady"
(1978).

In the 1980s Richie has taken what might be
called "'a total performance view' in his
composing. The words must be dramatic enough to
survive adaptation to other media. Rather than
take the purist's point of view that a song should
be played as it is originally conceived, Lionel has
discovered the challenge of fine-tuning his work to
the stage, to videos, and perhaps, in the future,
feature film" (pp. 113-114). Of Richie's songwriting the author writes, among other things, that
"Lionel took the word _easy_, made it the title,
expanded it to the phrase, 'I'm Easy,' and realized
he was being led into the body of the song. 'After
that I work on the mood that paints a picture, that
opens up the song so that it breathes'" (p. 116).
In 1983 Richie launched his solo career, producing
the hit albums _Lionel Richie_ and _Can't Slow Down_
and making a world tour. In the following year,
1984, he made another world tour and reached the
pinnacle of his career.

In telling this fascinating story, the author
also writes of Richie's early frugality and
stinginess; his wife's participation in his career;
his relationship to Motown mogul Berry Gordy, Jr.;
how he learned to write songs and his development
as a songwriter; his Grammy, American Music, and
People's Choice awards; the making of his hit song
"Endless Love"; the method the Commodores used to
choose members' songs for their LPs; the
circumstances surrounding the disintegration of the
Commodores; the making of Richie's musical ideas;
and the choreographing of his act. Appended to the
book is a list of awards and nominations.

Review: Billboard 97:51 Ja 19 '85

Lionel Richie

SELECTIVE DISCOGRAPHY

Can't Slow Down. Motown 6059-MD, 1984.
Commodores Greatest Hits. Motown M4-912, 1978.
Endless Love Soundtrack. Motown 5309, 1981.
Lionel Richie. Motown 6007-MD.
Midnight Magic. Motown 5348, 1980.

Paul Robeson

Gilliam, Dorothy Butler. <u>Paul Robeson: All American</u>. Washington, D.C. New Republic, 1976. x, 216 pp. photographs. bibliography. play/filmography. index.

One of the two most perceptive, penetrating, and honest of the Robeson biographies, this work treats many of the events in Robeson's life, glossed over in other accounts, with depth and specificity, and it covers activities and practices often not mentioned in other accounts. We learn, for example, that

Using his voice to earn money for law school, Paul sang with "The Four Harmony Kings," which included jazz bandleader Fletcher Henderson, in the fabulous <u>Shuffle Along</u>, and at the Cotton Club in a show with the diminutive and dynamic Florence Mills. Another job during law school was playing professional football with the Akron Indians and later the Milwaukee Badgers, on week-ends. Occasionally, during his rare moments of leisure, he would drop by Harlem's Lafayette Theater to catch the plays by the stock company, particularly enjoying sensuous Abbie Mitchell and an intense actor named Charles Gilpin (p. 25).

We learn also that Robeson's circle of friends included "the most promising members of the Harlem Renaissance" and that he frequented the soirees of

Harlem's Dark Tower (p. 39). By 1932 Robeson was an international celebrity, his entire career being detailed in the British Who's Who (but still absent from the American edition). By 1934 Robeson had developed his philosophy of culture and had become proficient in several languages. By the late forties, he had become a "Cold Warrior" (p. 123), fighting for his civil rights in his own land as he was investigated and harassed by agencies of the federal government and protected by "several young budding actors and entertainers, some of whom would later become black superstars--Sidney Poitier, Harry Belafonte, Ossie Davis, Leon Bibb, and Julian Mayfield" (p. 161).

The book's nineteen chapters treat such topics as "All-American," "Ascent to Fame," "A Marriage in Trouble," "Birth of a Political Artist," "The Moor," "Cold Warrior," "An Artist Beseiged," "A Prisoner in His Own Land," and "Free at Last," all having to do with Robeson's application of his art to social issues and concerns and the impact of this practice on his career. The work also discusses or mentions his roles in plays and films, including: All God's Chillun Got Wings, The Emperor Jones, Taboo, Black Boy, Shuffle Along, Simon the Cyrenian, Porgy, Show Boat, Othello, Borderline, The Hairy Ape, Sanders of the River, Basalik, Stevedore, The Song of Freedom, King Solomon's Mines, Toussaint L'Ouverture, Big Fella, Jericho (Dark Sands), Plant in the Sun, Proud Valley, and Tales of Manhattan. It also tells of his singing of songs that would be musically or culturally important events: "Ol' Man River" and "Ballad for Americans."

Reviews: America 136:424 My 7 '77; Best Sellers 37:11 Ap '77; Book World pH4 D 5 '76; Booklist 73:1082 Mr 15 '77; Choice 14:543 Ju '77; Christian Science Monitor 69:26 Ja 14 '77; Kirkus Reviews 44:877 Au 1 '76; Journal of Popular Culture 11:372 Fall '77; Library Journal 101:2166 O 15 '76; Negro History Bulletin 41:29 S '78; New York Times Book Review p29 F 12 '78; Progressive 41:61 My '77; West Coast Review of Books 3:31 Mr '77

Graham, Shirley. Paul Robeson: Citizen of the World. Foreword by Carl Van Doren. 1946. Reprint. Westport, Conn.: Negro Universities Press, 1971. [viii], 264 pp. photographs. bibliography. index.

Paul Robeson

This book, written for juveniles, contains dialogue created by the author from basic research or conjecture and evocative descriptions of events in Robeson's life. It begins with Robeson's childhood and covers his college career, his marriage to Eslanda Goode Robeson, and his acting and concert careers until his 46th birthday in 1944. The reader gains a feeling for the Harlem Renaissance through verbal pictures of figures such as Carl Van Vechten, J. W. and J. Rosamond Johnson, the writing team of Sissle and Blake, and authors Claude McKay, Vachel Lindsay, and W.E.B. DuBois.

Review: Kirkus Reviews 39:818 Au 1 '71

Hamilton, Virginia. Paul Robeson: The Life and Times of a Free Black Man. New York: Harper & Row, 1974. xvi, 217 pp. bibliography. index.

> Cornbread was regularly his dinner, breakfast and lunch, along with nourishing mustard greens or dandelion greens. Happily, Paul passed in and out of aunts', cousins' and friends' households. He attended segregated black schools in Princeton and lived totally within a black world. No blacks were allowed to attend the Princeton High School. Paul's brother Bill had been forced to go to Trenton eleven miles away in order to attend high school (p. 12).

This was what singer/actor Paul Robeson's early world was like. He graduated from high school in 1915, at seventeen. He had been "an honor student, a talented singer, a superb debater, and an outstanding athlete" (p. 29). Then he attended Rutgers, where he became a star athlete but "shunned the glee club out of fear of the color line." Next he earned a law degree at Columbia University.

By 1924 he was playing the leading roles in All God's Chillun Got Wings and The Emperor Jones and had "grown to manhood at a time when the inner mood and artistic spirit of his people had come into its golden age. And his ability to reveal that mood and spirit at will to others marked him as an intuitive actor" (p. 29). Then he met Lawrence Brown, the musician who with Robeson would form "one of the most superb collaborations in musical history" (p. 30). In 1928 Robeson "became an overnight sensation in London" when he played the part of Joe, singing "Ol' Man River" (p. 38). He and his wife became the "darlings" of the British upper class and were widely known and admired in society circles. The early 1930s "brought his steady mastery of his art, and his continued fame as an individual artist on concert tours in England and the United States. But in the U.S., unrecognized in small towns, Paul was the object of prejudice and discrimination as was the rest of his race" (p. 48).

In 1933, having made England his home (temporarily), he visited the United States and starred in the movie version of <u>The Emperor Jones</u>. In the meantime, "Nazism, anti-semitism, the plight of Jewish refugees, had made him sensitive to world affairs. And still changing, still growing, he was now willing to discuss the 'Colour Question'" (p. 52). He expanded his repertoire from Afro-American spirituals to embrace the folk songs of many nations, and he learned several new languages. For socialists, "he <u>was</u> the symbol of emerging darker peoples and clearly a new man bringing forth a new society" (p. 53). In 1934 Robeson and his wife traveled to the Soviet Union. Stopping briefly in Berlin, his encounter with the hatred of Nazi storm troopers crystallized his growing political point of view, and he was then "bound to fight intolerance wherever he found it" (p. 60). In the Soviet Union, however, Robeson felt "like a human being for the first time since I grew up. Here I am not a Negro but a human being. . . . You cannot imagine what that means to me as a Negro" (p. 62). While in Russia, he sang as "Russians looked on with awe at this giant black man and stood to applaud him" (p. 63). Early in 1935 Robeson returned to London. By 1937 he was thinking

first about the world and then only about himself. Where were freedom and equality--for the world, not just for himself? And where was peace--not only for himself? The great celebrity concerts he had once given to the upper and middle classes of England seemed pompous and futile now. For he had been transformed by his study of Marxism and his concern for oppressed Africans, Spaniards, Jews, into making a crucial change in his life (p. 73).

During the turbulent years of the late thirties Robeson sang in many countries, devoting himself and his art to the cause of the working classes and antifascists. In 1939 he returned to live in the United States; soon thereafter, when he broadcast and recorded "Ballad for Americans," "he experienced immense love and popularity from his countrymen, the first black American ever to be thus flattered. The press sought him out, demanding his comments on a wide range of subjects" (p. 85). His audiences began to grow larger and larger as he performed across the country; for example, "13,000 people at New York's Lewisohn Stadium. Tall, dark and superbly at ease in the spotlight, he was near the peak of his fame. More than ever now, he stood out before the public, impressing it and influencing it with his artistry" (p. 89). There were 30,000 in Hollywood, 150,000 in Chicago. In 1944 <u>Othello</u> became his "greatest triumph" (p. 97). After the performance, "the Schubert Theater echoed the applause for twenty minutes after the last scene . . . and the production ran two hundred and ninety-six performances, the longest run on Broadway for any Shakespeare play" (pp. 97-98). The play traveled to and appeared in forty-four American cities until it closed in Chicago in April, 1945. For his Othello role Robeson won the "American Academy of Arts and Sciences award for the best acting performance in 1944" (p. 99). Following World War II, he formed a trio and went to Europe, giving five concerts a week for five weeks.

By 1947, however, reaction had set in against Robeson's political views and outspokenness, and "those who opposed him both as a black man and as a man of ideas succeeded in stopping the public from hearing him" in concert (p. 113). "The year 1949 marked the end of America's enthrallment with Paul Robeson. For some of his countrymen evidently thought they could no longer safely enjoy the magnificence of his great voice. The man had become dangerously 'subversive' and the man, along with the voice, had to be stilled" (p. 134). By the late fall of 1949 his records could no longer be found; he would not sing in American concert halls again for another decade. In 1950 his passport was canceled, and he was "confined to the United States for the next eight years" (p. 156). Throughout the decade he suffered "hateful and absurd" harassment and hounding by the United States government and by a large number of his fellow Americans, in spite of vigorous support from peoples and governments from all over the world (p. 157). By 1958, though, he had returned to the concert halls, his voice still "the greatest baritone of all time" (p. 181). His passport was restored, allowing him to travel abroad. But his voice and his health began to decline until, in 1963, his health broke permanently. In 1964 Freedomways, the Negro quarterly, organized a "Freedomways Salute to Paul Robeson" for which people came from all over the country. By 1967 he was in full retirement. Paul Robeson had been years ahead of his time. It was only in the 1970s that the society in which he lived came to think as he did in the 1940s.

In this work, some accounts in Robeson's life differ from those same accounts in Eslanda Goode Robeson's biography; details are provided here and entire events are presented that are not discussed in Goode-Robeson. In addition, developments that are compressed in Goode-Robeson are treated more fully here. Moreover, unlike Goode-Robeson, this work encompasses the whole of the great singer's life. It treats Robeson's life and career in the context of the cultural, social, political, and economic movements, events, and conditions of his time, including World War I and World War II, the Great Depression, the rise of totalitarianism and the growth of socialism, the Harlem Renaissance, McCarthyism and the Cold War, and the Peekskill incidents. It treats also of Robeson's making such films as Song of Freedom and King Solomon's Mines, in which he tried to "reverse the image of the shuffling, bug-eyed blacks shown in too many Hollywood movies" (p. 70); his campaigning for presidential candidate Henry Wallace for the Progressive Party ticket; the disappointment felt by the black leadership because of his political views; and the government's attempts, but inability, to intimidate him.

Reviews: Best Sellers 34:474 Ja 15 '75; Book World p6 D 15 '74; Book World pE2 Jy 8 '79; Booklist 71:35 S 1 '74; Booklist 71:766 Mr 15 '75; Center for Children's Books Bulletin 28:130 Ap '75; English Journal 69:95 F '80; Horn Book Magazine 51:159 Ap '75; Human Events 39:10 Au 25 '79; Kirkus Reviews 42:1208 N 15 '74; Kirkus Reviews 43:13 Ja 1 '75; Kliatt Young Adult Paperback Book Guide 13:30 Fall '79; Library Journal 99:3054 N 15 '74; New York Times Book

Paul Robeson

Review p8 D 22 '74; Publishers Weekly 206:58 Jy
29 '74; Publishers Weekly 216:160 Jy 23 '79

Hoyt, Edwin P. Paul Robeson: The American Othello. Cleveland and New York: World Publishing Co., 1967. ix, 228
pp.

After a section that treats Robeson's parentage and
childhood, this book discusses his entrance into
Rutgers University on a four-year scholarship; his
becoming a member of the football team and his
initial difficulties with his white fellow
athletes; his graduation from Rutgers in 1919 and
his entrance into the Law School at Columbia
University in the following year; his theatrical
debut in 1920 in Simon the Cyrenian; his marriage
to Eslanda Goode Robeson; his 1922 performance in
Taboo in London; and his graduation from Columbia
in 1923. The author portrays Robeson as being
"lazy" in waiting for an employment opportunity to
appear.

During the two years following his graduation,
Robeson performed for a short time at the Cotton
Club with Florence Mills, in the Broadway
production of Shuffle Along, and in two plays--All
God's Chillun Got Wings and The Emperor Jones. The
author states that, early in his acting career,
Robeson's acting skills were not well developed but
that he exhibited a great presence on stage and
played himself in his acting roles. In 1925
Robeson met Lawrence Brown, a pianist and arranger
of spirituals; together they presented the first of
many concerts that would span the next thirty-five
years. A short European concert tour provided
experiences in an atmosphere free of racial
prejudice, in contrast with a concert tour the
following year in the United States. During the
American tour, Paul's wife Essie served as his
personal manager; we are informed that "she was
becoming increasingly radical and increasingly
critical of the native land that promised so much
and delivered so little even to an extremely
talented Negro" (p. 46). In 1930 Robeson appeared
in Shakespeare's Othello and was highly successful
in that role. Talk of staging Othello in New York
with Robeson in the title role unleashed so much
criticism that the project was abandoned.

Beginning in 1932 Robeson became more and more
politically aware. The following year he participated in a performance of All God's Chillun Got

Paul Robeson

<u>Wings</u> to benefit Jewish refugees from Nazi Germany.

> From this point in 1933 . . . can be
> traced the beginning political awareness
> that led to beliefs that would grow ever
> stronger, and ever more firm. Eventually
> politics would pit Paul Robeson against
> the vast majority of his own countrymen.
> Paul Robeson's political beliefs were,
> and remained, exceedingly simple: he
> believed in the equality of mankind. He
> was willing, from this day forward, to
> take risks and speak out for that
> equality. . . . Paul's political aware-
> ness was furthered at home by Essie, in
> whom the fires of Negro and Jewish
> awareness of persecution burned
> brightly. Essie was more intellectual
> than Paul. She was more political than
> he. She <u>stated</u> the arguments that he
> <u>felt</u>, she put them into a semblance of
> logic; all of which strengthened Paul's
> emotional devotion to the Negro cause
> (pp. 59-60).

In 1934 Robeson visited Russia via Germany, where he experienced the open racism of the Nazis.

The late 1930s and early 1940s were a time of great recognition for Robeson. He was awarded honorary degrees from Hamilton College, Rutgers University, and Morehouse College and was awarded the Spingarn Medal by the NAACP. He became more and more publicly militant in his advocacy of Negro rights, and he refused to sing concerts where audiences were segregated. He spoke out in support of Russia because he had seen and felt a lack of prejudice against Negroes there. This growing political activity caused concerts halls to be canceled for his engagements in Peoria, Illinois, and Albany, New York, in 1947. His concert reper-toire was increasingly composed of folk songs from around the world that dealt with freedom. In 1947 he gave up his concert career to devote his time to political activism.

The author portrays Robeson as a "political adolescent" who did not fully comprehend the meaning of events and who was used by the American Communist Party to further its own ends. Robeson's political activity culminated in the Peekskill, New York, riots, where hundreds of concertgoers were injured by a local mob led by the American Legion. In 1950 his passport was canceled, and his opportunities for continuing his concert career were thereby curtailed. Groups in England supported concerts where he sang via transatlantic cable and worked on his behalf with the U.S. State Department. His passport was restored in 1958. In that same year, Robeson published his autobiography, Here I Stand. His concert career ended in 1960. The book concludes with the death of his wife in 1965. Robeson himself lived until 1976.

Reviews: AB Bookman's Weekly 41:488 F 5 '68; Booklist 64:480 D 15 '67; Best Sellers 27:291 N 1 '67; Kirkus Reviews 35:629 My 15 '67; Kirkus Reviews 35:704 Ju 15 '67; Library Journal 92:2558 Jy '67; New York Times 117:35 D 21 '67; New York Times Book Review 72:28 N 12 '67; Publishers Weekly 191:65 Ju 26 '67; Punch 255:417 S 18 '68

Robeson, Eslanda Goode. Paul Robeson, Negro. New York and London: Harper Brothers, 1930. 178 pp. photographs. appendix.

This early work on singer/actor Paul Robeson treats of "The Negro Preacher," "The Rev. William Robeson and His Boy," "Paul at College," "Harlem and the Negro," "Groping: Law, Theatre, Music," "London," "Voice-Help," "Two Pauls," "London Again," and "Finding Himself." Special attention is given to details of Robeson's academic ability; his athletic prowess and participation; the matter of social equality between the races; the phenomenon of "passing"; his personality, character, and easy interactions with others; his European vacation; his wife's (the author herself) perception of, devotion to, and relationship with him, including her support of his career; and his preparation for his first encounter with Othello. We learn that in his boyhood days he was the most popular boy at school, thoroughly happy in his interactions with blacks and whites alike; and that he attended Rutgers University, where he was an outstanding athlete in several sports, winning All-America honors in football and a Phi Beta Kappa key. After graduating from Rutgers, he entered the Columbia Law School and graduated from there, also with honors. Following law school, he joined a large and successful law firm in New York. "But eventually the clerks and other members of the firm objected to the constant presence of so conspicuous a Negro in the office, and Paul felt forced to withdraw" (p. 75).

This turned out to be a break, however, for he almost immediately joined the Provincetown Players, landed leading roles in two Eugene O'Neill plays--All God's Chillun Got Wings and The Emperor Jones--and was "immediately acclaimed by the leading dramatic critics in New York as one of America's finest actors" (p. 81). His first solo recital, in 1925, was a sold-out affair which was the first recital of entirely "Negro" music in the country; his first recital tour took place the following year. Also in 1925, Emperor and its cast went to London, and so did Robeson's recitals. On his return he started voice lessons and improved his vocal technique considerably. In 1928 he went to London again to sing "Ol' Man River" in the musical Show Boat, and settled "permanently" in England (p. 142).

Reviews: Booklist 27:63 O '30; Boston Transcript pl Au 9 '30; Cleveland Open Shelf pl51 D '30; New Republic 63:345 Au 6 '30; New York Herald Tribune Books pl Ju 29 '30; New York Times p5 Jy 13 '30; New York World pll Ju 25 '30; Outlook 155:350 Jy 2 '30; Pittsburgh Monthly Bulletin 35:86 D '30; Saturday Review 150:27 Jy 5 '30; Spectator 145:230 Au 16 '30; Times Literary Supplement p432 My 22 '30

Robeson, Paul. Here I Stand. Preface by Lloyd L. Brown. 1958. Reprint. Boston: Beacon Press, 1971. xx, 121 pp. appendix.

"A statement of defiance and bold power" by "the best known American on Earth" in the 1950s, Here I Stand is not a biography but a statement of the singer/actor's position on human rights and politics and how it was formed from his earliest years (pp. ix, x). Robeson here tells of his birth into a family of six in 1898 and of a childhood in which he was "imbued" with the concept of "Loyalty to Convictions" and was the only child at home during his father's years as a widower, yielding to his quiet discipline (p. 8). Robeson grew up in a secure and comfortable home and close-knit, hard-working, but largely poor, Afro-American community in Princeton, New Jersey, a town that was fraught with Jim Crow traditions. Robeson's community was an enclave of "songs of love and longing, songs of trials and triumphs, deep-flowing rivers and rollicking brooks, hymn-song and ragtime ballad, gospels and blues, and the healing comfort to be found in the illimitable sorrow of the spirituals" (p. 15). Early identified and treated by his father and his community as one who must become "a credit to the race," Robeson excelled in both academic and extracurricular activities but shied away from most social affairs (p. 16). "There was always the feeling that--well something unpleasant might happen; for the two worlds of white and Negro were nowhere more separate than in social life" (p. 19). In this context he learned to protect himself from the cruelties of personal and institutional racism.

In 1915 Robeson won a scholarship, against significant odds, to attend the then-exclusive Rutgers College. From Rutgers he matriculated at the Columbia University Law School. From these roots Robeson would proudly take political and philosophical stands that would offend the American Establishment and would lead to its unfair and severe suppression and curtailment of his freedom. Believing that this oppression was a result partly of misunderstandings and distortions of his views, Robeson devoted his book to setting the record straight. It all began when he first traveled abroad.

> Having begun my career as a concert singer and actor in the United States, I first went abroad, like many other Negro performers, to work at my profession. . . . It was in London, in the years that I lived among the people of the British Isles and travelled back and forth to many other lands, that my outlook on world affairs was formed. This fact is a key to an understanding of why I may differ in certain attitudes from many of my generation in Negro life (p. 32).

It was in London, among African students, that he discovered African culture. He was in London twelve years (1927-1939), and his discoveries there led to a close and deep study of African culture. That led, in turn, to a study of the culture of the Soviet Union, where "I came to believe that the experiences of the many peoples and races in the Soviet Union--a vast country which embraces one-sixth of the earth's surface--would be of great value for other peoples of the East in catching up with the modern world" (p. 37). But also in London he "came to feel a sense of oneness with the white working people whom I came to know and love. This belief in the oneness of humankind, about which I have often spoken in concerts and elsewhere, has existed within me side by side with my deep attachment to the cause of my own race" (pp. 48-49). Traveling to Spain to witness the "antifascist struggle" there and the participation in it of American volunteers--black and white--he resolved to return to the United States.

In his chapter on "Our Right to Travel" Robeson explains that his fight for "Negro Rights" was at the heart of the court case in which he sought his right to travel freely. He then discusses the possibilities of achieving "Negro Rights" in the 1950s and the struggle that still lay ahead. As his narrative develops, Robeson also tells of his association with pianist/composer/arranger Lawrence Brown; the heavy inclusion of Afro-American folk songs in his repertoire; his concept of international brotherhood; his open-air concerts at the American-Canadian border, the first of which drew "30,000 Canadians from many miles to hear me" (p. 55); and his transatlantic telephone "concerts" during his enforced restriction from travel abroad.

Reviews: Booklist 68:278 N 15 '71; Booklist 68:329 D 1 '71; Black World 21:85 Jy '72; Library Journal 96:3601 N 1 '71; Negro History Bulletin 34:167 N '71; New York Times Book Review p40 O 21 '73; Publishers Weekly 200:53 Jy 26 '71

Seton, Marie. Paul Robeson. Foreword by Sir Arthur Bryant. London: Dennis Dobson, 1958. 254 pp. photographs. index.

This book, written by a personal friend of Robeson who shared his philosophical point of view, begins with Robeson's childhood and ends in the late 1950s with Robeson effectively barred from expressing his views or practicing his art in the United States and abroad. It is the story of a man who, early in his life, achieved recognition among his white contemporaries for his athletic and intellectual abilities. In 1915 he earned a scholarship to Rutgers University, where, even in the face of the segregationist practice of the time, he played on

the varsity football team, participated on the
debate team, and was elected to Phi Beta Kappa at
the end of his junior year. He graduated from the
Law School at Columbia University in 1923.

During his graduate studies Robeson made his
acting debut in _Simon the Cyrenian_; performed in a
play called _Taboo_, which was directed by Augustin
Duncan, the brother of Isadora Duncan; and spent
the summer of 1922 in England playing the lead in
the same play under a new name--_Voodoo_. Following
his graduation, Robeson played the lead in _All
God's Chillun Got Wings_ and _The Emperor Jones_, and
he performed at the Cotton Club in New York with
Florence Mills. His concert career began in 1925,
when he sang a program of spirituals at the
Greenwich Village Theatre, accompanied by Lawrence
Brown; Brown served as Robeson's accompanist and
arranger for all of his concert career. In the
years preceeding World War II he performed in
productions of _The Emperor Jones_ and _Showboat_ and
made concert tours in the United States and Europe.

In 1933 Robeson donated his services to a matinee
performance of _All God's Chillun Got Wings_ to
benefit Jewish refugees from Hitler's Germany. "He
began to see a parallel between the position of the
Jewish people in Nazi Germany and the position of
his own people in the United States. In later years
he referred to this matinee as the beginning of his
political awareness" (p. 69). Robeson's travels
during the late 1930s included visits to Moscow,
where he experienced an absence of discriminatory
practices against Negroes. In 1939 he returned to
the United States from England, where he had lived
and worked for a decade. He continued his concert
career, refusing concert engagements where the
audience was to be segregated. He made his first
appearance in Shakespeare's _Othello_ in 1942--the
first casting of a black actor in that role in the
United States. In the early 1940s Robeson was
awarded an honorary doctorate from Morehouse
College in Atlanta; other honors he received during
that time included the Spingarn Medal.

Robeson's strong political stand against
increasing segregation and violence against black
Americans and his verbal support of the lack of
such discrimination in the Soviet Union led to his
being labeled a Communist and to the cancellation
of his concert dates in 1947. In 1949-1950 his
United States concerts were canceled wholesale.

His continuing to speak out against govern-
ments--including the United States government--
whose policies were discriminatory to blacks the
world over culminated in the riots at his
performances in Peekskill, New York, in 1949, led
by members of the American Legion and observed by
local law-enforcement officers. The book ends with
the revocation of Robeson's passport in 1950 and
the efforts of his friends in England to support
him by bringing his singing to audiences in England
via telephone and tape recording. Robeson's
attitude toward his concert career is summed up in
this statement: "he thought he was more articulate
through the songs he sang than anything he ever
said; that his singing was the truest expression of
himself as a man as well as an artist; that song
had always been a form of speech for him"
(pp. 232-233).

Review: Melody Maker 33:10 Au 9 '58

SELECTIVE DISCOGRAPHY

The Essential Paul Robeson. Vanguard 73110.
Paul Robeson. Scandalize My Name. Vanguard Recording
  Society 30-5647, 1976.

Sonny Rollins

Blancq, Charles. Sonny Rollins: Journey of a Jazzman.
Boston: Twayne Publishers, 1983. [xii], 142 pp.
photograph, musical examples. chronology. bibliography.
discography. index.

This is a chronicle and analysis of jazz styles in
general and of Rollins's recorded output; although
sketchy, the narrative effectively relates the
former to the latter, giving a good picture of
Rollins's position in jazz history. The author
shows how "the combination of phonograph
recordings, a smattering of formal instruction, and
a musical family . . . played a part in shaping
Rollins the young musician," with the "most significant stimulation [coming from] the neighborhood
environment and the rich musical tradition that it
provided" (p. 3). The reader is informed about
Rollins's bout with drugs and his cure in 1959; his
early association with Clifford Brown and Max
Roach; the two sabbaticals Rollins took from public
performance, the first during 1959-1961, the second
during 1969-1971; his friendships with John
Coltrane and Ornette Coleman; and his entry into
the avant-garde.

The author mentions Rollins's study of yoga and
Hindu philosophy, exposure to Indian music, and
exploration of the potential of pop/jazz. He
discusses and explores the nature of jazz
improvisation. The emphasis is on Rollins as the
individual who changed the nature of melodic
improvisation from episodic to unified melodic

- 245 -

Sonny Rollins

statement. Consequently, the book contains succinct treatments of thematic and non-thematic
improvisation, figuration, motivic development,
melodic sequence, modal and pentatonic scales as
the basis for improvisation, and related matters.
Rollins is presented as perhaps "the first to have
expanded his improvisations by the creation of new
themes" (p. 71), with the author discussing, in
turn: the changes in Rollins's creative outlook
when he "ceases to be a melodic player and joins
the avant-garde" (p. 88); "The Free Jazz Years";
and Rollins's participation in the jazz/rock fusion
movement.

Reviews: Jazz Times p16+ Au '85; Library Journal
108:1365 Jy '83

SELECTIVE DISCOGRAPHY

The Bridge. RCA LPM-2527, 1962.
Don't Ask. Milestone M-9090, 1979.
Freedom Suite. Riverside RLP-12-258, 1958.
Graz 1963 Concert. Jazz Connoisseur JC-108, 1978.
Horn Culture. Milestone M-9051, 1973.
Milestone Jazz Stars in Concert. Milestone M-55006, 1978.
More from the Vanguard. Blue Note BN-LA475-H2, 1957.
Moving Out. Prestige LP-7058, 1954.
Saxophone Colossus and More. Prestige P-24050, 1956.
Sonny Rollins' Next Album. Milestone MSP-9042, 1972.
Stuttgart 1963 Concert. Jazz Connoisseur JC-106, 1978.
Tenor Madness. Fantasy FCD-638-7047, 1956.
Way Out West. Mobile Fidelity MFCD-801.
Worktime. Prestige LP-7246, 1955.

Diana Ross

Brown, Geoff. <u>Diana Ross</u>. London: Sidgwick & Jackson, 1981. 144 pp. photographs. discography. index.

This is a career sketch of singer/entertainer Diana Ross, integrated with a capsule history of Motown Records and, of course, the Supremes. Ross's career is traced through the hit songs, movies, albums, and technical developments of Motown and of the industry in general. The story begins with the formation of Motown and the development of the Gordy "game-plan"; progresses to a treatment of Ross's early days in Detroit and the formation of the Primettes, soon to become known as the Supremes; and development of the Motown sound and the reign of the Supremes. In 1970 Ross left the Supremes to begin a solo career. Between 1970 and 1973

> Diana had negotiated the first three years of solo work with great commercial success and no small amount of artistic acclaim. Her screen performance had been nominated for an Oscar for Best Actress . . . and she had won many other awards and trophies--a Golden Globe award for Best New Star, for instance, and <u>Cue Magazine's</u> Entertainer of the Year title. And she had found time to marry, set up home in Beverly Hills and have two daughters (p. 69).

By 1981 she had arrived as a complete entertainer.

The author also discusses the development of Ross's career by Berry Gordy, Jr.; the effects on Ross of songwriter-producer teams Holland-Dozier-Holland, Ashford and Simpson, Deke Richards and Hal Davis, and Bernard Edwards and Nile Rodgers; how Ross's output was received in the United States and in the United Kingdom; her tours of Britain and Europe; her relationships with the other members of the Supremes and with other Motown stars; and the making of the films in which she has starred: <u>Lady Sings the Blues</u> (1972), <u>Mahogany</u> (1975), and <u>The Wiz</u> (1978).

Reviews: Billboard 95:36 Ap 23 '83; Booklist 79:852 Mr 1 '83; Library Journal 108:502 Mr 1 '83; Publishers Weekly 223:365 F 4 '83

SELECTIVE DISCOGRAPHY

<u>The Boss</u>. Motown 923, 1979.
<u>Diana</u>. Motown 936, 1980.
<u>Eaten Alive</u>. RCA AFL1-5422.
<u>Everything Is Everything</u>. Motown 724, 1970.
<u>Farewell</u>. Motown 708, 1970.
<u>Greatest Hits</u>, 2 vols. Motown 663, 1967.
<u>Greatest Hits</u>, Vol. 3. Motown 702, 1969.
<u>Greatest Hits</u>. Motown 869, 1976.
<u>I Hear a Symphony</u>. Motown 643, 1966.
<u>Meet the Supremes</u>. Motown 606, 1963.
<u>Ross</u>. RCA PCD1-4677.
<u>Swept Away</u>. RCA PCD1-5009.
<u>20 Golden Hits</u>. Motown EMTV, 1979.
<u>Where Did Our Love Go</u>. Motown 621, 1964.

Philippa Schuyler

Schuyler, Philippa Duke. <u>Adventures in Black and White</u>. Foreword by Deems Taylor. New York: Robert Speller & Sons, 1960. xv, 302 pp. photographs. index.

This concert pianist and composer gives a view of the concert world and the world at large as she sees them, detailing her adventures in other lands as a young touring artist and the intrigues and machinations of concert promoters, impresarios, producers, reporters, writers, and strangers she met in other lands. Especially intriguing are her accounts of her many tours of numerous foreign countries, her unselfconscious encounters with a wide variety of individuals in her travels and her fascinating discussions with them, and her unwise practice of mingling and traveling, on the spur of the moment, with strangers in the lands she visited. In the foreword to this autobiography, Deems Taylor sums up the phenomenon of Philippa Schuyler thus: "She is the child of a mixed marriage--a Negro newspaper man and a white Texan. Her mother had taught her to read and write simple words by the time she was two years old. . . . Tested at New York University, she was found to have an I.Q. of 185 and an E.Q. (Educational Quotient) of 200. . . . By the time she was four she had composed ten pieces, thus breaking Mozart's record of only one at that age" (pp. xiv). <u>Rumplestiltskin</u> was her first composition, followed by the tone poem <u>Manhattan Nocturne</u> and by <u>Rhapsody of Youth</u>. Schuyler's description of her visit to Dr. Albert Schweitzer's compound in Lambaréné and

the informative photographs are memorable features
of   the   book.   Notably   absent is any   significant
discussion of music.

Reviews: Chicago Sunday Tribune   p5   Jy 29 '62;
Kirkus   Reviews 30:143 F 1 '62; Library   Journal
87:1144 Mr 15 '62; New York Herald Tribune Books
p11 Ju 17 '62; San Francisco Chronicle p29 Ju 10
'62

Bobby Short

Short, Bobby. <u>Black and White Baby</u>. New York: Dodd, Mead, 1971. 304 pp. photographs.

Short makes us aware that he is

> a Negro who has never lived in the South, thank God, nor was I ever trapped in an urban ghetto. I grew up in Danville, Illinois, where my family always lived on a pleasant street, in a pleasant neighborhood where the houses had front yards and back yards, with flower beds and vegetable gardens. Many of our neighbors were white. This book is a collection of memories from those days and from the two years when I was a child star on the vaudeville and nightclub circuit, out on stage in a white suit of tails, playing the piano and singing (p. 3).

Short's narrative carries the reader from his ancestry and birth to his graduation from high school. A candid exposition of his retrospective and contemporary views of life, this sketch touches on Short's first exposure to music through Tin Pan Alley and coon songs and on his relaxed, permissive, musical, but impoverished childhood, during which he sang and played the piano intuitively, "reciting pieces at Sunday school or singing 'Trees' on Arbor Day or playing 'Shanty Town' at a school party" (p. 91). He also performed "at the country club, the Kiwanis Club, luncheons, teas, the Elks Club and YMCA functions, dressed for my performances in a gleaming white tuxedo" (p. 84). Later, he performed in a not-so-pure environment, playing as a single and as a member of a local band--The Dukes of Swing--in Danville saloons as early as age nine.

As a professional child performer, sought after for engagements all over Illinois and Indiana, he was "a representative of the Negro people and to move so freely among whites as an entertainer was a double albatross around my neck. Everyone demanded that I be immaculate in thought, word, and deed, because I had a chance that other colored children did not have. I was the emissary sent into the white camp" (p. 93-94). Billed in the 1930s as "The Miniature King of Swing" and known as "The Boy Wonder," "The Budding Fats Waller," "The Youthful Duke Ellington," and so on, Short went on the road at twelve, performing on the regular vaudeville circuit, where he had encounters with such black artists as Cab Calloway, Fats Waller, and Fletcher Henderson and with such white performers as Bunny Berigan, Mildred Bailey, Henny Youngman, and Judy Garland (p. 236-237); he performed alongside mature vaudeville stars of the day, including Moms Mabley, Pigmeat Markham, Timmie Rogers, Ella Fitzgerald, and the Chick Webb Band. His tenure in vaudeville provided him with insights into the world of show business and its intricacies, including a look at the workings of America's major black theatrical houses of the period--Harlem's Apollo Theater, Chicago's Regal Theater, Washington, D.C.'s Howard Theater, and Detroit's Fox Theater, with additional peeks at locales in Atlantic City, Kansas City, and Covington and Louisville, Kentucky. Short also comments on racial segregation and racial progress in Danville, in Illinois, in the Midwest, and on tour in other sections of the country.

Reviews: AB Bookman's Weekly 47:949 Mr 22 '71; Black World 21:97 D '71; Christian Science Monitor 63:9 My 25 '71; Jazz Digest 1:18-19 Ap/My '72; Kirkus Reviews 39:97 Ja 15 '71; Library Journal 96:1970 Ju 1 '71; Music Journal 29:68 S '71; New York Times Book Review p6 Ju 20 '71; Publishers Weekly 199:70 F 1 '71

Bobby Short

SELECTIVE DISCOGRAPHY

<u>Bobby Short Live at the Cafè Carlyle</u>. Atlantic SD2-609, 1974.
<u>Bobby Short Celebrates Rogers and Hart</u>. Atlantic SD2-610.
<u>Mabel Mercer and Bobby Short at Town Hall</u>. Atlantic SD2-604.
<u>Bobby Short Is K-Ra-Zy for Gershwin</u>. Atlantic SD2-608.

Noble Sissle

Kimball, Robert, and William Bolcom. <u>Reminiscing with Sissle and Blake</u>. New York: Viking Press, 1973. 256 pp. photographs, music facsimiles, posters, charts. appendixes.

This "story of great musical theater," as told by Noble Sissle and Eubie Blake and as elaborated on by the authors, begins with a brief sketch of the history of black musical theater. It treats Sissle and Blake's development from a two-man vaudeville act into Broadway showmen and composers; matters pertaining to <u>Shuffle Along</u>--its plot, its music, its initial tour, its success on Broadway; and information about the development and plots of other black musicals of the period. Included are reprints of letters and news clippings; large and striking photographs of significant events, groups, and individuals; and an appendix which includes lists of compositions, productions and films, a rollography, and a discography.

Reviews: Best Sellers 33:113 Ju 1 '73; Jazz Journal 26:16 My '73; Jazz Report 8:32 n4 '73; Kirkus Reviews 41:378 Mr 15 '73; Library Journal 98:1822 Ju 1 '73; Music Journal 31:10 Annual '73; Newsweek 81:81 Ap 30 '73; Publishers Weekly 203:56 Mr 12 '73; Variety 271:43-44 Au 8 '73

Noble Sissle

SELECTIVE DISCOGRAPHY

<u>Sissle and Blake: Early Rare Recordings</u>. 2 vols. Eubie
   Blake Music EBM-4/7.
<u>Sissle and Blake's "Shuffle Along</u>." New World
   Records NW-260, 1976.
<u>Songs from "Shuffle Along</u>." RCA Victor LPM-3514, EPA-482.

Bessie Smith

Albertson, Chris. Bessie. paperback. New York: Stein and Day, 1982. 253 pp. photographs. bibliography. discography. index.

This is "the story of a woman who was black and proud long before that became the acceptable thing to be," one who "had vocal abilities no one in her field could equal, and . . . a gift for showmanship to match . . . [who] danced, and did comedy routines with a skill that evoked the envy of other performers" (pp. 12, 24). She was born in low circumstances in 1894. As a child Bessie sang "for nickles and dimes on Chattanooga's North Street," and in 1912 she entered show business, joining "a traveling show as a dancer and comedian" (p. 26). In about 1913 she made Atlanta's "81" Theater her base, touring from there on the Theater Owners' Booking Association (T.O.B.A.) circuit and with minstrel shows. In 1921 she moved to Philadelphia and by 1922 was playing at Atlantic City's cabarets and at venues all along the Eastern seaboard. In 1923 Smith was married, made her first record--"Down Hearted Blues"/"Gulf Coast Blues"-- and by December of that year had made numerous theater and cabaret dates and "140 performances in the studio" (p. 59). In 1924 she toured more widely, traveling again to the South, where she appeared at "Nashville's all-white Orpheum Theater on January 15 and 16" (p. 64). From Nashville she toured on to Memphis, Atlanta, Cincinnati, Detroit, Pittsburgh, and Philadelphia. Later that year she made another tour, traveling to Chicago and

Indianapolis. In the years to come she would make
numerous such tours.

Knowing "every drinking joint from New Orleans to
Detroit," Smith partied excessively during her
periods at home and while on tour (p. 77). By 1925
"she could rightly feel that she had 'arrived.' She
had enjoyed a year and a half of prominence and
prosperity; she had earned billing as 'the Greatest
and Highest Salaried Race Star in the World'; she
was supporting her family in a fashion she had
never thought possible; she was married, and she
was still running around" (p. 83). In June, 1925,
Bessie took her <u>Harlem Frolics</u> show South,
"traveling in her own personal railroad car. . . .
"Seventy-eight feet long, the car was large enough
to carry the entire show. It had seven state-
rooms--each one comfortably sleeping four--
kitchen, bathroom with hot and cold running water,
and a lower level accommodating as many as
thirty-five people" (p. 94). In 1926 she adopted a
son, moved her relatives from Chattanooga to
Philadelphia, squandered a great deal of money,
slowed down her professional activities, and became
involved in sexual liaisons with at least two of
the female members of her troupe. In 1927 Smith
was as professionally impressive as ever, still "in
a class by herself" as "an actress, comedienne,
dancer, and mime as well. And in all these guises
she had no equal in her ability to communicate with
an audience, to command its involvement in whatever
she was doing, and to control and even shape its
responses" (p. 135).

By 1928 Bessie and her husband, Jack Gee, each
seemed "unable or unwilling to adjust to the
other. They fought incessantly, tolerated each
other's promiscuities to a certain extent, and
spent most of their married life playing a
nerve-wracking game of hide and seek" (p. 148).
Later that year they were separated permanently.
Also in 1928 Smith cut what some consider to be
"the finest record she ever made"--"Poor Man's
Blues," toured with her show <u>Steamboat Days</u>, and
produced and performed in "her best show to date"
(pp. 148, 152). By 1929 "Bessie's brand of blues
had definitely lost its broad appeal, and the
talking picture was beginning to strangle
vaudeville" (p. 153); she performed in the Maceo
Pinkard-produced Broadway show <u>Pansy</u> and starred in
the film <u>St. Louis Blues</u>.

Smith began the decade of the thirties "with what
was to be her last Theater Owners' Booking
Association (T.O.B.A.) tour. She had sold the
railroad car, her salary had gone down from a peak
of two thousand dollars a week to half that amount,
but in 1930 Bessie was still making what was
considered a great deal of money" (p. 168). Her
career would take an upturn in 1933, when she began
recording again. "Her repertoire now consisted
mainly of popular tunes like 'Smoke Gets in Your
Eyes' and 'Tea for Two,' but she still sang the
blues when her audience demanded it" (p. 189). In
1936 "Connie's Inn brought Bessie a whole new
audience, and what they heard was a new Bessie
Smith; gone were the blues--except for an
occasional request--and that powerful voice belted
out the popular songs of the day with an
accompaniment that now featured the 'modern' swing
beat" (p. 199). By 1937 she had completely
transcended the blues idiom and "slipped graceful
into the Swing Era" (p. 212). In September of that
year she died from injuries suffered in an
automobile accident. In telling Smith's story the
author debunks previous myths about her life and
discusses her generosity and her free-spending
ways; her "uninhibited sexual appetite" (p. 77);
the effects of the Great Depression on her life and
career; the large number of revues she produced and
in which she starred; her numerous tours of the
East Coast, South, and Midwest; and her
professional relationships with Ma Rainey, Fletcher
Henderson, Louis Armstrong, Ethel Waters, Alberta
Hunter, Clara Smith, Clarence Williams, James P.
Johnson, pianist Porter Grainger, Carl Van Vechten,
Will Marion Cook, and others.

Reviews: Black World 23:95 N '73; Blues
Unlimited n101:19 My '73; Booklist 69:1041 Jy 15
'73; Books & Bookmen 18:75 Jy '73; Crawdaddy
n27:80 Au '73; Footnote 4:17-18 n5 '73; Guardian
Weekly 108:24 Ju 2 '73; Hudson Review 26:765
Winter '73/'74; Jazz Digest 2:16-17 Mr '73; Jazz
Forum n24:63 Au '73; Jazz Journal 26:7 F '73;
Jazz Journal 26:18 Ju '73; Jazz Research
5:169-171 '73; Kirkus Reviews 40:1328 N 15 '72;
Library Journal 98:71 Ja 1 '73; Library Journal
98:274 Ja 15 '73; Listener 90:222 Au 16 '73;
Music Journal 31:4+ Ap '73; New Music Council
Bulletin 33:28 n2 '73; New Statesman 86:28 Jy 6
'73; New York Times Book Review p28 F 18 '73;
New Yorker 49:128 F 24 '73; Newsweek 81:92 Ja 22
'73; Observer (London) p37 My 27 '73; Orkester

Bessie Smith

Journalen 41:2+ Mr '73; Publishers Weekly 202:59
N 20 '72; Saturday Review 1:81 Ap 7 '73; Second
Line 25:21 Fall '73; Stereo Review 31:12 O '73;
Times Literary Supplement p1593 D 28 '73;
Variety 269:56 Ja 31 '76; Village Voice 18:21 Jy
12 '73

Albertson, Chris. <u>Bessie Smith: Empress of the Blues</u>. New
York: Schirmer Books; London: Collier Macmillan, 1975. 143
pp. photographs, musical examples. discography. index.

Although photographs and sheet music constitute the
bulk of this book, the biographical and stylistic
information included are valuable. The reader
learns that this classic blues singer was born in
1894 in Chattanooga, Tennessee, in "abject poverty
and under unspeakable living conditions, . . .
began singing for small change on street corners,"
and attended school through the "eighth or ninth
grade" (p. 7). In 1912 Smith left Chattanooga with
the Moses Stokes minstrel troupe, later moving to
the Silas Green Show and Pete Werley's Florida
Blossoms, touring throughout the South. She made
her first record in 1923 ("Down Hearted
Blues"/"Gulf Coast Blues"), "a sensational hit with
780,000 copies sold in the first six months,"
making her the "highest paid black entertainer of
her day" (p. 9). In this position, "In an era when
many blacks sought white acceptance by adopting
their mannerisms, speech and life-style, Bessie
often went out of her way to emphasize them"
(p. 11). Proclaimed the "Empress of the Blues," she
toured both independently and on the Theater
Owners' Booking Association (T.O.B.A.) circuit and
by early 1926 had made more than a hundred
recordings. But the growth of talking pictures
and, later, the stock market crash slowed and ended
her period of glory, causing her to play "to
half-empty houses for a fraction of her previous
fee" (p. 16). By the mid-1930s Bessie was moving
toward swing, playing, by 1937, New York's famed
Connie's Inn. But she died later that year from
injuries suffered in an automobile accident. In
addition to such biographical information, the
author presents a brief examination of Smith's
singing style (by Gunther Schuller), a large number
of impressively striking photographs, and sheet
music for thirty of Smith's recorded compositions.

Moore, Carman. <u>Somebody's Angel Child: The Story of Bessie
Smith</u>. Women of America, edited by Milton Meltzer. New
York: Thomas Y. Crowell, 1969. [xi], 123 pp. photographs,

Bessie Smith

music illustrations. list of compositions. discography.
bibliography. index.

Born in Chattanooga, Tennessee, near the turn of
the century, Bessie Smith early began performing on
the stage and on the street. She made her
professional debut at the Ivory Theater, where she
"earned her eight dollars that week and did what
her nine-year-old heart told her. She bought a
brand new pair of ball-bearing roller skates"
(p. 11). She was never to learn to care for money,
being generous to anyone who asked for help and
spending money as quickly as she earned it. When
she was eleven she was "kidnapped" by the famous Ma
Rainey and joined the Rabbit Foot Minstrels, where
Rainey taught her to sing the blues and to survive
in show business. Three years later she was again
kidnapped, this time by Charles P. Bailey, owner of
the "81" Theater in Atlanta. Smith was the featured
performer there for nearly a year before she began
to travel, performing with the Florida Cotton
Pickers on the Theater Owners' Booking Association
(T.O.B.A.) circuit in the South. Also performing
with this group was pianist/composer Clarence
Williams, who was to become an important part of
Smith's professional life in later years. Several
years passed, with Smith performing in the South
and East as a blues singer. In 1920 she met Jack
Gee in Philadelphia; she would marry him three
years later. In the meantime, she began her
recording career with "I Wish I Could Shimmy Like
My Sister Kate," with its composer, Clarence
Williams, acting as her accompanist. She was to
make many successful blues recordings over the next
few years, with such talented and famous men as
Fletcher Henderson, Louis Armstrong, and James P.
Johnson. Gee soon became her manager and directed
her singing tours. Bessie drank increasingly,
becoming mean when she was drunk. In 1930 she and
Gee separated. Bessie continued to perform, though
the Depression and the passing of the blues as the
most popular and demanded music of the period meant
that her fortunes were reduced and that times were
hard. In 1937 she was on tour in Mississippi when
she was involved in a car accident. She was
seriously injured and died shortly after reaching a
hospital.

Reviews: Book World 4:10 My 10 '70; Book World
4:10 My 17 '70; Center for Children's Books
Bulletin 23:164 Ju '70; Commonweal 92:250 My 22
'70; Down Beat 37:27 Au 6 '70; English Journal

Bessie Smith

59:731 My '70; Grade Teacher 88:99 Mr '71;
Kirkus Reviews 37:1327 D 15 '69; Library Journal
95:1641 Ap 15 '70; Music Journal 28:82 D '70;
New York Times Book Review p26 My 10 '70;
Orkester Journalen 39:16 My '71; Publishers
Weekly 197:278 Ja 26' 70; Saturday Review 53:40
Mr 21 '70; Storyville n31:6-7 O/N '70

Oliver, Paul. Bessie Smith. Kings of Jazz. New York:
Barnes and Noble, 1959. xi, 92 pp. photographs. bibliography. index.

This first book on Bessie Smith is a career sketch
of "the greatest Negro recording artist of her day
and one of the most outstanding figures in the
whole history of American music. Bessie Smith was
a complex woman: heavy, truculent, she was coarse
in conversation, earthy in her humor, ugly in her
manner when she was in her cups" (p. ix). Smith was
early inspired by a little-known singer named Caro
Fisher and by W. C. Handy. Traveling in minstrel
and vaudeville shows as a child, she was, in her
teens, of striking and matronly presence. By 1923
she was recording successfully, covering and
improving on the songs of other blues singers who
had previously established themselves as recording
artists. Compared to her most outstanding
predecessor, Ma Rainey, Smith carried blues singing
away from its folk roots toward professional
entertainment, carefully refining her art so that
every phrase, every pause was impeccably timed and
turned. In this, she came to be "unrivalled as a
jazz singer" (p. 48). By 1927 Smith had reached the
peak of her career and had had professional
interactions and relationships with Clarence
Williams, Fletcher Henderson, Joe Smith, Louis
Armstrong, James P. Johnson, Porter Grainger, Tommy
Ladnier, inventor Thomas Alva Edison, and other
individuals of fame and legend. By 1931 "Gin and
the Depression" had affected her voice and her
delivery, and they and she languished in a
depressed blues market (p. 66). Smith died in 1937,
leaving as her legacy her art and her legend. Her

origins in poverty, the rise to the
heights of her profession, the years of
success, the search for an elusive
happiness, the fall from fame, the final
years of hope and disappointment working
in squalid shows, the sudden brutal end
at the moment when recovery seemed
possible: the life and death of Bessie

Bessie Smith

Smith has all the elements of high drama and great tragedy. As an historic figure alone she has heroic stature, but her importance in jazz far exceeds the facts of her life (p. 71).

Reviews: Jazz Hot 26:9 Ju '60; Jazz Journal 12:33 D '59; Jazz Monthly 5:29-30 Ja '60; Melody Maker 34:13 O 17 '59

SELECTIVE DISCOGRAPHY

Any Woman's Blues. Columbia G-30126.
Bessie Smith: World's Greatest Blues Singer. Columbia GP-33.
The Bessie Smith Story. 4 vols. Columbia CL-855/6/7/8.
The Empress. 2 vols. Columbia CG-30818, 1924-1928.
Empty Bed Blues. Columbia G-30450.
Nobody's Blues But Mine. Columbia CG-31093, 1925-1927.
World's Greatest Blues Singer. GP-33.

Willie the Lion Smith

Smith, Willie "The Lion," with George Hoefer. <u>Music On My Mind: The Memoirs of An American Pianist</u>. Foreword by Duke Ellington. Introduction by John S. Wilson. First paperback edition. New York: Da Capo Press, 1978. xvi, 318 pp. music bibliography. discography. index.

This account of the musical life of one of the most important figures in jazz history is also an insider's view of "the relatively unreported jazz life on the East Coast" from about 1914 (p. [iii]). With a "colorfully convincing mixture of braggadocio and fact," Smith begins by discussing his childhood, the influence of his family and neighborhood on his personal and musical growth and development, and how he began playing the piano "by ear" at about age six (p. [ii]). Then he tells how, at sixteen, he met the pianist and composer Charles Luckeyeth Roberts in Newark, how he met Eubie Blake in Atlantic City in 1913, and how he met James P. Johnson, who became his closest personal friend, in 1914 (or 1916). We also learn that he spent his early years as a pianist/entertainer in Atlantic City and are introduced to older East Coast ragtime pianists, such as One-Leg Willie Joseph, John "Jack the Bear" Wilson, Jess Pickett, Richard (Abba Labba) McLean, and Thad (Snowball) Wilkerson. We learn of the black migration to Harlem from downtown just after the turn of the century and of Smith's World War I army experience, including how he came by his nickname.

Willie the Lion Smith

Smith tells of how he made his headquarters, for a time, at Leroy's, a well-known Harlem night club; his version of how the first blues record, on which he appeared and led the band, was made; his brief flirtation with "the road," during which he spent "eight or nine months" in Chicago, "taking charge" at the Fiume Cafe (p. 126); etiquette, operations, and interactions of night-club entertainers; the strider's wardrobe and attire in the days of high fashion; his working for "big shots" such as Jack "Legs" Diamond, Larry Faye, Thomas Guinan, and others; and his knowledge of Arthur (Dutch Schultz) Flagenheimer, Big Frenchy DeMange, Vincent (Mad Dog) Coll, and Lucky Luciano. There is a brief chapter on the house-rent-party phenomenon, including details of arrangements, food, music, personalities, and carving contests. Some of the "musicians from downtown" who came to hear the music in Harlem cabarets are also discussed. Smith subsequently writes of his engagement at Helbock's, a speakeasy on New York's 52nd Street, and "the beginning of Fifty Second Street as 'the cradle of swing'," the subsequent development of the Street in the early 1930s (p. 203), and his first and only trip to Europe in 1949, when he performed in the "French provinces; Antwerp, Belgium; Barcelona, Spain; Switzerland; and all over North Africa-- Tangiers, Algiers, Casablanca" (p. 270).

The book is sprinkled with casual references to, and in some cases portraits of, friends and acquaintances, such as Clarence Williams, Bessie Smith, Jelly Roll Morton, Sidney Bechet, Andy Razaf, Fats Waller, and many others, as Smith discusses partying with Waller on Park Avenue and their playing for publishing, literary, television, film, and social celebrities at parties and other social occasions; his encounters with communist groups that sought to exploit or convert him; and his becoming a cantor, serving at a synagogue at 122nd Street and Lenox Avenue in Harlem. He mentions pianists who studied with him, including Mel Powell, Howard Smith, Milt Raskin, and Mel Gross. Hoefer's four brief documentary interludes effectively place Smith's comments in historical and cultural perspective. The list of Smith's compositions, the discography, and the excellent index, together with the engaging narrative, all make this autobiography a valuable source.

Reviews: Book Week p40 D 6 '64; Choice 2:234 Ju '65; Christian Science Monitor p5 Jy 30 '64;

Kliatt Young Adult Paperback Book Guide 13:34 Ja
'79; Library Journal 89:3301 S 15 '64; New York
Times Book Review p4   Au 16 '64; Observer
(London) p26 Ap 25 '65; Saturday Review 47:50 S
12 '64; Times Literary Supplement p993 O 19 '67

SELECTIVE DISCOGRAPHY

The Legend of Willie "The Lion" Smith. GA-368, 1958.
The Lion Roars. Dot 3094, 1957.
The Lion Steps Out. London H-APB1017, 1953.
Live at Blues Alley. Chiaroscuro CR-104.
Luckey and "The Lion": Harlem Piano. Good Time Jazz
  S-10035, 1958.
The Piano Album. Meritt 004, 1978.
Willie "The Lion" Smith. Commodore XFL-15775, 1938-1939.
Willie "The Lion" Smith. GNP Crescendo GNPS-9011.

William Grant Still

Arvey, Verna. In One Lifetime. Introduction by B. A. Nugent. Fayetteville: University of Arkansas Press, 1984. xii, 262 pp. photographs. glossary. music bibliography. appendixes.

This memoir by the composer's wife--a pianist, composer, and author herself, as well as an intense devotee--provides insights into the growth of Still's compositional style, into his method of working, and into the writing and production of such works as the operas Troubled Island and Highway 1, U.S.A., the multiforce And They Lynched Him on a Tree, and the Afro-American Symphony. The book begins with a vivid portrayal of Still's ancestry and with details of his childhood activities and training in Little Rock, Arkansas, including schooling, leisure, entertainment, and family interactions. We learn that he "attended the Cole and Johnson shows . . . whenever they came to town. Afterwards, at home, [he and his step-father] would describe the music, relate the plots and laugh again at the jokes" (p. 29). He also studied the violin and witnessed and experienced racial incidents that would become part of his consciousness. Generally, however, the community of Little Rock was "one of the most enlightened he would ever know, among colored people and among many white people. There, cultural and intellectual pursuits were held in esteem; Negro achievement was praised; Negro artists were engaged to give public programs. Clarence Cameron White,

the composer gave a violin recital. . . . Mme.
Azalia Hackley . . . gave a vocal recital" (p. 37).

Still's college years were spent at Wilberforce
University, where "there was much more musical
activity . . . than [he] had ever known before.
. . . His violin playing was enjoyed" by the
college community (p. 3); he learned to play the
clarinet and other instruments; and "he attended
concerts and opera in nearby towns" (p. 40). At
Wilberforce his primary music professors were
Florence Cole Talbert and composer Clarence Cameron
White. He began to compose music, his earliest
model being Samuel Coleridge-Taylor. In the spring
of 1915 he entered the world of commercial music,
where jazz and folk idioms began to complement his
formal training. He played in a park orchestra in
Cleveland, joined a National Guard band, and played
oboe and violin in various orchestras in Columbus.
Later that year he was married; still later he
joined W. C. Handy's band as cellist, oboist, and
arranger. In 1917 Still attended the Oberlin
Conservatory, and the next year he joined the Navy.
On discharge in 1919 he eventually returned to
Columbus, where he joined the Whispering Orchestra
as its violinist and briefly continued his studies
at Oberlin.

The next step was New York, where he again joined
W. C. Handy; then, in 1921, he joined Shuffle
Along's pit orchestra, playing oboe, and began to
study composition with George W. Chadwick. In 1923
Still became a student of Edgar Varese; thereafter,
his career as an orchestrator and composer
accelerated. Performances of Darker America, La
Guiablesse, Log Cabin Ballads, Africa, Sahdji, and
Afro-American Symphony had been achieved by 1930,
and in that year he became arranger and
orchestrator for the radio program "Deep River
Hour," later becoming the conductor of its
orchestra. In 1934, upon receiving a Guggenheim
Fellowship, he left the show and moved to Los
Angeles, settling down to compose a new opera. As
he began to gain acclaim, Verna Arvey started to
handle his public relations and promotional chores
and, in 1939, became his second wife. Thereafter,
the composer's craft reached a point of considerable refinement, and more successes followed.

Soon, however, Still and Arvey confronted a
period of ostensible suppression and persecution.
For example, "we tried so hard to reach Marian

Anderson, to ask if she would be willing to examine some of Billy's songs, with a view to including a Still work on her concerts. We were not able to get near her--nor indeed, to any of the top Negro singers of the day, when their attention would have helped so much" (p. 126). A paranoiac fear and disdain of communism are apparent throughout the book. Combined, the latter two concerns reflect the author's contention that circumstances were seldom in Still's favor and that conspiracies constantly threatened and inhibited his acceptance and his progress. The book is also sprinkled with comments about psychic perceptions, spiritual experiences, jealousies, and plans to "try and thwart us" and about the experiences of their interracial marriage and with disparaging remarks about "modernist" composers (p. 105). In spite of these traits, however, the book does provide valuable information about Still the man and the composer.

Reviews: Black Perspective in Music 13:122-124 n1 '85; Central Opera Service Bulletin 26:53-54 n1

Haas, Robert Bartlett, ed., Paul H. Slattery, Verna Arvey, William Grant Still, Louis and Annette Kaufman. _William Grant Still and the Fusion of Cultures in American Music_. Forewords by Howard Hanson and Frederick Hall. Los Angeles: Black Sparrow Press, 1972. xi, 202 pp. photographs, musical examples, figures. catalogue of works. discography. bibliography. sample programs. author biographies.

Consisting of a series of short essays or discussions, this book presents a picture of the life and career of William Grant Still. The authors, who include the composer and his wife, touch on topics ranging from Still's early life experiences to analytical discussions of his works and philosophy of composition. Mention is made of Still's performing on a variety of instruments in his college days at Wilberforce University; a band concert at Wilberforce whose program was made up entirely of compositions by Still; his study with George W. Chadwick and Edgar Varese; his work as an orchestrator, arranger, and conductor in New York in the 1920s; and the special awards and honorary degrees the composer received over the course of his lifetime. Still himself writes of his childhood in Little Rock, Arkansas, including his introduction to Afro-American folk music; his having heard Clarence Cameron White and E. Azalia Hackley in his hometown; his selection of the violin as his first musical instrument; and his later adoption of a "racial form of expression" (p. 80). He also discusses briefly his method of composing, the nature of his inspiration, the stages in his development as a composer, the distinction between idiom and style, his membership and experiences with the W. C. Handy band in Memphis in 1916, his views on matters of race, and his encounters with black militants in the 1960s and early 1970s.

Throughout the book, the reader is reminded of Still's intolerance of the musical avant-garde and of avant-garde thought. "A comprehensive portrayal of William Grant Still, the man, his style of musical composition, his compositional philosophy, and his place in the historical style continuum of American music," the book presents discussions of Still's major compositions, with two of them--the First Symphony (Afro-American) and the Fourth Symphony (Authocthonous)--treated to analysis and comparison (p. 10). The catalogue of Still's compositions is a valuable resource for scholars interested in his work. It is organized by genre, each entry containing the following information, as appropriate: title, date, duration, publisher or an indication that the piece is still in manuscript, movement names, first performance, and a brief annotation. The sample programs consist of suggestions for ten performances consisting of Still compositions; they are accompanied by suggested program notes.

Reviews: Black Perspective in Music 1:83-84 nl '73; Choice 9:1600 F '73; Library Journal 97:3715 N 15 '72; Music Educators Journal 59:87 Mr '73; Music Educators Journal 60:73-74 O '73; Music Journal 30:49 D '72; Symphony News 24:31 n5 '73

SELECTIVE DISCOGRAPHY

Afro-American Symphony. Columbia M-32782, 1974.
Darker America/From the Black Belt. Turnabout TV-S-34536, 1974.
Ennanga, Songs of Separation, Song for the Lonely, Danzas de Panama. Orion ORS-7278, 1972.
Festive Overture. CRI SD-259, 1970.
Lenox Avenue. New Records NRLP-105, c1950.

Sahdji. Columbia M-33433, 1975.
Seven Traceries. Orion ORS-78305/6, 1978.
Suite for Violin, Pastorella, Summerland, Carmela,
  Here's One. Orion ORS-7512, 1971.
Three Visions. Desto DC-7102/3, 1972.
William Grant Still, 1895-1978. North Arkansas Symphony
  Orchestra Records WGS-001, 1984.

Donna Summer

Haskins, Jim, and J. M. Stifle. <u>Donna Summer: An Unauthor-ized Biography</u>. Boston and Toronto: Little, Brown, 1983. 136 pp. photographs. discography. index.

This book for young people tells of the singer's birth in 1949 into a Boston family of nine, her early attraction to singing, including her singing in her church choir, and her teaching herself to sing by listening to records of Mahalia Jackson's performances. We learn that she was later inspired and influenced by the Motown sound, that she began to skip school to hang around recording studios, and that, at seventeen, she became interested in white rock & roll music, forming, with white friends, a group called "Crow," which quickly disbanded. She then began to sing with other rock groups, quit school, and moved to New York in 1968, with the intention of breaking into musical theater. She quickly landed a role in a European production of the rock musical <u>Hair</u> and, when it closed in 1970, chose to remain in Germany, appearing in productions of <u>Porgy and Bess</u>, <u>Show Boat</u>, and other stage shows, "singing backup on studio recordings, appearing in productions of <u>Godspell</u> and <u>The Me Nobody Knows</u>" (p. 34).

At twenty-three Summer was married to another struggling actor--an Austrian--and gave birth to a daughter, but she was divorced in 1974. In that year she also made her first records:

soon, all three records were being played throughout Europe, and two became major hits. "Hostage" became the number-one record in Holland and Belgium, number two in France, and in the top ten in Spain and Scandinavia. Within six weeks after its release, it was a certified gold record (having sold 500,000 copies). "Lady of the Night" was almost as popular, and it too went gold within six weeks of its release. All over Europe people were wondering about this new black singer with the haunting voice (p. 41).

In 1975 her first album was released in the United States and immediately went gold, with its "A" side, "Love to Love You, Baby," placing "number one on Billboard magazine's Hot 100" (p. 60). On her return to the United States "she felt culture shock. . . ; the pace of life was different, people talked so fast and used expressions that were foreign to her, Americans whites looked at her differently than European whites did" (p. 61). And she was immediately "panned by the critics [and] lacerated by self-styled moralists" (p. 74). In 1976 her second album, Love Trilogy, was produced; like her first, it went gold and yielded a gold single. In 1978 she became dependent on drugs, brought members of her family into her tour entourage, set out to win the night-club audience, starred in the movie Thank God It's Friday, made a South American tour, and topped the pop-music charts with her album Live and More. Her 1979 double album Bad Girls achieved "a perfect blend of German Eurodisco and American rock and soul that ultimately transcends the disco environment" (p. 103). Also in 1979 Summer was named "Top Disco Artist of the Year" "for the fourth year in a row" and became a born-again Christian (p. 106).

In 1980 the "Donna Summer Alive and More" television special was aired, she was married for the second time, had a second child, and made a new record album--The Wanderer--that reaffirmed her "position over rivals Barbra Streisand and Diana Ross as the most consistent and adventurous female record maker in the pop mainstream" (p. 116). The year 1982 brought another successful album--Donna Summer--and her third child. Whereas Summer's early records had been infused with sexual innuendo, now her audiences were weaned from such

content with offerings that contained "no sex or
violence or killing or hatred" (p. 126). The
authors relate the details of Summer's sense of
humor; her early self-consciousness; the estrange-
ment from her family when she joined the cast of
Hair; the lean early years of her show-business
career; her private concerns, fears, and
motivations; her association with two European
producers and their production of her first hit
record; the growth of her musicianship and musical
sophistication through the release of her albums;
her "intense" relationships with the men in her
life; and her collaboration with Quincy Jones.

Reviews: Booklist 79:1331 Ju 15 '83; Children's
Book Review Service 11:138 Jy '83; School
Library Journal 30:168 O '83; Voice of Youth
Advocates 6:153 Au '83

SELECTIVE DISCOGRAPHY

Bad Girls. Casablanca S2-7150.
Cats without Claws. Geffen GHS-24040-2.
Donna Summer. Geffen GHS-2005-2.
Love to Love You, Baby. Oasis 5003.
Love Trilogy. Oasis 5004.
She Works Hard for the Money. Mercury 812-265-2.
The Summer Collection. Mercury 826144-1.
Walk Away. Casablanca 810-011-2.

Fats Waller

Fox, Charles. Fats Waller. Kings of Jazz. New York: A. S.
Barnes, 1961. 87 pp. photographs. discography.

    Pianist Thomas "Fats" Waller was a "gay irreverent
comedian at the piano, a symbol of good fellowship,
a kind of latter-day Pickwick with a taste for
whiskey instead of claret and a decidedly bawdy
sense of humor. But the personality which Fats
paraded before the public was really a gross
over-simplification of the man, as well as
something of an obstruction to his work as an
artist" (p. 4). In high school Waller read "Nick
Carter novels as well as books on musical theory"
and studied piano privately with Carl Bohm and
Leopold Godowsky (p. 11). Soon he quit school and
went to work as organist at Harlem's Lincoln
Theater, accompanying silent films. His first job
as a pianist was at Leroy's Cabaret in Harlem. In
1922 Waller started making piano rolls,
approximately twenty over the next few years, then
began making records. "During 1929 Fats Waller
recorded some of his very finest piano solos"
(p. 36). In 1932 he began a series of radio
programs on Cincinnati's WLW. In 1935 he continued
to record and took part in two Hollywood
films--Hooray for Love and King of Burlesque. His
most productive year for recording--with eight
sessions--was 1936; in that year Waller also began
to earn large sums of money. Between 1939 and 1941
Waller made a large number of records and appeared,
together with his band, in four film shorts. In
1943 he became sick and disbanded his group; in

December he died. At the height of his career, "a typical image of Waller . . . would have had him sitting at the piano, his derby hat tilted on one side, winking and leering at his audience as he butchered yet another sentimental lyric with a chuckle and some salty innuendo" (p. 70).

Kirkeby, Ed, in collaboration with Duncan P. Scheidt and Sinclair Traill. Ain't Misbehavin': The Story of Fats Waller. New York: Da Capo, 1966. 248 pp. photographs. discography.

This is a biographical study of a great American pianist/composer/entertainer who, according to the author, "was able to reap a harvest of fame . . . first through piano rolls, then, as the way opened up, through gramophone records and lastly through the night clubs" (p. 75). Waller changed the course of piano jazz and American popular songwriting. The author recounts the early days of Waller's parents' settlement in New York, first in Greenwich Village, then in Harlem, one of the first black families to settle there before World War I; the parents' establishment of a religious and musical household; Waller's brief period of piano lessons in childhood and his first professional job as a movie-theater organist; and his introduction to James P. Johnson.

The author gives details of Waller's apprenticeship with Johnson; the Striders and piano rolls and the procedure for making the latter; the relationship of the Striders to the music-theater activities of the 1920s; Waller's gastronomic and alcoholic appetites and feats; episodes with process-servers, judges, and jail for avoidance of alimony and child-support payments; his stay in Chicago, where he played at the Vendome Theater with the Erskine Tate Orchestra; his Cincinnati radio show; and his performance of James P. Johnson's Yamekraw, for piano solo and orchestra, at Carnegie Hall in 1928. There are good discussions of the rent-party phenomenon and the Harlem gladiator-pianists; Waller's professional collaborations and personal associations with Andy Razaf, J. C. Johnson, Edgar Dowell, Spencer Williams, Fletcher Henderson, Louis Armstrong, Bill "Bojangles" Robinson, Willie the Lion Smith, and Una Mae Carlisle. Also discussed or mentioned are Waller's study of piano and advanced harmony with Leopold Godowsky and Waller's last days and death in 1943. Woven into the text are brief career sketches of James P. Johnson, Willie the Lion Smith, and a few others. Especially informative and revealing are the insider's views of preparations for revue productions.

Reviews: Down Beat 34:37-38 Ja 12 '67; Guardian Weekly 95:11 Jy 14 '66; Jazz Journal 19:16 Jy '66; Jazz Journal 20:42 D '67; Jazz Monthly 12:22-23 Jy '66; Jazz Report 5:3 n5 '67; Library Journal 91:4119 S 15 '66; Library Journal 92:1335 Mr 15 '67; National Review 18:1234 N 29 '66; New York Times 116:49M O 26 '66; New York Times Book Review 71:74 D 11 '66; Observer (London) p22 Jy 17 '66; Publishers Weekly 190:340 Au 29 '66; Saturday Review 50:61 F 11 '67; Second Line 17:160 N/D '66; Times Literary Supplement p993 O 19 '67

Vance, Joel. Fats Waller: His Life and Times. Chicago: Contemporary Books, 1977. viii, 179 pp. photographs. bibliography. index.

Vance portrays his subject as "a master of music and life" and tries to give readers some idea of the pianist/songwriter's musical abilities and contributions (p. 6). He sets the stage by discussing events and conditions that must have shaped Waller's life and then presents a brilliant musical/character sketch of the great musician. Information is given regarding Waller's early musical influences and training; Waller on the house-rent party circuit; Waller as the object of "diligent pursuit by shyster lawyers" who attempted to serve him with legal documents related to defaulted alimony payments (p. 55); the character, quality, and nature of Waller's musical compositions; and Waller's "casual, negligent attitude toward the commercial and artistic value of his compositions, coupled with the exploitation of black composers by white (and black) music publishers of the 1920s" (pp. 62-63). Discussed, in addition, are Waller's relationships with such contemporaries as James P. Johnson, Willie the Lion Smith, Mary Lou Williams, Art Tatum, Louis Armstrong, and others; and Harlem's 1920s "establishments of note," including the Cotton Club, Barrons, Big John's Cafe, Connie's Inn, and Pod & Jerrys. Two important features present here that are absent from the other works on Waller are analyses of Waller's recorded output in the 1934-1942 period and of the motivations behind Waller's "brave and resolutely carefree mask"

(p. 170). Previously undocumented claims are debunked in light of better information; in some cases, information about certain events is merely presented differently, with no increase in its reliability.

Reviews: AB Bookman's Weekly 61:697 Ja 30 '78; Billboard 89:54 N 19 '77; Booklist 74:656 D 15 '77; Cadence 3:39 Ja '78; Choice 15:411 My '78; Christian Science Monitor 70:20 Ja 6 '78; Coda n164/165:36 F 1 '79; Jazz Journal International 32:21 O '79; Kliatt Young Adult Paperback Book Guide 13:34 Fall '79; Library Journal 102:2502 D 15 '77; Music Journal 36:38 Mr '78; New York Times 127:19 F 11 '78; New Yorker 54:110 Ap 10 '78; Orkester Journalen 47:12-13 F '79; Saturday Review 5:56 D 10 '77; School Library Journal 24:105 Ap '78

Waller, Maurice, and Anthony Calabrese. <u>Fats Waller</u>. Foreword by Michael Lipskin. New York: Schirmer Books; London: Collier Macmillan, 1977. xix, 235 pp. photographs, musical examples. discography. rollography. music bibliography. index.

This is a remarkably balanced account of the life of jazz pianist and songwriter Thomas "Fats" Waller, written by one of his sons. It is the story of

> a jazz piano stylist with a touch that influenced the course of the pop and jazz keyboard, a composer of hit songs and Broadway musicals, and an energetic performer capable of bringing happiness to thousands during the mid-Depression and early World War II years as they listened to his hundreds of recordings, heard him on network radio, or had the special pleasure of seeing him live with his band "Rhythm" (p. ix).

> The Fats Waller story is not just one of contrast between public entertainer and serious pianist-composer, but also that of a prodigy. Fats started playing piano as soon as he discovered what it was--when he was six years old. . . . He quit high school to work as a movie theater-organist accompanying the silents, and recorded his first piano solos for Okeh records when he was eighteen.

His first work was published when he was nineteen, and by twenty-five he had highly original piano solos on discs, and was in demand as an accompanist for blues singers (pp. x-xi).

The book also touches on Waller's use and making of piano rolls, records, and radio broadcasts; musical prowess in composition and performance; participation in the house-rent party circuit; character problems; running feud with the courts for his continuing failure to pay alimony to his first wife; writing of songs and scores for revues and musicals, such as, for example, Hot Chocolates and Early to Bed; encounters with discrimination on tour and at home; his life at home and away with his family; and his musical and personal relationships with James P. Johnson, Willie the Lion Smith, Count Basie, Clarence Williams, Spencer Williams, Duke Ellington, Andy Razaf, Eva Taylor, Don Redman, Fletcher Henderson, Louis Armstrong, Bill "Bojangles" Robinson, Perry Bradford, Rev. Adam Clayton Powell, Jr., Mary Lou Williams, Art Tatum, Una Mae Carlisle, and others. Some of the dishonest machinations of music managers, producers, lawyers, and others in the 1930s and 1940s are revealed here, as well as some of the means musicians used to counter them.

Reviews: AB Bookman's Weekly 61:697 Ja 30 '78; Booklist 74:656 D 15 '77; Cadence 3:39 Ja '78; Christian Science Monitor 70:20 Ja 6 '78; Choice 15:411 My '78; Contemporary Keyboard 4:6 Ap '78; Economist 269:120 N 4 '78; Jazz Forum n53:52 '78; Jazz Magazine (US) 2:61-62 n4 '78; Kirkus Reviews 45:1135 O 15 '77; Library Journal 102:2349 N 15 '77; Music Journal 36:38 Mr '78; New Yorker 54:110 Ap 10 '78; New York Times 127:19 F 11 '78; New York Times Book Review p13 N 20 '77; Orkester Journalen 47:12-13+ F '79; Publishers Weekly 212:136 S 19 '77; Saturday Review 5:56 D 10 '77; Saturday Review 5:40 Au '78; Swinging Newsletter 8:8 n35 '78

SELECTIVE DISCOGRAPHY

Ain't Misbehavin'. RCA Victor LPM-1246.
The Complete Fats Waller. Bluebird ANX2-5511/AXN2-5575/ AXM2-5583.
Fats Waller Piano Solos. 2 vols. RCA-Bluebird AXM2-5518, 1929-1941.

Fats Waller's Jam School. Forgate Discs WOP-69.0.
Handful of Keys: Fats Waller and His Rhythm. RCA Victor
    LPM-1502, 1957.
One Never Knows, Do One?. RCA Victor LPM-1503, 1957.
Piano Rolls. 3 vols. Biograph BLP-1002Q/1005Q/1015Q.

Ethel Waters

Waters, Ethel, with Charles Samuels. His Eye Is on the Sparrow. 1950. Reprint. Westport, Conn.: Greenwood Press, 1978. 278 pp. photographs.

Tracing her family from her maternal grandfather, "Albert Harris, a native of India" and her great-grandmother, "a slave, but very fair" (p. 1), singer/entertainer Ethel Waters tells of the circumstances of her birth in 1900 and her subsequent rather dismal childhood that was "like a series of one night stands," in which she was "shuttled among relatives, boarded out, continually being moved around to Camden, Chester, and Philadelphia homes" (p. 8). Growing up in a "wasteland of violent emotions and exploding egos" (p. 40), she gained experience in social and what would later be professional endeavors. For example, while she was still a teenager she taught dancing at "a respectable dance hall" and "won many prizes in dancing contests (p. 41). She could also "sing, and do the split" (p. 47). At thirteen she was married, and at fourteen she was "separated and on my own," working "in hotels as a substitute for dishwashers, cleaning women, waitresses, or bus boys" (p. 64). Waters began to move toward being an entertainer by imitating roles she had seen played by Negro stock companies. By seventeen she had a "sweet, bell-like voice" and was "a really agile shimmy shaker" (p. 71); and it was then that she went on the vaudeville stage as a professional, first playing Baltimore's Lincoln Theater, then other houses on the East Coast, in the South, and across the Midwest.

The first woman to sing W. C. Handy's "St. Louis Blues," Waters's first record was "Down Home Blues"/"Oh, Daddy" for Pace & Handy's Black Swan label; she went on to make other records that are now collector's items. Waters "can't read music, never have. But I have almost absolute pitch. My music is all queer little things that come into my head. I feel these little trills and things deep inside of me, and I sing them that way. All queer little things that I hum" (p. 147). In her early days she "was scared to work for white people. I didn't know very much about them, and what I knew I didn't like. The very idea of appearing on Broadway in a cast of ofays made me cringe in my boots" (p. 148). But that, of course, was to change.

The first show in which she appeared as a name performer was Oh, Joy, a revue, in the 1920s. In the late twenties she starred in an edition of Lew Leslie's Blackbirds and, in 1931, his Rhapsody in Black. As Thousands Cheer followed--"a smash hit on Broadway." With that show, Waters became "the highest paid woman performer on Broadway" (p. 223). In 1935 she co-starred in the play At Home Abroad, and in 1936 came Mamba's Daughters, in which "I was to prove I was an actress as well as a blues singer" and which "made my reputation on the American legitimate stage" (pp. 235-236). With Mamba's Daughters she also became "the first colored woman, the first actress of my race to be starred on Broadway in a dramatic play," and received rave reviews for her acting (pp. 246-247). In 1940 she starred in Cabin in the Sky; then moved on to a series of films, including Tales of Manhattan, in which she played opposite Paul Robeson, Cairo, and the film version of Cabin in the Sky; then to the revue Laugh Time. Waters had established herself--in theaters, movies, and night clubs. With her recording of it, the song "'Dinah' had been the first international song hit to come out of a night club. 'Stormy Weather,' which might have been the theme song of my life, was proving to be the first dramatic song hit out of a night club" (p. 221). Then came an eclipse of several years, a depressing period during which she "hit bottom" until 1949, when she got the role of Granny in the film Pinky (p. 268). Then, in 1950, the play The

<u>Member of the Wedding</u> opened with Waters in the leading role.

In the course of Waters's narrative she communicates many details of her personal and professional experiences, including accounts of theater incidents; her experiences on tours on the Theater Owners' Booking Association (T.O.B.A.), Keith, and Orpheum vaudeville circuits; her early predilection for strong profanity; her initial insecurities as a professional; her billing as "Sweet Mama Stringbean"; her saloon work, including her transformation of Harlem's Edmond's Cellar from a "low class dump" to a "high class dump" (p. 132); her experiencing of the cruelty of racism in the South and in the North; her visits to Paris and London; her philanthropic gestures; her touring with the Mallory band; and her relationships with other important figures of the period, including Bessie Smith, Fletcher Henderson, heavyweight boxing champion Jack Johnson, and William Grant Still.

Reviews: Atlantic 187:79 Mr '51; Booklist 47:235 Mr 1 '51; Bookmark 10:156 Ap '51; Canadian Forum 31:47 My '51; Chicago Sunday Tribune p5 Mr 18 '51; Christian Science Monitor p9 Mr 10 '51; Commonweal 53:652 Ap 6 '51; Kirkus Reviews 19:16 Ja 1 '51; Library Journal 76:868 My 15 '51; Manchester Guardian p4 N 27 '51; Nation 172:303 Mr 31 '51; New York Herald Tribune Book Reviews p5 Mr 4 '51; New York Times p3 Mr 4 '51; New Yorker 27:119 Ap 7 '51; Publishers Weekly 191:99 Ap 24 '67; San Francisco Chronicle p22 Mr 23 '51; Saturday Review 34:18 Mr 24 '51; Survey 87:232 My '51; Time 57:104 Mr 12 '51; United States Quarterly Book Review 7:131 Ju '51; Wisconsin Library Bulletin 47:87 Ap '51

Waters, Ethel. <u>To Me It's Wonderful</u>. Introduction by Eugenia Price and Joyce Blackburn. New York: Harper & Row, 1972. ix, 162 pp. photographs.

This is the biography of a singer whom "the most influential critics of the fifties considered . . . [also as] one of the four top-ranking actresses in the world of American drama" (p. vii). Waters introduced songs such as "Dinah," "Stormy Weather," and "St. Louis Blues," all in 1925; was the first black performer in an all-white cast for a Broadway show, singing "Heat Wave" and "Supper Time" in Irving Berlin's <u>As Thousands Cheer</u>; made a number of hit records before 1927; and starred in the Broadway shows _Africana_, _Mamba's Daughters_, and _Cabin in the Sky_ and in the movie _Pinky_.

The book begins with Waters at the age of sixty-one, in 1957, with her feeling troubled by her overweight condition, "trapped in all that fat" and unable to function properly because of the discomfort it brought (p. 11). The condition caused her to reminisce about her childhood in Chester, Pennsylvania, where she learned, in church, the song "His Eye Is on the Sparrow," where she was a ring leader of "street gangs and street life in the slums" at twelve, and where she experienced a religious conversion at the same age (p. 15). Waters connects her childhood religious experience with the religious renewal that came with her first attendance at a Billy Graham Crusade meeting in 1957: "the more he said, the more I knew that what I felt when I first walked in was that my Lord was calling me--me, Ethel Waters, His child--to come on back home" (p. 23). She tells of her introduction to stardom in the 1920s; her meeting of and relationship with such celebrities as Carl Van Vechten, Rev. Billy Graham and members of his crusade, and Richard Nixon; and her once-corpulent condition and how she related to it. The major portion of the book is devoted to her participation in the Billy Graham Crusade and her religious orientation and beliefs.

Reviews: AB Bookman's Weekly 50:12 Jy 3 '72; Booklist 69:21 S 1 '72; Booklist 69:140 O 1 '72; Library Journal 97:2196 Ju 15 '72; Publishers Weekly 201:115 F 21 '72

SELECTIVE DISCOGRAPHY

Ethel Waters' Greatest Years. 2 vols. Columbia PJ-31571, 1925-1934.
Jazzin' Babies Blues. Biograph BLP-12026.
Oh Daddy! Biograph BLP-12022.
On Stage and Screen 1925-1940. Columbia CL-2792.

Dicky Wells

Wells, Dicky, as told to Stanley Dance. <u>The Night People:
Reminiscences of a Jazzman</u>. Foreword by Count Basie.
Boston: Crescendo Publishing Co., 1971. vi, 118 pp.
photographs. glossary. index.

This is an autobiographical reminiscence of "an
individualist, and one of the great trombone
soloists [who] might be described as inimitable,
. . . a pace-setter in his profession during the
era of the big bands" who worked with "Benny
Carter, Charlie Johnson, Fletcher Henderson, Teddy
Hill, Count Basie, Sy Oliver, Earl Hines, and Ray
Charles over the course of his career" (p. v). The
book contains brief comments on Wells's childhood:
his musical start in "kids'" bands in Louisville,
Kentucky; his association with and exposure to
early boys' bands and to such young and older
musicians as Jonah Jones, Jimmie Harrison, the
Kansas City Monarch Band, Helen Humes, Big Green,
Doc Cheatham, Louis Armstrong, the Fletcher
Henderson Orchestra, and the Alphonso Trent
Orchestra. The treatment of his professional career
begins with his move to New York and his performing
in bands there in cabarets and ballrooms. It
progresses to discuss his life on the road; his
trips to Europe; bus and dressing-room conversation
among jazz musicians, and cutting contests. The
glossary is a dictionary of jazz jargon.

Reviews: AB Bookman's Weekly 48:1239 O 25 '71;
Black World 23:96 N '73; Booklist 68:96 O 1 '71;
Crescendo International 10:17 D '71; Down Beat

38:14 N '71;   High Fidelity/Musical America
21:MA30-31 N '71; Hip 10:13 n5 '71 Jazz and Pop
10:10 Jy '71; Jazz Hot n273:22 Ju '71; Melody
Maker 46:40 O 16 '71; Music Journal 29:68 S '71;
Music Educators Journal 58:85+ Mr '72; New
Statesman 83:117 Ja 28 '72; Notes 29:34+ S '72;
Point du Jazz n8:84 Ap '73; Popular Music and
Society 2:167-168 n2 '73; Publishers Weekly
199:69 Mr 8 '71

SELECTIVE DISCOGRAPHY

Classic Tenors. Contact CM-3, 1943.
Dicky Wells in Paris, 1937. Prestige 7593, 1937.
The Lester Young Story, Volume 2. Columbia JG-34837,
   1977.
Louis Armstrong, Roy Eldridge: Jazz Masterpieces. Frank-
   lin Mint Record Society FM-004, 1982.

Bert Williams

Charters, Ann. Nobody: The Story of Bert Williams. New York: Macmillan, 1970. 157 pp. photographs, drawings, music, reproductions of sheet music covers and advertising posters. discography. index.

"Bert Williams was a man who hated the stigma of his color, but the only way he had found to succeed in the theater was by wearing the minstrel show mask of burnt cork. He had struggled and worked to perfect his great gifts as a comedian, but he was expected to appear in blackface, and the role became as impossible to abandon as his own shadow" (p. 138). He was born of West Indian parents in the mid-1870s. He began his stage career in San Francisco in 1892 and met his future partner, George Walker, there a few years later. The two young men joined forces and soon went to Chicago in the hope of performing in John Isham's Octoroons, an all-black show.

They began to differentiate their roles more sharply. Walker continued to tell the jokes and act the comedian, but he also emphasized his flair for clothes. He became the dandy, the "Broadway Swell," the standard minstrel show dude characterization. He dressed in flashy street clothes, exaggerated peg top trousers, silk cravats, vests, and two-toned button shoes, with colors and patterns all beyond the standards of careful taste but definitely guaranteed

to attract attention. He played the bold
and carefree sport who was so self-
possessed and triumphant that his
posturing verged on the preposterous. In
contrast to Walker's flamboyant
arrogance, Williams put on his oldest
trousers and a mis-matched jacket. He
had a larger build than Walker, and it
seemed natural for Bert to emphasize the
awkwardness of his long arms and legs.
He shuffled on stage and played straight
man to George's clowning before starting
to sing his dialect songs (p. 28).

Within a short time, they were called to New York
to play in a show titled The Gold Bug (1896). There
followed several such revues, for example, The
Policy Players (1900), The Dramatic Mirror (1900),
Sons of Ham (1900-1902), In Dahomey (1902-1905),
including a European tour, In Abyssinia (1905), and
Bandana Land (1908-1909). George Walker was forced
to retire in 1909 due to ill health, and the famous
Williams and Walker team was dissolved.

As a single act, Williams toured on the
vaudeville circuit and, in 1910, starred in a
short-lived production, Mr. Lode of Koal. At this
turning point in his career,

> he debated endlessly with himself the
> best course to follow. . . . As the top
> ranking comedian in the United States, he
> could do anything he wished--stay in
> America or return to England, where he
> had found less flagrant social humilia-
> tion. He could organize his own company
> again, stay in vaudeville as a single, or
> he could accept a very challenging offer
> that had recently been suggested to him.
> He decided to try something new, and in
> May, 1910, newspapers announced that Bert
> Williams would be a feature in Florenz
> Ziegfeld's Follies of 1910 (p. 109).

He was to appear with the Follies on an irregular
basis until his death in 1922. In 1908 Bert
Williams was instrumental in founding the Frogs, a
professional organization for black actors. In
addition to Williams and Walker, the charter
members of this group included "Bob Cole, Lester A.
Walton, Sam Corker, James Reese Europe, Alex
Rogers, Tom Brown, J. Rosamond Johnson, Jesse

Shipp, and R. C. McPherson" (p. 94). An unusual
feature of the book is the inclusion of complete
sheet music of eleven songs that were associated
with Bert Williams during his career, including
"Nobody," "I'm a Jonah Man," and "Good Morning
Carrie."

Reviews: Black World 20:90 Ja '71; Library
Journal 95:4251 D 15 '70; Music Clubs Magazine
50:76 n4 '71; Music Journal 29:60-61 Ja '71;
Western Folklore 30:147-149 n2 '71

Rowland, Mabel. <u>Bert Williams: Son of Laughter</u>. Preface by
David Belasco. New York: English Crafters, 1923. xvii, 218
pp. photographs, drawings.

This book is described on the title page as "A
Symposium of Tribute to the Man and to His Work, by
His Friends and Associates." It is not organized
chronologically except in its broadest outlines;
rather, it consists of a string of reminiscences by
Williams's friends and acquaintances, interspersed
with the lyrics of songs associated with or
composed by Williams. Supporting commentary by the
author provides facts, a more or less orderly
progression through Williams's life, and the
logical connection between the reminiscences. From
these sources we learn that Bert Williams was born
and spent his early childhood in Antigua, West
Indies. As a child he exhibited a gift for mimicry
and a love for animals and nature. He moved with
his family to San Francisco in mid-childhood.
There he began to work as a singer in restaurants
and other establishments in the late 1890s. "He did
not at first specialize in any particular kind of
song, but sang any and everything. However, as
time went on and he decided to make a specialty of
the southern darky he adopted 'cork,' as the black
make-up is known, and he depicted a type of this
southern darky which required slow, deliberate
treatment to express a melancholy nature and an
unlucky slouch" (p. 14).

In 1889 Williams met and formed a partnership
with George Walker. Six years later they went to
Chicago and played in "The Six Octoroons." The year
1898 saw their move to New York to appear in "The
Gold Bug." In the years following, the pair
appeared in several shows in New York and were
among the first black comedians to be featured on
Broadway in such highly successful reviews. Their
shows included <u>The Policy Players</u>, <u>Sons of Ham</u>, <u>In</u>

Dahomy, Bandana Land, and In Abyssinia. In Dahomey
was taken to England, where it was presented in a
command performance for British royalty and enjoyed
great success during its entire run. One of its
features was the introduction of the cakewalk to
England. During the tour of the British Isles,
Williams was inducted into the Masonic order, thus
fulfilling a long-time desire. The career of
Williams and Walker as a starring duo was ended
with the retirement of George Walker. Williams
joined the company of the Ziegfeld Follies in 1910
and performed there for the next ten years. His
last show was Under the Bamboo Tree. Among the
songs written by Williams whose lyrics are quoted
in the book are: "Jonah Man," "That's a Plenty,"
and "Nobody" (lyrics by Alex Rogers). Throughout
the book, Williams is portrayed as a gentle,
considerate, and peace-loving man by the author and
the various persons quoted: "He craved harmony all
the time; harmony of environment, harmony of sound
and of every condition. If he saw or sensed the
slightest argument going on, he would cross the
street to avoid it. The easiest way, the way of
least resistance, that was the keynote of his
temperament" (p. 17).

SELECTIVE DISCOGRAPHY

"Brother Low Down." Columbia A-3508, 1921.
"I'm Sorry I Ain't Got It, You Could Have It If I Had It
  Blues." Columbia A-2877, 1919.
"It's Nobody's Business But My Own." Columbia A-2750,
  1919.
"Lonesome Alimony Blues." Columbia A-2979, 1920.
"Nobody." Columbia A-302, 1906.
"Unexpectedly." Columbia A-3508, 1921.
"Unlucky Blues." Columbia A-2941, 1920.

Stevie Wonder

Haskins, James. <u>The Story of Stevie Wonder</u>. New York: Lothrop, Lee & Shepard, 1976. 126 pp. photographs. discography. index.

Born Steveland Morris in Saginaw, Michigan in 1950, Wonder became permanently blind almost immediately after birth. While still very young, although his family "was not especially musical," Wonder revealed "strong musical interest and ability" (p. 17). The family moved to Detroit when Stevie was a preschooler, and he "was enrolled in special classes for the blind in the Detroit public school system" (p. 19). In listening to the black solo singers and groups of the fifties over the radio, little Stevie "would sing the words of the songs quietly to himself. He would hum the tunes. He would tap out the beats on his toy drum and try to play the melodies on his four-note harmonica" (p. 29). By the age of seven, in spite of his family's poverty, he owned a set of drums, a harmonica, and a piano. He began to sing in his church choir and became a junior deacon before he was ten. Heard by and recruited for the record company Hitsville, USA (later to be named "Motown") in 1960, Wonder was hired immediately by the company president, Berry Gordy, Jr. His first two records were undistinguished, but in 1963, at the age of twelve, he made "Fingertips," which became a smash hit. At Hitsville "he spent most of his time with adults," learned the Motown formula, and collaborated with the label's writers (p. 44). Between 1968 and 1970 he had a string of hits, including "For Once in My Life," "My Cherie Amour," and "Signed, Sealed, and Delivered, I'm Yours." By 1970, at twenty, he himself had produced two records and was married; and on his twenty-first birthday the money that had accumulated in a trust fund that was early established for him became available. Now "he could afford to hire a recording studio and produce his own records, and that is exactly what he decided to do" (p. 66). He also voided his contract with Motown and struck out on his own, renting a recording studio in New York and buying studio equipment for the production of his records. This allowed him to make tracks on which he played most of the instruments himself, making possible total control of his product. This was the beginning of his most fertile period. The first result was the album Music On My Mind. In 1972, while promoting the album on tour as the opening act for the Rolling Stones, his audience became national. By 1974 he had accumulated a number of gold singles and albums, two platinum albums, and more than five Grammys. As this youth book progresses, the reader learns: how Wonder coped with his blindness in childhood, using his "sonar" to "see" objects (p. 13); how he was taught to live effectively in a sighted world; his condition of living totally immersed in a world of sound; about his automobile accident from which he had a long recovery; about his two marriages; and about what it means to be sightless.

Reviews: Booklist 73:30 S 1 '76; Booklist 73:38 S 1 '76; Center for Children's Books Bulletin 30:125 Ap '77; Catholic Library World 48:405 Ap '77; Journal of Reading 27:521 Mr '84; Kirkus Reviews 44:604 My 15 '76; Kliatt Young Adult Paperback Book Guide 13:30 Fall '79; Reading Teacher 31:22 O '77; School Library Journal 23:92 Ja '77; School Library Journal 26:39 Ap '80

SELECTIVE DISCOGRAPHY

Alfie. Motown 5298, 1968.
For Once in My Life. Motown M5-234, 1968.
Greatest Hits. Tamla SLP-282.
In Loving Memory. Motown M5-207.
In Square Circle. Tamla 6134-TL, 1985.
Innervisions. Tamla T7-326, 1973.
My Cherie Amour. Motown M5-179, 1969.
Signed, Sealed, Delivered. Motown M5-176, 1970.

Stevie Wonder

<u>Stevie Wonder's Greatest Hits</u>. 2 vols.   Tamla T7-282/313.
<u>12 Year Old Genius</u>. Motown M5-131, 1963.
<u>Woman in Red</u>. Motown 6108, 1984.

Index

Index